Technology for Literacy Teaching and Learning

WILLIAM J. VALMONT
Director of Technology
Professor of Language, Reading, and Culture
College of Education, the University of Arizona

HOUGHTON MIFFLIN COMPANY
Boston New York

Editor in Chief: Patricia A. Coryell
Senior Sponsoring Editor: Sue Pulvermacher-Alt
Senior Development Editor: Lisa Mafrici
Senior Project Editor: Kathryn Dinovo
Cover Design Manager: Diana Coe
Manufacturing Manager: Florence Cadran
Marketing Manager: Nicola Poser

Cover Image: © Jason Hawkes/Stone

Printed in the U.S.A.

Library of Congress Control Number: 2001133360

ISBN: 0-618-06855-4

123456789-DOC-06 05 04 03 02

Contents

CHAPTER 3

CHAPTER 4

Preface

I wrote this book to help prospective and practicing teachers learn about the many resources available to help their students develop literacy capabilities during interactions with technology, such as computers, CD-ROMs, and the Internet. It takes time, something busy educators often lack, to identify appropriate software for literacy development and to find good web sites with exciting examples of the materials practicing educators have placed online. During the creation of this book, I discovered very helpful resources founded on practical, authentic classroom strategies, and I examined the changing nature of literacy brought about by technological developments. In this book, I share them with you. Because students have access to a great deal of unfiltered information, I became more convinced than ever that we, as educators, must help students develop critical thinking and literacy capabilities. This book encourages the use of thinking strategies during literacy development.

Specifically, what I want this book to accomplish is to help future and current teachers:

- understand how the technology of literacy is changing from print text to electronic text accompanied by multimedia features, and thus redefining what it means to be literate today and in the future
- use computers, software, and the Internet to help students develop language and visual communication capabilities
- discover ways to integrate technology and literacy in authentic learning experiences
- help students in understanding and constructing both verbal and nonverbal electronic messages
- prepare young students to take great responsibility as critical thinkers and consumers of electronic messages
- become familiar with CD-ROMs and web sites and with ways to use them to help students develop literacy capabilities

National, state, and local standards guide teachers, and some of the standards deal specifically with helping students use technology wisely. We believe there are appropriate ways to integrate technology and literacy using thematic units that lead to productive standards-based outcomes.

The International Society for Technology in Education (ISTE) and the International Reading Association (IRA) each have standards that dovetail, and you will learn how to design literacy experiences that fit together nicely with both sets of standards.

Audience

This book can be used as the basic text in technology or literacy methods courses at the graduate and undergraduate school levels. It demonstrates that technology can be valuable when used as a tool to meet curriculum needs.

This text can serve as a supplemental text for reading and language arts courses for pre-service teachers seeking certification. Literacy is fundamental to all aspects of learning, and this text illuminates ways to integrate technology with the language and visual arts. It explains in depth several literacy strategies that other current literacy texts pass over lightly, such as the Directed Reading-Thinking Activity (DRTA), related Seeing- and Listening-Thinking Activities, and instructional uses of the cloze technique.

This text can be a valuable resource for individual teachers or groups engaged in in-service education about integrating technology into daily classroom experiences. Even if you are computer savvy, you will learn about many useful, practical strategies.

Content and Organization

We start by looking at "Contexts for Literacy and Technology Interactions in Your Classroom" (chapter 1). We explore what it means to be literate in the electronic age and begin to make literacy-technology connections. Using thematic units is encouraged.

"Putting Technology to Use in Your Classroom" (chapter 2) discusses several of the basic procedures you can use to involve students with technology. Real-life examples illustrate what creative teachers are already doing in their classrooms.

"Managing Technology in Your Classroom" (chapter 3) presents thoughts about district-wide and classroom considerations that you must think about if you wish to use technology efficiently and effectively.

"Using Technology to Develop Reading and Thinking Strategies" (chapter 4) explores literacy further and describes the Directed Reading-Thinking Activity (DRTA) as a major strategy for helping students become self-sufficient, critical readers.

"Using Technology to Develop Word Recognition, Vocabulary, Reference, and Study Skills" (chapter 5) and "Using Technology to Develop Writing Abilities" (chapter 6) demonstrate how you can use online resources to help students develop these basic but important literacy capabilities.

"Using Technology to Develop Listening and Speaking Abilities" (chapter 7) highlights how you can help students develop these important language arts capabilities through making formal presentations and learning to be effective listeners.

Students' exposure to visual messages has increased dramatically in recent decades, and visual literacy is closely intertwined with verbal literacy. "Using Technology to Develop Graphic and Visual Literacy" (chapter 8) is a unique chapter that examines these connections.

Reading is a process—not a subject—and the verbal and nonverbal content of CD-ROMs and the Internet is what students see, hear, and interpret. "Using Technology with Children's Literature" (chapter 9) reviews several genre of children's literature and identifies where you can find some excellent online materials.

"Assessment of Student Learning and Achievement" (chapter 10) looks at the use of standards for assessment and evaluation of student progress, and it discusses the need to attend to both literacy and technology standards.

"Where Is Technology Taking Us?" (Epilogue) encourages all of us to prepare for significant new developments in technology that will cause us to redefine literacy even further.

Special Learning Features

We have worked hard to give this book a user-friendly writing style and tone. We know you are very busy teachers or students who will quickly understand the suggestions offered and who will "run with" ideas and generate many other creative ways to integrate technology and literacy. We have included descriptions of practical classroom uses of Internet and software features you can use starting today, and we have located hundreds of web sites—the tip of the iceberg, so to speak—to alert you to some readily available electronic resources. All the web addresses for these sites were accurate at the time this book went to press. We firmly believe that authentic teacher-created projects will continue to proliferate on the Web as more and more educators freely share their teaching ideas and strategies with the world.

To support the practical nature of this text, we have included special features throughout the book and on this book's web site. Most are **Teaching Tips** that describe, in teachers' own words, how they use technology for literacy development. Some of the tips explain how to create learning experiences that use technology for teaching. **Student Projects** are examples of projects that students have created, and **Tech Tips** are designed to help you better understand a term or use of technology, such as the Tech Tip explaining the term *ring* (as in Literature Ring) on the World Wide Web.

Almost every chapter contains **Webliographies,** lists of web sites we encourage you to explore—as well as descriptions of CD-ROMs you can examine for possible use. All of the chapters conclude with suggested activities that can help you extend your exposure to ways of integrating technology and literacy as well as software and further reading recommendations. We have also included margin notes to point out important ideas and defined key terms in the end-of-text glossary.

This Book's Web Site

Throughout the book you will see a marginal web site icon, and a suggestion for you to visit this book's web site. Houghton Mifflin and I have designed a web site on which we have placed additional instructor and student materials that we could not place on the pages of the print version of this book, such as short discussions that extend topics in the printed book, additional teacher-prepared classroom suggestions, materials for chapter review and study, and several PowerPoint presentations. We have also included additional Uniform Resource Locators (URLs) of web sites we believe you might find pertinent to the topics included herein. Please visit the web site for updates and to learn about additional ideas and activities that will help you integrate technology and literacy. The students' section of the site can be accessed from **http://education.college.hmco.com/students/**, and the instructors' section from **http://education.college.hmco.com/instructors/**.

Acknowledgments

I wish to thank the many people associated with Houghton Mifflin who contributed to the production of this book. Loretta Wolozin, the senior sponsoring editor at Houghton Mifflin, traveled to a technology conference to get acquainted with me and encourage me to create a proposal for this book. Her enthusiasm for my initial ideas about the natural connections between technology and literacy led to the basic contents of the book. Merryl Maleska Wilbur became the development editor of the project. Though we never met in person, Merryl and I worked extremely well together, using e-mail, electronic attachments, and express snail mail, and we communicated through occasional phone conversations. Her strong support and outstanding grasp of content and organization made the writing and rewriting of this book very enjoyable experiences. Nancy Benjamin, my project editor, shepherded me through the final stages of the book's production, and Bryna Fischer made many helpful suggestions during copyediting. From the beginning to the end of production, Lisa Mafrici, senior development editor for education, guided the book's development and gave thoughtful help and support. I give many thanks to these fine, highly professional people.

During a sabbatical leave from the University of Arizona, I visited schools in southern Arizona to observe firsthand how teachers were using technology in their classrooms. During these visits I saw many creative strategies being employed—sometimes with very limited resources—and I have made note of some of them in this book. Later, as chair of the International Reading Association's Technology, Communications, and Literacy Committee for three years, I interacted with scores of literacy teachers and learned about their authentic projects involving technology and literacy. In some cases, you will read their personal accounts in this book; in other cases I have described their exciting projects for you. Many thanks to all of the terrific educators whose words and ideas appear in this book and on this book's web site.

I want to give a very special thanks to Dr. Marian Stauffer Langerak for permitting me to quote heavily and to reprise ideas from Dr. Russell G. Stauffer's classic work, *Teaching Reading as a Thinking Process.* This seminal work has inspired countless literacy educators to help students learn to be critical, thoughtful, self-directed readers. His ideas and strategies for helping students become intelligent, self-reliant readers have never been more important than they are in today's high-tech communications world.

Thanks to the Instructional Technology Facility staff—Rich Frost, Brian Grove, Michael McVey, J. David Betts, and Carol Karlen—who supported my work, as well as Daylene Moss, who provided essential clerical assistance. Thanks also to the faculty and students in the Department of Language, Reading, and Culture who offered suggestions and acted as sounding boards for some of my ideas. In addition, I would like to acknowledge the following reviewers who contributed ideas to strengthen the book: Gloria Antifaiff, Qu'Appelle Valley Shared Services, Regina, Canada; Jay Blanchard, Arizona State University; Karla Broadus, University of Texas, San Antonio; Gwen McAlpine, University of West Georgia; Daniel Matthews, University of Illinois at Springfield; Susan Tancock, Ball State University; and Paul Zimmer, University of West Georgia.

Last, but definitely not least, my deep thanks to my extraordinary wife, Sharon Hale Valmont, for her loving support and encouragement throughout the project and to our wonderful children and grandchildren.

CHAPTER 1

Contexts for Literacy and Technology Interactions in Your Classroom

INTRODUCTION

Definitions of what it means to be literate change as technological developments alter how communications are delivered. Traditionally, literacy has referred to the ability to read and write. But today, a new type of literacy is developing. People must become **telecommunications literate.** Individuals who can quickly locate, collate, analyze, and act upon electronic messages, as well as construct new ideas and electronic messages, exemplify the newest literate people of the world. Telecommunications literacy implies much more than the ability to operate a computer and its ancillary technologies (e.g., printers, modems, power supplies, and so forth). Rather, telecommunications-literate people can use the unique features of digital technologies both to construct meaning for themselves and to create communications for others. People who lack these abilities will be telecommunications illiterate.

Constructing meaning as you read printed words alone is quite different from constructing meaning as you interact with multimedia, from which you construct meaning not only from words but also from graphics, photographs, animations, audio, and video almost simultaneously. Historically, according to McKenzie (1999),

> we tended to equate literacy with reading text, but a multimedia world requires more than a dozen literacies. If we expect students to convert information into value, they must be able to interpret data in many different formats, whether it be photographs, charts, paintings, spreadsheets, or video clips. (p. 32)

To be literate as we discuss it in this book includes having the ability to use effectively any of the body's senses for the reception, interpretation, and construction of meaning for oneself and others.

Major developments in communications technology have created a tremendous potential for helping more people than ever become literate. At the same time, new communications technologies will leave behind those people who fail to—or cannot—take advantage of such developments. Students who use the new technologies effectively will be the new literacy "haves," while those do not will be literacy "have-nots." As educators, we must be prepared to help all students become proficient in using advanced technologies in their development of literacy and thinking capabilities. In other words, we must do all we can to help our students become telecommunications literate. The goal of this book is to help elementary and middle school educators do so.

Change is ongoing, and you should not feel overpowered by it. Chances are you know a great deal about helping students develop traditional literacy capabilities. With a bit of effort, you can take steps today to help students learn to use technology to improve their ability to (1) locate messages quickly and efficiently, (2) use messages thoughtfully, and (3) construct verbal and nonverbal messages productively and creatively.

The Literacy-Technology Connection

Telecommunications instruments send multiple, complex messages.

Technology, in the broadest meaning of the word, enables literacy through its ability to communicate messages. Today's telecommunications instruments are capable of rapidly sending multiple, complex messages, but earlier instruments that permitted the delivery of messages could not. We need to consider how a given technology's capabilities impact literacy.

THE NEW TECHNOLOGIES

People sometimes use the word *technology* in a broad sense to mean the use of any device, manufactured or not, that permits one person to communicate with other people. This definition of technology incorporates the ability of a society to apply its current body of knowledge to fashion many kinds of instruments for communicating. Communication is the cornerstone of teaching and learning, and it is the foundation on which literacy rests. Using this broad definition, we realize that people have used technology to communicate since ancient times. They scraped symbols in the earth with sticks (primitive technology) and scratched drawings on cave walls with stones (also primitive). Clay tablets, tree bark, rag paper, quill pens, pencils, ballpoint pens, chalk, slate boards, typewriters, and books are just some of the older technologies teachers have used to communicate with students. Some of these technologies, such as printing and photography, made teaching and learning possible for the masses; other such technologies have emerged over time. Instructional materials became abundant and more beautiful. More important, they became inexpensive enough that many people could afford them. Schools purchased books and, later, films, sound and video recordings, and other ancillary materials and technologies (such as overhead projectors) to aid teaching and learning. Today, when we hear someone say "technology," we likely think of computer technology because computers connected to the Internet have made a major impact on our ability to communicate with one another. *In this book, we generally use the term* **technology** *to mean computers and the technologies that enable the Internet and World Wide Web (WWW).*

People want to believe that printed books will be around for a long time, but even today there are massive movements by governments, libraries, universities, businesses, school districts, book publishers, and others to make materials that were once available only in print form into digitized materials that will be widely available only electronically. Therefore, it is imperative for students to understand electronic materials. We need to help students recognize that **e-materials** (various electronically based materials) have features that print materials lack. Most notably, electronic materials can almost instantly and simultaneously present sounds, animations, line graphics, photos, and video, as well as text, to computer users. Furthermore, electronic materials, through hyperlinks, can be interactive; that is, the user can choose the order in which he or she looks at parts of the information or even how much information to access. Students must understand the unique features of the new technologies to profit from using them.

E-materials have features that print materials do not possess.

Recent technology has made communicating easier and faster than ever before. People talk on their cellular phones (often annoying those around them), work or play at their computers, and use the World Wide Web for business or pleasure. The stimulation of all of our human receptive systems (seeing, hearing, tasting, touching, and smelling) will increase as new technologies emerge. For instance, people are developing electronically triggered e-mail perfume ads that you can smell (Milner, 2000), and virtual reality systems that mimic "real reality" are being refined.

New technologies are being tested today that will redefine what literacy will mean in the foreseeable future. For example, people are developing electronic paper that can be updated instantly, and Microsoft's recent advances in the appearance of electronic print makes reading digitized e-books a different reading experience. People can quickly reformat text in a variety of ways. Even some clothes may soon have built-in sound, text, and graphics. Change is a reality, and we must realize that as the technology of literacy changes, we must help students intelligently deal with those changes.

A NEW LOOK AT LITERACY

It is difficult to determine precisely how literacy will continue to change because new, digital technologies are changing very rapidly. We can think about some of the physical, psychological, and social contexts of the changing nature of literacy, however. For example, physical interactions with electronic communications tools are needed to manipulate hypertext. Psychological forces are at work when you instantaneously deal with multiple sign systems. The international social contexts of literacy come into play because of the ease of telecommunicating with people anywhere they are. New developments will continue to impact literacy in the future.

Visual literacy and media literacy are important for students to learn today.

Educators are now beginning to recognize the importance of **visual literacy,** which is the ability to identify and interpret visual messages as well as construct visual messages. In fact, **media literacy,** the ability to interpret and construct in multiple communications formats (e.g., video, music, art) is becoming more critical as people are bombarded with ideas in news, entertainment, and instructional formats.

In this book you will learn that developing literacy capabilities is much more than helping students read from books and other materials printed on paper. Reading print is only one kind of literacy, and in view of the various ways people can receive and construct messages today, it is a limited kind of literacy.

EVOLVING LITERACY CONVENTIONS

Technology and literacy have a history of being linked together because as technologies change, so does the nature of reading. Clearly, a technology's properties influence how we construct meaning. For instance, a hundred or more years ago students used a **hornbook,** a primer consisting of a sheet of paper or parchment covered by a sheet of transparent horn. Hornbook technology delivered few messages. Computers, on the other hand, can deliver huge amounts of multimedia messages. As we will discuss below, one recent development, called **hypertext,** permits instantaneous access to new information. The ability to rapidly access various formats of information almost simultaneously influences comprehension. International access is influencing the content and context of literacy, and the independent use of technology is bringing about new responsibilities for learners to act with critical thinking abilities.

Hypertext

You can read electronic materials from the beginning to the end of a passage—just the way you probably do with print on paper. However, when you click on specially coded words or graphics in electronic text, you can instantly access (be linked to) a different portion of verbal text, sound, or visual material located elsewhere in the same document, on another web site, or in another file. You can choose to *ignore* all or some of the links you see, *click on* all or some links, or—when those links have other links *move elsewhere* completely away from the original text. Using (or not using) hypertext gives you, the reader, active control over the way you act upon electronic materials. An analogous behavior when reading printed text occurs when you stop reading to look up a word in the glossary or skip backward or forward looking for some information related to the current portion of text.

Hypertext enables students to have active control over visual and verbal messages.

Temporal Contiguity

The speed and ease of linking to other texts or searching through electronic materials are unique features of electronic materials that affect comprehension, the heart of literacy. **Temporal** means "time" and **contiguity** means "proximity." **Temporal contiguity** means observing two or more things together at nearly the same time. The speed with which you are able to juxtapose two or more pieces of electronic information influences the likelihood of making and understanding connections between (or among) them.

You can make available information in electronic formats to enhance students' capabilities to profit from temporal contiguity. For instance, you can have students examine two web sites simultaneously by opening two web browsers and letting students compare information about a topic. You can create links to other web sites that can help students make meaningful connections of ideas as they rapidly visit one site after another. Fast access to—and control over—electronic materials can influence comprehension.

Reacting to Multiple Texts at Once

With today's technologies, students may process multiple "texts" at once.

When information is presented in a multimedia format, students react to multiple sign systems almost simultaneously. It was no accident that silent movies were accompanied by piano music in order to add **affective** (emotional) layers of meaning to the written words and physical actions shown on movie screens. Audiences constructed meaning evoked by the music and had no trouble sensing danger or excitement, interpreting love scenes, and so forth. The music sign system enhanced the movie's visual action and written messages, and it evoked additional meaning in people's minds. Creators of online electronic materials are increasingly making use of all of the features of multimedia to generate ideas in multiple formats, and students are learning to comprehend these complex multifaceted presentations. Creating meaning while attending to simultaneous verbal and nonverbal polysymbolic messages is now affecting literacy.

Changes in the Context of Literacy

Historically, most students dealt mainly with materials created in their own cultural milieu. Additionally, the content was generally about their society or country. Now, partially because students can send and receive communications internationally, the context of literacy is changing: the context is now global. You and students in all grades can access information from around the world in many languages. You can hear, online, words spoken in other languages; you can compare online newspapers written in yours and another language; and you can study graphic images to determine whether pictures, illustrations, or other graphics convey different slants on the news. You can also analyze art and artifacts from other cultures. Daily literacy events are now possible on a global level.

Computer programs permit you to translate a web page written in one of several languages into your own language; likewise, students in other countries can translate your web page into their language using online translation engines. Students can even communicate person-to-person with students from other cultures via these online translation engines, and this changes the context of literacy. Figure 1.1, for instance, shows my home page as translated into French by a translation engine. While the translation is not 100 percent perfect, native French speakers could learn things about me from reading the page in their own language.

Learner Responsibility for Constructing Meaning

The amount of information available today is mind boggling! There is too much information for teachers, librarians, professional organizations, or

FIGURE 1.1

Valmont's Web Page in French

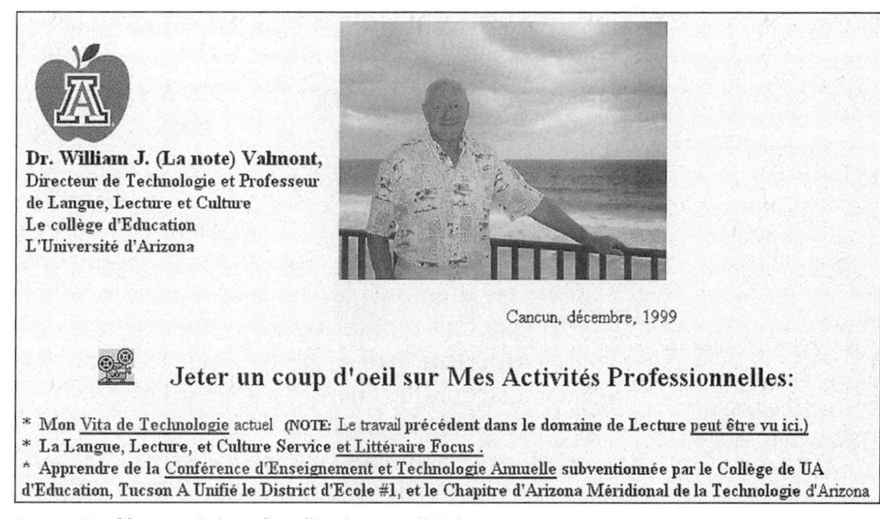

publishers to screen, let alone know about in depth. The amount of information—good and bad—on the Internet is far more extensive than predicted, and it is growing tremendously as more nations put materials online. The bad news is that anyone can place any materials on the Internet and the WWW. But that is also the good news, because despite the reluctance of traditional information gatekeepers (e.g., governments, publishers) to give up their ability to shape and screen materials for people, you and students can readily publish on the Web.

Students must learn to make careful, intelligent choices and decisions about information.

Technology makes more sources of information possible, and therefore making critical decisions about content of information on the Internet and WWW is extremely important. Students *must* develop learning strategies to enable them to make the most intelligent choices and decisions about information they encounter. This calls for you to introduce strategies to help students be selective, critical, and intelligent consumers of the resources available electronically. You cannot be the gatekeeper of knowledge for students. In and out of school, *they* must be responsible for their interactions with electronic materials. Students today must be intellectually critical of everything they encounter online, become skilled in using a variety of resources to verify or refute ideas, and act wisely using self-directed strategies.

Fortunately, there are a number of well-respected, time-tested literacy strategies such as the Directed Reading-Thinking Activity (DRTA), K-W-L (see page 106), and scaffolding, to name a few, that can help students learn to be more self-directed, critical readers and thinkers. Effective strategies can help students locate, evaluate, and use evidence, make predictions as they set purposes, and determine how well they comprehend when engaged in literacy activities. The DRTA and related strategies are described in several places throughout this book. (See chapters 4, 7, and 8.) Because students can spend so much time independently using computers and the Internet, because traditional ways of screening or validating information are not followed by all Internet authors, and because new literacy strategies are emerging as technology evolves, students need to assume responsibility for their own learning, and you can help them learn to do so.

A polysymbolic learning environment promotes a strong literacy-technology connection.

To conclude, computers, the Internet, and the World Wide Web have led to the creation of a polysymbolic learning environment that affects literacy instruction. There is a strong literacy-technology connection, particularly when we think of literacy as the ability to read and listen to the verbal, language-based alphabetic symbolic world as well as the ability to interpret signs, signals, and codes within other, nonverbal symbolic literacy worlds. Likewise, the literacy-technology connection is strong when we think of literacy as including not only writing and speaking but also constructing meaning for others using multiple sign systems. Tremendous technology is built into today's communications devices and systems, and the possibilities for teaching and learning are vast. The next part of this chapter suggests ways you can use some technology resources today in the teaching and learning of literacy.

Using Literacy-Technology Connections in Your Teaching Today

In an interview (Norman, 2000), Don Tapscott, author of *Growing Up Digital: The Rise of the Net,* noted:

> In schools today, kids know more than their teachers about the most powerful learning invention of all time. This is the first generation to grow up interacting with media rather than simply being broadcast to. Because children are authorities on digital technology, things are different. Our wired kids are no longer interested in an education model that has teachers simply being factoid fountains at the front of the class. (p. 50)

The advent of computers and of students who quickly learned to use them in and out of school ushered in several changes in the teaching and learning strategies used by many teachers. For one thing, teachers increased the

Constructivism and collaboration work well in technologically rich environments.

amount of time that students worked together in collaborative groups. Students working around a limited number of computers made cooperation imperative. Also, teachers capitalized on the intrinsic motivation exhibited by students pursuing their own interests online by increasing the use of inquiry strategies. In addition, **constructivism** gained in popularity. Constructivism is based on the idea that "meaningful learning occurs when people actively try to make sense of the world—when they construct an interpretation of how and why things are—by filtering new ideas and experiences through existing knowledge structures" (Snowman & Biehler, 2000, p. 291). Learn more about constructivism on this book's web site.

If you are new to using technology for literacy teaching and learning, you can start by exploring the web sites referenced in this chapter. If you already use computers, software, and the Internet (including the Web), you may learn about some useful sites you have not already encountered. Sites listed below are grouped to help you become familiar with certain things you can learn and do.

- You can learn to conduct efficient searches using metasearch engines.
- You can learn the language of the Internet and Web to help you communicate with students, and you can explore online technology glossaries to get up to speed with **techspeak** (sometimes called geekspeak), meaning the use of esoteric technology-related terms.
- You can use online teaching ideas and lessons, usually by adapting them to your own school context and classroom needs. Teachers, as well as libraries, institutions of higher education, and publishers, have placed many fine ideas and lessons online.
- You can guide students to fun online resources that can help them pursue their interests while engaging in literacy learning experiences.
- You can get support and advice about teaching and learning. You can go online and network with other teachers and access the opinions of experts.
- You and students can work with teachers and other students almost anywhere in the world by engaging in **telecollaborative** activities.
- You can help students publish original works online.
- You can learn how to find, evaluate, and use software effectively. You can visit several web sites, commercial and noncommercial in nature, to learn about specific software products and to read reviews of current software.
- You can locate web sites for parents that will engage them in your literacy efforts and introduce them to other resources they can use at home.
- You can enhance your professional knowledge when you access online professional sites to learn about teaching practices, research, and activities. Information produced by organizations interested in literacy can provide valuable support as you integrate literacy instruction and technology.

METASEARCH ENGINES

Learning about web sites and software will help you promote technology in school.

You and students will need to find things on the WWW quickly because instructional time is fleeting; ineffective surfing of the Internet just to see where the trail leads can be a major waste of time. Fortunately, web pioneers realized that systems for finding information had to be developed, so **search engines** were created to help people locate web sites more efficiently. To use a search engine, you type in one or more keywords central to your quest for information, and the search engine locates matches for those words and reports the findings to you. Search engines can find the titles, **Uniform Resource Locators** (**URLs**), and **headers** (coded identification information placed at the top of web pages) of sites, or they can search the full text of a web page. The parts of a URL are described on this book's web site.

Newer **metasearch engines** (also called metacrawlers) are designed to search several other search engines in parallel and report results from each of those engines, thereby giving you more information. Experiment with several metasearch engines to determine which ones you prefer. Also, if you do not get results with one metasearch engine, try another. The World Wide Web is extremely large, and no single metasearch engine contacts all of the web servers in the world. Here are some to try.

WEBLIOGRAPHY

- **Beaucoup!**
  http://www.beaucoup.com/1metaeng.html
  This metasearch engine searches ten other engines at once and reports back each one's findings. More than twenty other search engines are linked from this site (e.g., WebCrawler, Dogpile).

- **Langenberg.com**
  http://www.langenberg.com/
  At this amazing site you can locate people and businesses in the white pages and in the yellow pages. You can conduct metasearches of the WWW and dazzle students by translating a web page into English, French, German, Dutch, Danish, Spanish, Finnish, Czech, Italian, or Portuguese. When you engage in collaborative projects with students in countries who speak those languages, you can work in English, and they can read your web site in their own language.

- **ProFusion**
  http://www.profusion.com/
  This powerful metasearch engine site contains tips for conducting searches of the World Wide Web. It reports results from nine other search engines. We used ProFusion to locate most of the web sites we list in this book and on its web site.

ONLINE TECHNOLOGY GLOSSARIES

Years ago, several literacy textbooks contained lists of "survival words" that the authors thought everyone should be able to read in order to function in society. *Explosives, danger, poison,* and similar words were on such lists. Technology has spawned a huge new vocabulary. You and students will encounter computer terminology that you might not understand and need to have defined. You can use online references to learn about *cybersquatters, lurkers, transit spam,* and other recent terms. Online glossaries act as models for electronic glossaries you and students might create. Technology terms are the new survival words of today and tomorrow.

WEBLIOGRAPHY

- **FOLDOC (The Free Online Dictionary of Computing)**
  http://foldoc.doc.ic.ac.uk/foldoc/index.html
  You can type in a word inspired by technology and learn its meaning, making this a very fast resource for defining terms.
- **Internet & Technology Terms**
  http://www.ed.arizona.edu/lrc320/A_vocabulary/vocab2/vocab.htm
  Using frames, you click on a term and instantly see its definition.
- **NetLingo**
  http://www.netlingo.com
  You can find concise definitions for technology terms at this site.
- **Webopaedia**
  http://www.webopaedia.com/
  This is an online dictionary and search engine about computers and Internet technology. You can read and discuss the "Term of the Day" on a routine basis.

FINDING TEACHING IDEAS AND LESSONS

Many excellent lessons and suggestions to foster literacy exist on the World Wide Web.

Because you and students can access information and communicate with people around the world, you can engage in recently developed strategies that make use of telecommunications. WebQuests (see page 43), scavenger hunts, e-pal exchanges, and chats are just a few online activities in which you and students can participate. Gigabytes of online information about these strategies already exist because educators have placed a multitude of lessons and lesson plans on web sites. Some online activities can be used intact; others will give you ideas for creating your own. It is a little-applauded fact that classroom teachers, librarians, professors, and others often share their ideas freely to help teachers make instruction valuable and fun for K–adult students. Educators seem to have a natural desire to help others, and nowhere is that more clear than online, where so many creative teaching ideas are emerging. Below are a few sites. Hundreds of other sites that should be helpful to you in your teaching are identified elsewhere in this book and on its web site.

WEBLIOGRAPHY

- **A to Z Teacher Stuff**
  http://www.atozteacherstuff.com/
  This web site contains more than 1,000 pages of resources and lesson ideas. You can submit your own lesson ideas to this site.
- **ERIC Clearinghouse on Reading, English, and Communication**
  http://www.indiana.edu/~eric_rec/
  The Educational Resources Information Center (ERIC) is a major source of information for literacy educators that has articles, links to other educational sites, and many lesson plan ideas.
- **The Gateway to Educational Materials**
  http://www.thegateway.org/
  At this web site you can search for lesson plans and resources by grade level, subject, keyword, or title. After you complete a search, you will see a list of activities. Click on one to learn about its creation, or click on the title to see the actual lesson.
- **LessonPlanZ.com**
  http://lessonplanz.com/
  You can view more than 3,000 K–12 lesson plans at this site, which includes a breakdown of language arts lessons by grade level. There are also lessons incorporating songs and poetry.

- **K–12 Schools on the Web**
  http://www.tenet.edu/education/exemplary.html
  This site links to several school sites and explains why those sites are effective.

- **The Miss Rumphius Award**
  http://www.reading.org/awards/rumphius.html
  Members of the RTEACHER mailing list (see page 23) nominate exceptional sites that are noncommercial and have been created by educators. Figure 1.2 shows links to class or school web pages that have received the award. Technology expert Donald Leu, creator of the RTEACHER listserv, also originated this award.

FIGURE 1.2

The Miss Rumphius Award

Source: Screenshot reprinted by permission of The International Reading Association and Donald Leu. All rights reserved.

- **Mrs. Silverman's Webfolio**
  http://www.kids-learn.org
  Susan Silverman won a regional award in the International Reading Association's Presidential Award for Literacy and Technology, 1999, for her project titled "Winter Wonderland: A Thematic Literature Collaborative Internet." You will find many excellent examples of collaborative projects at this site.

- **Teachers.Net**
  http://teachers.net/
  This site contains numerous references and links. You can find lesson plans, chat with other teachers, and seek help.

- **Web66: International School Web Site Registry**
  http://web66.coled.umn.edu/schools.html
  From this site you can link to school web sites throughout the United States, as well as to sites in Australia, Canada, Europe, Japan, and elsewhere. Register your school's web site and use the directory to find schools with which you would like to work collaboratively.

FINDING FUN ACTIVITIES FOR STUDENT LEARNING

Students can find intrinsically interesting literacy activities online.

A variety of online materials exist that introduce students to fun and educational activities. You can tie these sites to communication and literacy activities and help students make the most of the free resources available online. Here are just a few sites we think are useful.

WEBLIOGRAPHY

- **AwesomeCards.com**
  http://www.marlo.com/
  Students, who often lack money to purchase printed cards, can send electronic cards to relatives and friends for birthdays or holidays. Model social graces for students by sending them personalized e-cards on special occasions.
- **Discovery Channel Online**
  http://www.discovery.com/
  This site contains information about the Discovery Channel, as well as news and features. It has hundreds of interesting topics to discuss, write about, or use in constructing electronic messages.
- **Map Machine**
  http://plasma.nationalgeographic.com/mapmachine/
  You can see enhanced satellite views of various areas of Earth. Type in your city and see a view of the area. Students can locate their community and neighboring towns at this site or see where their e-pals live.
- **Marshall Brain's HowStuffWorks**
  http://www.howstuffworks.com/
  Students will be able to use this site to learn about many things of interest to them. Descriptions and illustrations make this a valuable source of information.
- **Scholastic News Zone**
  http://teacher.scholastic.com/newszone/index.asp
  At this site, students can find recent news and features about various events, such as the very popular Iditarod dogsled race.

- Weekly Reader Galaxy
  http://www.weeklyreader.com/
  The site contains activities similar to those in the popular school magazine. There are sections for students, teachers, and parents. Teachers can print classroom calendars and read short articles about teaching. Students can try to figure out a mystery sound or photo, participate in a poll, or find out how well they know current events. (See Figure 1.3.)

FIGURE 1.3

Weekly Reader Galaxy

Source: Screenshot reprinted by permission of Weekly Reader Corporation.

- YAHOO! Acronyms and Abbreviations
  http://dir.yahoo.com/Reference/Acronyms_and_Abbreviations/
  This is a major reference site that links you to sources of acronym definitions. If you think there are too many TLAs (three-letter acronyms), you are probably right.

GETTING SUPPORT FROM ONLINE RESOURCES

You can communicate with people through e-mail or chats, read articles, and learn how to integrate technology into the countless lessons you can find online. Take advantage of the abundance of ideas that were created by educators, students, and others interested in helping students gain literacy capabilities.

WEBLIOGRAPHY

- 700+ Great Sites
  http://www.ala.org/parentspage/greatsites/amazing.html
  Compiled by the Children and Technology Committee of the Association for Library Service to Children, a division of the American Library Association, this site includes links to literature and language sites.

- AskERIC
  http://ericir.syr.edu/
  Ask questions, submit lesson plans, and read lesson plans at this site, which is produced by the Educational Information Resources Center.

- Bobby
  http://www.cast.org/bobby/
  Run by the Center for Applied Special Technology (CAST), this site lets you check other web sites online or download free software to analyze sites and determine their accessibility to people with disabilities. You should ensure that any web pages you and students create are as accessible as possible, not only because of legal considerations but because features recommended by CAST are educationally sound for all students. (See Figure 1.4.)

FIGURE 1.4

Bobby Screen Capture

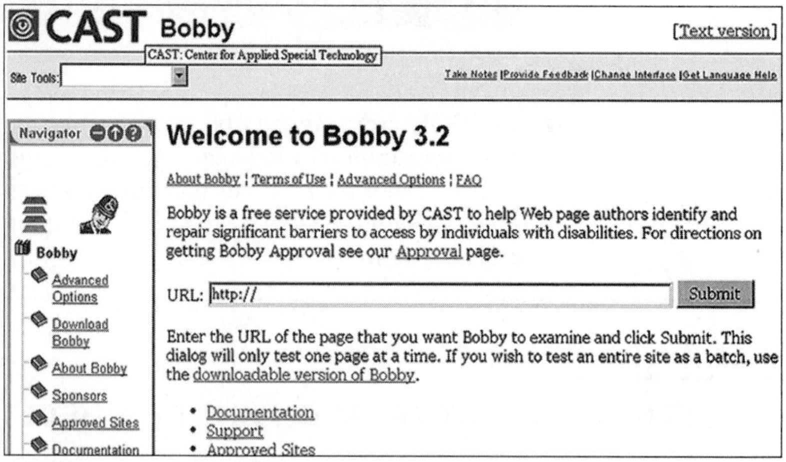

Source: Screenshot reprinted by permission 1999–2000 from CAST. All rights reserved.

- Education World
  http://www.education-world.com
  This is a huge, comprehensive database of education links. There are countless archived lessons and activity ideas for teaching and learning language arts and literature.

- **Hot Potatoes Half-Baked Software (University of Victoria Language Centre)**
  http://web.uvic.ca/hrd/halfbaked/
  Download the freeware Hot Potatoes suite, which includes applications (computer programs) that help you create multiple-choice, short-answer, jumbled-sentence, crossword, matching, ordering, and gap-fill exercises to place on the Internet.

- **Kathy Schrock's Guide for Educators**
  http://school.discovery.com/schrockguide/index.html
  This highly acclaimed site offers a wealth of information for teachers interested in using technology in teaching. Ms. Schrock is the district technology department head for the Dennis-Yarmouth Regional School District, Cape Cod, Massachusetts.

- **KLICK! (Kids Learning in Computer Klubhouses)**
  http://www.klick.org/website/index.asp
  Supported by grants from the U.S. Department of Education and the C. S. Mott Foundation and coordinated by Michigan State University, this consortium of Michigan schools helps teachers design online projects. Register as a guest.

- **Teacher Zone**
  http://www.techtv.com/callforhelp/teacherzone/
  Learn a variety of ways to use technology in teaching. Short, informative articles deal with topics such as repetitive strain injury, safe surfing on the Internet, and essential software for teachers (e.g., virus protection, web filters).

USING TELECOLLABORATIVE LEARNING EXPERIENCES

Telecollaborative learning experiences enable communication and cultural exchanges.

Teachers often like to work with other teachers, and students often like to work with other students. Advances in telecommunications have made working with people who reside elsewhere in the world easy to accomplish. The value of communicating with students in other schools, states, or countries can be enormous. Worldwide communication can help people understand one another better, and students can learn about countries, cultures, and the similarities and differences among people. Sites exist that will help you plan telecollaborative projects and contact others to engage in such projects.

WEBLIOGRAPHY

- **Buddy Project**
  http://www.buddyproject.org/default.asp
  Sign up at this site to participate in collaborative projects around the world and to gain access to collaborative activities for students.

- **Cooperative Learning: Some Basics and Online Resources**
  http://atozteacherstuff.com/articles/cooperative.shtml
  This article, found on the previously mentioned A to Z Teacher Stuff web site, discusses some of the basics of cooperative learning, including suggestions for language arts collaborative activities.

- **Cyberkids**
  http://www.cyberkids.com/
  At this site, young students can interact with others, play games, get help with homework, and submit original art and stories for publication.

- **The Global Schoolhouse**
  http://www.gsn.org/
  Free membership lets you learn about a large number of worldwide collaborative projects. The "Professional Development" section tells how to make and find collaborative projects. Some activities require paid membership.

- **In the Kitchen—Designs for Telecollaboration and Telepresence**
  http://ccwf.cc.utexas.edu/~jbharris/Virtual-Architecture/Telecollaboration/
  Judi Harris defines and links to examples of three kinds of telecollaborative activities: (1) interpersonal exchanges, (2) information collection and analysis, and (3) problem-solving activities. (See page 39.)

- **KEYPALS**
  http://www.keypals.com/
  This site helps you find classrooms in other schools to communicate with about a variety of topics. You can arrange for your class to participate in activities. "Internet Safety Tips," at **http://www.epals.com/help/safety_en.html,** is worth studying and sharing with parents. The Keypals site identifies ways for teachers and students to communicate with others. Some of the sites that Keypals links to require teacher passwords to access.

HELPING STUDENTS PUBLISH ONLINE

It has become easier and easier to create materials and place them on a school or district web server. Word-processing software such as Microsoft Word and Corel WordPerfect allows you to create a document and save it in HTML format; you can then post the document to a web site that people can visit. Even kindergartners can become published authors! Just one site is given here because chapter 5 discusses using technology for writing activities.

WEBLIOGRAPHY

- **Incredible Story Studio**
  http://www.storystudio.com/
  Students can submit stories for publication at this site.

FINDING AND EVALUATING LANGUAGE ARTS SOFTWARE

You sometimes hear about new software from friends and other pre- or in-service teachers, or you might see ads in magazines or journals and want to learn more about a product. You can find information about, and reviews of, computer software products online. Also, if you want to contact a company, you can locate its snail mail address, e-mail address, or web site's URL. The sources listed here can help you quickly find and learn about software. You can learn more about software evaluation from Warren Buckleitner on this book's web site.

WWW

WEBLIOGRAPHY

- **Diskovery**
  http://www.diskovery.com/
  This is a site for locating software by title or publisher using a search engine. You can compare price quotes at this site with those at Amazon.com (a major online store).
- **Kids Domain**
  http://www.kidsdomain.com/
  This site contains brief reviews and articles about educational software programs. An alphabetical listing of software reviews appears also, and you can

WEBLIOGRAPHY (continued)

check indexes by age and subject matter. In addition, you can download some free shareware.

- **Nerd's Heaven: The Software Directory Directory**
  http://boole.stanford.edu/nerdsheaven.html
  This site is a major source of information about dozens of computer software directories on the Web.

- **SoftSearch**
  http://www.softsearch.com/
  This site, which bills itself as the "world's largest software database," is extremely helpful for finding software products and company information. You get contact information (i.e., mailing address, e-mail address, and a URL) and a listing of a company's products. You can also read about a product's features.

- **Software and Information Industry Association**
  http://www.siia.net/
  This group tracks software piracy worldwide and instigates legal action against software thieves. You and students need to know the consequences of illegal copying.

SOFTWARE TO ENHANCE LITERACY

It is most important to learn about and evaluate software for use in literacy instruction.

At the end of most of the chapters in this book, we have included references to some pertinent software you may wish to examine and possibly have students use during literacy learning experiences. Listed here are several general reference software programs that you can use in a wide range of classrooms. We also list the publisher and recommended grade levels.

American Heritage Children's Dictionary	Houghton Mifflin Interactive	2–6
Compton's Encyclopedia 2000 Deluxe	Compton's/Mattel Interactive	K–8
Compton's Interactive World Atlas	The Learning Company	3–12
Encarta	Microsoft	5–12
Encyclopedia Britannica Multimedia Edition	Encyclopedia Britannica	4–12
Eyewitness Children's Encyclopedia	DK Family Learning, Inc.	2–6
Grolier Multimedia Encyclopedia 2000 Deluxe	Grolier Interactive, Inc.	5–12
Ultimate Children's Encyclopedia	The Learning Company	2–6
2000 World Book Reference Suite	World Book	4–12

When considering the use or purchase of any software, you should enlist other teachers, librarians, and technology personnel to help evaluate their features. School purchasing policies must apply, also. Some publishers provide preview copies or demonstration disks you can have students try in your effort to evaluate the software.

WEB SITES FOR PARENTS

As a teacher, you encourage parents and guardians to read to students, take them to the library, and buy them books. Most caregivers *want* to help children do well in school. You can enlist their aid in supporting your efforts to integrate technology and literacy activities by helping them (1) understand what you are trying to accomplish, (2) learn to be comfortable online themselves, and (3) learn about resources they and their children can use. In chapter 9, "Using Technology with Children's Literature," you will find dozens of web sites to share with parents and guardians. We suggest that you routinely share many of the fine educational things you find online with parents and make software recommendations to them that support your classroom literacy experiences.

WEBLIOGRAPHY

- **Berit's Best Sites for Children**
  http://www.beritsbest.com
  This site presents more than 1,000 sites divided into categories such as "Just for Fun," "Holidays," "Serious Stuff," and "Creatures Great and Small."
- GetNetWise
  http://www.getnetwise.org/
  Parents (and teachers) will find this to be a helpful site for becoming more sophisticated about being on the Internet.
- **Kids Domain Review: Internet Safety**
  http://www.kidsdomain.com/review/features/safety.html
  The article at this site offers Internet safety advice for parents, including information about software programs that block access to web sites that parents may not want their children to visit.
- **The LYCOS 50 Daily Report**
  http://50.lycos.com/
  Links to the fifty most popular sites for the week are listed at this site. Parents can see what is popular with young people and decide which sites their

WEBLIOGRAPHY (continued)

own children may visit. Sites dedicated to popular stars and singers, holidays, sports and athletes, as well as books and authors are often on the list.

- **Thinking Critically about World Wide Web Resources**
  http://www.library.ucla.edu/libraries/college/help/critical/index.htm
  This is a primer of awareness factors to consider when using the WWW. It links to a related site, "Thinking Critically about Discipline-Based World Wide Web Resources." These sites are both sponsored by the UCLA college library.

PROFESSIONAL ASSOCIATIONS

Professional organizations have valuable online resources for you to use.

Below are some of the professional associations that deal with literacy and have an online presence. These organizations provide valuable online support and information not only to their members, but also to anyone interested in helping students learn to be literate.

WEBLIOGRAPHY

- **American Library Association** (ALA)
  http://www.ala.org/
  This is the professional organization's main web site. You can read about ALA's conferences, activities, and membership services. Various news releases and articles are also available.
- **The International Reading Association** (IRA)
  http://www.reading.org/
  IRA is the prime professional organization for dealing with the many facets of literacy. More than 72,000 individuals worldwide are members of IRA, which promotes research and disseminates information about literacy in its publications and conferences. IRA cosponsors, with The Learning Company, the IRA Presidential Award for Reading and Technology, which is presented at its annual convention. You can learn about the award at **http://www.reading.org/awards/awardtech.html.**
- **International Society for Technology in Education** (ISTE)
  http://iste.org/
  The organization's web site contains articles from *Learning & Leading with Technology,* a journal that contains many practical ideas and suggestions across the curriculum. ISTE is a leader in developing national technology standards and showing teachers how to integrate technology with all subject areas.

- The National Council of Teachers of English (NCTE)
  http://www.ncte.org/
  This site is aimed at teachers of students of all ages (K–college), and contains resources, articles, and also a section specifically for new teachers.
- Read Across America
  http://www.nea.org/readacross/index.html
  You can learn how to participate in the National Education Association's annual Read Across America event at this site. NEA also co-sponsors the National School Boards Association's annual technology learning conference that you can learn about at the organization's home page, **http://www.nea.org/**.
- Reading Online
  http://www.readingonline.org/
  Reading Online (see Figure 1.5) is the major electronic publication of the International Reading Association. You can read articles to learn about what practicing teachers are doing with technology in the "Electronic Classroom" section of the journal. That section also contains helpful "Web Watch" feature articles to increase your knowledge of web resources.

FIGURE 1.5
Reading Online Screen Capture

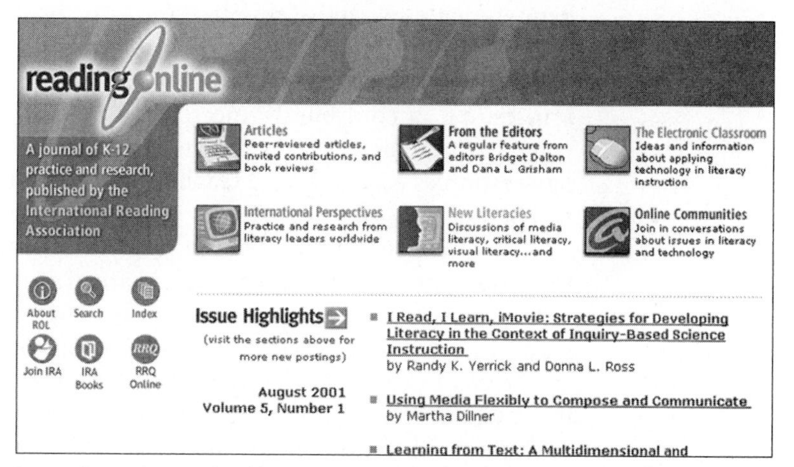

Source: Screenshot reprinted by permission of The International Reading Association.

- RTEACHER
  http://www.reading.org/publications/rt/rt_listserv.html
  RTEACHER is the mailing list for the International Reading Association's journal *The Reading Teacher*; sign up at this site. Readers of *Reading Teacher* use this Listserv to share ideas and educational strategies and otherwise support one another. You can read the comments, even if you do not read the journal.

Using Technology to Help Students Succeed

As you read this chapter, you probably came to the realization that you do not have to wait for special training to integrate technology into your strategies for helping students develop literacy capabilities. You might just need to know how to get started. Often teachers conduct needs assessments to determine what assets and liabilities are present that might affect their teaching. Carry out a technology assessment to determine the personal resources, hardware, and software available as well as the support you already have in integrating technology into your literacy-building activities (Thurlow, 2000). Start with a strong commitment to learning about and using technology with students as they develop literacy capabilities. Consider what you already know and what you need to learn in order to improve your knowledge of technology. Take stock of the hardware and software available to you at home and school. Also consider the support you may be able to get from the community, your district or school, family members, friends, and students to improve the use of technology for instruction (Thurlow, 2000). After finishing your assessment, help students use those resources already available and take steps to get whatever additional tools you need. If you have just one networked computer with a CD-ROM and a way to let groups of students see computer images (e.g., a computer projector or a hookup to a television monitor), you can immediately take advantage of many of the literacy and technology resources as well as the teaching and learning strategies described in this book.

Take advantage of the seemingly natural fascination with technology that young people have. Preschoolers are drawn not only to television and videos, but also to computer games, instructional CD-ROMs, and other software programs. Some students may have several years of experience and a great deal of knowledge about using computers, the WWW, and those CD-ROMs their parents have given them. Such students tend to like to share their computer and Internet knowledge with other people, so let them become your helpers and co-teachers.

Thematic units are helpful when integrating literacy and technology.

There is much for you to think about. Various technology leaders have recommended ways to integrate technology and learning experiences across content and across grade levels. One major instructional strategy involves developing broad thematic units with ample room within a given theme for creatively using technology to locate and share ideas and information with others in the class, school, or world. Some thoughts about using thematic units and an example of one well-designed unit appear in the final section of this chapter.

AN EXEMPLAR THEMATIC UNIT

The International Society for Technology in Education (ISTE) created a set of technology standards designed to guide teachers in the educational use of technology. (You will see them in chapter 3.) ISTE received funding to demonstrate how to integrate those technology standards into the daily learning experiences that students encounter every school day. In January 1999, a writing team gathered in Tempe, Arizona, and created sample thematic units for the book *National Educational Technology Standards for Students: Connecting Curriculum and Technology.* Beverly Chin from the University of Montana represented the National Council of Teachers of English (NCTE), and I represented the International Reading Association (IRA); our goal was to correlate the joint IRA/NCTE standards with the English language arts learning activities developed for this project. (The IRA/NCTE standards appear in chapter 3.) That experience helped me fully understand that standards, technology, and literacy learning can be naturally blended in effective ways. While all of the examples in the ISTE reference are excellent models, for this textbook we chose Figure 1.6: You Were There! because it is designed for intermediate-grade-level language arts. An examination of this unit should help you understand how you can create similar units for higher or lower grade levels. The unit is a fine example of the use of a common story structure element, **point of view (POV)**, which involves understanding something from various perspectives. POV is just one element that you can use to focus students' work while they integrate the use of technology into literacy activities.

As you examine the unit, think about or write responses to the following questions. You will need to consider these questions whenever you create thematic units of your own. In fact, to give yourself a sense of your growth in knowledge, it would be beneficial for you to revisit the questions after you have read this entire book.

1. What resources might you use to help determine the purpose for a thematic unit?
2. What is the value of creating a concise overview and description of a unit?
3. How would students' potential learning be affected if no technology were built into the unit? (In other words, how does technology allow students to do things they could not do without it?)
4. What additional uses of hardware, software, or the Internet, including the World Wide Web, do you see fitting within the unit?
5. Are ample opportunities for collaborative learning included?

FIGURE 1.6

An Exemplar Thematic Unit

You Were There!

English Language Arts

Intermediate Grades 3–5

Purpose

Students read for point of view (POV) as they study a historical fiction novel, original source documents, and other sources of information. Students produce both a written and visual account of an event that advances their own point of view.

Description

Note: Although the novel selected for this lesson sequence is appropriate for the fifth grade, consider examining the technology-related options to revise the sequence to fit a grade-designated core literature selection.

Using literature to enhance social studies units by adding personal stories is a way to hook students into understanding the point of view of people of a particular time. Students read about the Boston Massacre through the historical fiction novel *My Brother Sam Is Dead* by James and Christopher Collier, factual texts, and other documents related to the event. Students enjoy visiting Web sites to view actual documents from the period. After evaluating, analyzing, and synthesizing the information in the documents and sites, students (1) write an article for publication in a classroom political newspaper; (2) produce a multimedia eulogy for one of the Boston Massacre victims; and (3) develop and present a group video "on-the-scene" report of the Boston Massacre.

Activities	English Language Arts Standards	NETS Performance Indicators Grades 3–5
1. Begin this activity by reading together Chapter 1 in *My Brother Sam Is Dead* and discussing the characters' POV.	ELA 1, 6, 7, 8, 9, 11	1, 2, 3, 4
2. Assign or allow students to select a specific point of view of the incident. Investigate other accounts and documents at predetermined Web sites using each team's assigned POV.	ELA 2, 3, 7, 8	3, 6, 9, 10
3. Teams produce on-the-scene video accounts of the Boston Massacre. Either the "RBC" (Redcoat Broadcasting Company) or the "LTBC" (Liberty Tree Broadcasting Company) sponsors each group. As chair of the editorial review board, join board members (selected students) to screen all videos. The account should be from the POV of the reporter who represents the view selected for the group.	ELA 4, 5, 6, 8, 9, 11, 12	1, 4, 5, 9, 10
4. Have individual or groups of students produce a word-processed newspaper article that supports their political POV. Articles are to be published in one of two class newspapers: *Redcoat Daily Gazette* or *Liberty Tree Press.* The editorial review board will screen all articles.	ELA 4, 5, 6, 12	4, 5

	ENGLISH LANGUAGE ARTS STANDARDS	NETS PERFORMANCE INDICATORS GRADES 3–5
5 Students each draw the name of a massacre victim. Using multimedia software (e.g., HyperStudio, PowerPoint, or mPower), students develop several testimonials for their victim from the perspective of survivors who knew the victim well. Each stack should include the following: the victim's name, date of birth and death, image of the grave site (actual or student-visualized and -generated), drawing of the victim, and voice or text testimonials. At least one of the testimonials should be written from the POV of a surviving female (e.g., wife, sister, aunt) to help clarify the role of women in this event. The presentations can be part of a parent evening, shared with another classroom, or shared over the Internet with other students. (The violent nature of the deaths may be a concern to some students. The activity, however, should keep the focus on the humanness of each victim rather than how they died. The activity does involve violence, but when students see the victims as human beings like themselves and not as statistics, they are more likely to see violence for what it really is and less likely to glorify it.) Examples of researched information: *(1) Mr. Samuel Gray, killed on the spot by a ball entering his head; (2) Crispus Attucks, a mulatto, killed on the spot, two balls entering his breast; (3) Mr. James Caldwell, killed on the spot, by two balls entering his back; (4) Mr. Samuel Maverick, a youth of 17 years of age, mortally wounded; he died the next morning.*	ELA 4, 5, 6, 8, 12	1, 4, 5, 6, 9
6 Team members present their final products to various audiences (entire class, cross-grade-level classes, parents, interested community members).	ELA 4, 8, 11, 12	
7 Consider the following extensions:		
▸ E-mail with a class in the Boston area	ELA 8	
▸ Create a digital walking tour of grave sites	ELA 4, 7, 8	
▸ Do grave rubbings (be sure to get permission)		
▸ Create a market to exchange products	ELA 7	
▸ Write a song to a popular tune that tells the "real" story of the Boston Massacre	ELA 7	

Tools and Resources

SOFTWARE:

- Word-processing, multimedia-authoring, video-production

HARDWARE:

- At least one multimedia computer with audiovisual input-output capability, digital or analog video camcorder, presentation system

WEB SITES:

The Boston Massacre—A Behind-the-Scenes Look at Paul Revere's Most Famous Engraving:
www.earlyamerica.com/review/winter96/massacre.html

Anonymous Account of the Boston Massacre (background information, inflammatory first paragraph, list of the killed and wounded):
http://odur.let.rug.nl/~usa/D/1751-1775/bostonmassacre/anon.htm

FIGURE 1.6
(continued)

Find a Grave—Boston Massacre Victims (actual photos of grave sites):
www.findagrave.com/pictures/bostonmassacre.html
(select Crispus Attucks for a readable close-up image)

National History Day:
www.thehistorynet.com/NationalHistoryDay/
(The site changes from year to year depending on the topic of the History Day activities.)

Boston National Historical Park Virtual Visitor Center:
www.nps.gov/bost/home.htm

The Plumb Design Visual Thesaurus:
www.plumbdesign.com/thesaurus/
(Students can use online thesaurus to understand Web key concept words such as *massacre, patriotic,* and *loyal.*)

The Revolutionary War and Children's Literature (excellent activities and literature linked to the Revolutionary War):
www.carolhurst.com/subjects/ushistory/revolution.html

BOOK:

- Collier, J., & Collier, C. (1996). *My brother Sam is dead.* New York: Scholastic Inc.

Assessment

Evaluate individual student news articles based on a class-generated rubric that includes criteria such as: following the five W's and one H of a news article, writing from the POV of Loyalist or Patriot, and using period vocabulary. Create the rubric based on school or district guidelines, grade-level objectives for the lesson sequence, and a student assessment conducted at the start of the lesson sequence.

Evaluate student eulogies on a rubric. Criteria might include having a minimum number of cards or slides in a stack, design elements, ease of use, and including all elements required by the project.

Evaluate groups on their video production using a class-generated rubric that includes criteria such as clarity, creativity of the scene, and representing the perspective of the sponsoring agency.

Credits

Paula Conley, Coeur d'Alene District No. 271, Coeur d'Alene, Idaho
(pconley@sd271.k12.id.us)

Comments

I have used this unit in my classroom for several years. Infusing a required unit with technology never fails to produce highly motivated students. By the conclusion of these projects, the students understand the concepts of propaganda and point of view in historical events. The excitement generated by the activities even carries beyond the classroom walls: I have heard students planning and discussing their newspaper articles and videos out on the playground! History comes alive and the students are involved—a guarantee for success.

Source: Reprinted by permission from *National Educational Technology Standards for Students—Connecting Curriculum and Technology,* copyright © 2000, ISTE (International Society for Technology in Education), 800-336-5191 (U.S. & Canada) or 541-302-3777 (Int'l), iste@iste.org, www.iste.org. All rights reserved. Permission does not constitute an endorsement by ISTE. For more information about the NETS Project, contact Lajeane Thomas, Director, NETS Project, 318-257-3923, lthomas@latech.edu.

6. Is it likely that all students will find areas of the theme to explore that will be intrinsically interesting to them?
7. Are standards correctly correlated to the activities?
8. Do you agree with the choice of hardware and software suggested for the unit?
9. Do you agree that the web sites identified are appropriate to the unit?

We urge you to visit the web sites described in this book. Put into action the suggestions for using software, the Internet, and the WWW to help students increase all of their verbal and nonverbal literacy capabilities. Help students learn to construct effective electronic presentations of their ideas and to attend effectively to the presentations of other students. From classes, books, journals, and online sources, you are learning—or have already learned—many proven strategies to help students develop greater literacy capabilities. As you read the remainder of this book, tie in the suggested uses of technology to those strategies you already know and use. You should, with little trouble, be able to integrate technology and literacy development. You can use computers and other technologies today to help students learn and prepare for life tomorrow, outside school, so they become the telecommunications-literate people they must be to succeed both in school and in a polysymbolic world.

SUMMARY

- What it means to be a literate person has evolved over the centuries.
- Students need to become telecommunications literate.
- Technology that delivers communication influences what one must know and be able to use to be a literate person.
- Electronic materials have features that affect several aspects of comprehension.
- Tech-savvy students, cooperative learning strategies, and beliefs about constructivism have recently influenced classroom learning.
- Because unfiltered information is readily available, it is vitally important to help students become responsible learners and be thoughtful and critical of messages they encounter.
- A host of software and online literacy materials are available for you and students to use.
- Thematic units give you much leeway to integrate technology and literacy experiences.

ACTIVITIES

1. Use an online glossary to find five technologically related words that are new to you and use them in conversations several times in the next few days.

2. Locate and visit two classrooms that each have about six computers. Ask students what they may and may not do at the computers. Have students tell you how well they like being online and sharing what they learn with other students.
3. With a small group of pre- or in-service teachers, discuss the You Were There! unit in terms of its strategies, activities, or technology. Discuss other literacy strategies you could add.
4. Go on the World Wide Web and find five web sites that contain information about things you are interested in and would like to learn more about.

FOR FURTHER READING

Blanchard, J. (Ed.). (1999). *Educational computing in the schools: Technology, communication, and literacy.* Binghamton, NY: Haworth Press.

Cunningham, C. (Ed.). (1998). *Instructional technology for teachers.* Boulder, CO: Coursewise Publishing.

Grabe, M., & Grabe, C. (2001). *Integrating technology for meaningful learning* (3rd ed.). Boston: Houghton Mifflin.

Roblyer, M. D., & Edwards, J. (2000). *Integrating educational technology into teaching* (2nd ed.). Upper Saddle River, NJ: Prentice-Hall.

CHAPTER 2

Putting Technology to Use in Your Classroom

INTRODUCTION

When computers first made their way into schools, they were often placed only in computer labs, and technology lab aides or teachers were designated to teach students computer basics. Sometimes classroom teachers stayed in the lab to learn what was happening, and sometimes they went off to do other things. As more schools improved their technology infrastructures, classroom capabilities increased. Today, many more high-end, multimedia computers can be found in classrooms that have been Internet enabled. Teachers are now responsible for searching for instructionally valid learning experiences to use not only in one-computer classrooms, but also in classrooms that have six or more computers permanently installed. It is no longer just the computer teacher's responsibility to deal with computer instruction, it is every teacher's obligation to help students learn to use computer hardware and software, as well as the Internet, effectively.

You can structure your language arts curriculum in a fashion that creates both online and offline opportunities for students to use computer technology in literacy learning. As discussed previously, you can create broad thematic units that will give cohesion to the variety of learning experiences students undertake. In addition, you can model how to use technology to locate information, to demonstrate effective reading and thinking strategies, and to build online teaching and learning opportunities. When working with telecommunications, you can also call upon well-respected strategies such as **scaffolding**, which involves helping students until they can help themselves. For instance, when you locate web sites or online electronic materials for students before they are capable of finding them for themselves, you are providing scaffolding (Grabe & Grabe, 2000, p. 43).

You have probably discovered how easy it is to use a word processor that allows you to quickly revise your writings and to print out lessons, letters, recipes, or other documents. Ease of revision is probably why so many people quickly became enthusiastic about computers in the office and in the home. Also, you are most likely an e-mail user and probably have learned the good (ease of communication), the bad (unwanted e-mail), and the ugly (endless Listserv messages) aspects of being online. With a few basics, you can help students start to take advantage of technology.

Getting Set to Use Technology

You may or may not have started to use technology in your teaching. In this section we will look at getting started on the Internet, creating web sites, learning how to take advantage of the Internet's assets, and preparing to use software.

GETTING STARTED ON THE INTERNET

By now, most schools have their own **servers**—special computers and software—to handle e-mail, web sites, and other administrative electronic communications. If the school does not have such capabilities, advocate getting them because many of the students' opportunities to develop literacy skills will depend on your use of these and other electronic computer applications.

Establishing E-mail Accounts

If a school has limited Internet access, or if you teach kindergarten or first grade, you may have just one e-mail account to work with. While having just one account is not particularly desirable, you can make do by having students create messages in a word-processing program. You can then transfer the messages to a computer disk and cut and paste the messages into your e-mail account for transmission. Actually, any teacher whose students' parents would be uncomfortable with their child having access to his or her own e-mail account can use this technique. In either case, you should work closely with parents to obtain the e-mail addresses of those individuals parents authorize to correspond electronically with their child (e.g., a parent might not permit contact with a a former spouse if there are legal complications).

If possible, obtain e-mail accounts for each student through the school's system. Otherwise, there are online sites that will provide free Internet accounts to teachers and students. For example, see the Yahoo! GeoCities web site (**http://geocities.yahoo.com/**) and click on "Sign up now." Make sure you understand the conditions that are attached to using such free accounts, establish ground rules, and review with students and their parents any written school or district policies about the responsible use of e-mail. Be certain to obtain parental permission for students to have e-mail accounts.

Gaining Connectivity to the Internet

Advocate for Internet-capable classroom computers.

Most classrooms today have at least one Internet-capable computer. Ideally, each student should have considerable access to the Internet in order to take advantage of all that it has to offer. Even in classrooms that lack Internet connectivity, you can, through using programs such as Microsoft FrontPage, download a web site into a computer's memory and show the site to students in a classroom that has no Internet access. Again, if the classroom lacks a sufficient number of Internet-capable computers, you should advocate for additional Internet-capable multimedia computers so students can engage frequently in effective language and visual arts educational activities using Internet technology. **Web browsers**—software that lets you see web pages—such as Netscape Communicator and Microsoft Internet Explorer are free. Communication is at the heart of language arts learning, and you must have adequate technology tools to enable students to communicate frequently with the world outside the classroom.

CREATING WEB SITES

Many opportunities for learning language and visual arts exist when students develop web pages or sites. The planning and execution of such sites enable you to blend together technology and literacy in many authentic ways as students learn to communicate both visually and verbally. Students can contribute to either school or classroom web sites.

School Web Sites

Creating a school web site has been one effective mechanism some language arts teachers have used to engage students in authentic writing and other motivating communication activities. At first, it was a somewhat daunting task for users of the WWW to learn to use **HTML** (hypertext markup language) to create basic web sites. HTML is the code underlying the ability to place graphics, animation, and so forth, on the WWW. Now, thanks to programs such as Microsoft FrontPage and Knowledge Adventure's SiteCentral, the creation of web sites is relatively simple. Some knowledge of HTML is useful, however, when you run into problems creating a web page. Even modern word-processing programs such as Microsoft Word or Corel WordPerfect permit you to create word-processed documents and save them in HTML for publication on a web site.

Developing a school web site can be a beneficial collaborative project for students and language arts teachers. There are a myriad of choices that need to be discussed and decided on throughout the project. For instance, you and students must determine colors, page layouts, content, features, and icon designs. Endless opportunities to engage in language and visual arts arise during the production of school web sites. (See chapter 8 for specific advice about web site construction.)

Classroom Web Sites

You can ask students to participate in decisions about making a web site for the entire school, but you will help students best when you encourage them to develop web pages or web sites for their own classroom activities. Year after year, you and students can use a class web site as an outlet for creative narrative and expository publications. An excellent example of a teacher's use of her own web site is Susan Silverman's web pages. See "Mrs. Silverman's Webfolio" at **http://www.kids-learn.org** for a look at a variety of students' language arts projects. From publishing late-breaking news of a class's activities, to describing current assignments, to creating a showcase for students' projects, class web pages provide authentic and immediate publishing opportunities for students to display their very best, most polished works. In fact, teachers frequently comment that students are motivated to rewrite their work, proofread, verify spellings, and put forth their best efforts when they know the finished product will go online for anyone in the world to see.

Another example of a site that engages students in a variety of learning experiences is **www.globalclassroom.org,** created by Patricia Weeg, author of *Kids@Work: Math in the Cyberzone* (1999). Weeg's online projects are excellent examples of international communication efforts that engage students in a variety of activities. For some of the projects, you can easily combine math, literacy activities, and technology.

A class web site can be an effective public relations tool for you. It offers a direct avenue of communication with students' families. You can place your teaching philosophy and other ideas online, discuss your curriculum plans for the year, describe specific lessons or assignments, and place announcements about field trips or other matters online. You can make known ideas online that you would like parents to discuss either among themselves or with you at conference time. You can also recommend books or other materials for parents to read. Another feature that parents will appreciate is a **webliography**, which is like a bibliography except it contains the names and web addresses (URLs) of web sites you recommend that parents and their children visit. You can also share some web sites discovered by students while working on their various projects.

Publishing online can be an effective strategy for you to use in teaching and communicating with others. Back in the "Stone Age," students created many written projects that were placed on classroom walls or in school hallways—a practice that did not give students a great deal of incentive to expend much energy polishing their writings, given that only a few people would see the work. Now, however, technology gives language arts teachers a powerful tool to foster motivation to create better products not just online, but offline as well.

LEARNING HOW TO TAKE ADVANTAGE OF THE INTERNET'S ASSETS

You can use the Internet as a teaching tool to help students communicate with one another and interact with others at a distance.

Using the Internet Live While Teaching

Use the Internet's assets as a teaching tool.

There are many resources you can use live to foster reading and interpreting as well as the other language and visual arts. It is not uncommon for teachers to go online during a lesson to show students something they have found at a pertinent web site. You can show things either to small groups clustered around a computer or to the entire class through the use of a **computer video projector**, which projects computer images onto a screen. For instance, I frequently go online to show examples of well-designed and not-so-well-designed web sites for a course I teach about Internet authoring. My students discuss what they believe are the good and poor features of the sites, and together we reach an understanding of basic elements of web site design. You, too, can show web sites containing information that you want students to discuss; and from a class web site, students can share their own works or other web sites that pertain to a topic they are exploring.

Arranging for Communication

E-mail has proliferated wildly, and it is probably the online technology most used by students. Students can communicate with others worldwide in various ways.

- **Keypals (e-pals, net-pals):** Students communicate with one another informally.
- **Cross-classroom projects:** Students use e-mail for specific project development.
- **Student-mentor communication:** Students communicate with students in higher grade levels, with college students, or with or adults and experts who agree to work with them.
- **Teacher accounts:** Students who do not have their own accounts send and receive e-mail through teachers' accounts.
- **Discussion groups (often called Listservs):** Students join a discussion group where they read and contribute to discussions, usually about a specific topic.

If you are interested in helping students join a discussion group, or if you yourself want to subscribe to one for teachers, you can find a directory of pertinent groups at **http://www.topica.com.** Teachers.net hosts the "Teacher Mailring Center" at **http://teachers.net/mailrings/**, and it includes the "Project Center," which has discussion groups about classroom projects, pen pals, postcard projects, and more.

Encouraging Interactivity

Collaborative learning and the ease of Internet communications enable you to promote greater interactivity between you, students, and others. Depending on the capabilities of a school district's server, its software may be able to facilitate chat rooms that several students may use to communicate with one another, threaded discussions that you can initiate and then follow as students add their thoughts, or whiteboards that enable two or more students to work on a document or drawing at the same time from different computers (that may even be in different schools). As new technological developments occur, you will want to learn to use them as productive tools in fostering language and visual arts capabilities.

Making the Best Use of Specific Capabilities

The capabilities of the World Wide Web have grown at an astonishing rate since the 1990s. Not only can computers now handle electronic textual material with built-in links to other web pages or sites, but you can now create digital photographs with a digital camera or use a scanner to digitize images and photographs, all of which you can then place online. You can illustrate print with graphics and animations, and add audio and video. You can use the Web's capabilities to see and talk with other people online; for example, you can encourage students to correspond with today's well-known authors. You can use all of these electronic features in educationally sound ways to promote the growth of language and visual arts. Here are just some of the ways to use computers and the Internet in search of these goals.

- **Use online audio** to have students hear speakers of other languages. You can tune in a foreign-language radio station and have students listen to live broadcasts. One source of online audio is at Yahoo! Broadcast at **http://broadcast.yahoo.com/home.html.**
- **Use online video** to show students people (Martin Luther King, Jr.), places (the White House), and things (live news events). See Shockwave.com at **http://www.shockwave.com/sw/home/.**
- **Use online graphics** in online newspapers to explain a concept. One web site containing graphs of interest to educators is that of the National Center for Educational Statistics: K–12 Practitioners' Circle at **http://nces.ed.gov/practitioners/.** Another source of graphics is the "Snapshots" feature at the *USA Today* web site at **http://www.usatoday.com/snapshot/news/snapndex.htm.**
- **Use online animations** to instruct students in visually attractive ways. You can use free animations from the Animation Factory at **http://www.animfactory.com.**
- **Use online electronic print materials** that are not available in your school or community (e.g., the complete works of Shakespeare at the Bibliomania web site at **http://www.bibliomania.com/.**

Internet capabilities are now combined in ways that rival the capabilities of CD-ROM technology. For instance, you can read online stories silently or with accompanying RealAudio narration. Use *all* of the Internet's assets to help develop literacy abilities.

PREPARING TO USE SOFTWARE

While Web activities have become more and more valuable for encouraging active learning, there are also offline technology-driven activities of value to students who are developing literacy capabilities. CD-ROMs that cover a host of topics are available and serve as tutorials, reinforcement, and practice opportunities for students. Students can hear and read along with stories; click on words to access pronunciations or definitions; answer comprehension questions; and read related, supportive materials included with the main reading activity. There are programs that teach specific skills (Mavis Beacon Teaches Typing), educational games (Reader Rabbit's Ready for Letters), and references such as electronic encyclopedias (Britannica CD 2000 Deluxe) and other library resources. Of course, you can create your own learning activities and make them available on disk for students to analyze (e.g., use a spreadsheet or database program to report the results of a survey of students' hair color). Some districts or schools centrally purchase approved software to save money by using site licenses or to ensure continuity across classrooms or grades in the basic computer applications such as word processing or creating databases. You may want to request that a principal or school librarian purchase specific programs for use with your students. Some schools, in an attempt to ensure that only licensed software is being used, will not permit unauthorized software to be installed on school computers. Check with the school's technology office before installing any program on a school-owned computer.

Software evaluation is an important part of your planning for instruction.

It is crucial for you to evaluate programs to determine if they are (1) valuable to you in terms of your curriculum, (2) educationally sound, and (3) easy for students to use (user friendly). You can evaluate software by examining demonstration disks, asking for a trial-period use of a product before buying, finding other pre- or in-service teachers who have used or are using the product, or reading reviews of the products in magazines (such as *Technology & Learning*) that have software reviews in each issue.

You can also find information about prospective purchases online. For instance, Kids Domain (**http://www.kidsdomain.com**) and the other sites mentioned in chapter 1 contain reviews and articles about a variety of educational software programs. Many teachers or other people have written critiques of software programs and have placed that information online for your use. Be certain you analyze such reviewers' motives and credentials before you accept their advice without question.

Designing Classroom Projects

Countless web sites house literacy projects that you can use intact in your classroom, and CD-ROMs and other offline materials are available for use in literacy development. You may want to use these as you find them, but at some point you may want to become an instructional designer on your own. You might want to create your own literacy and technology connections and feel the pride of authorship of the multimedia projects you create. You know your students, your equipment, your situation, and your curriculum, so you are in the best position to create meaningful projects. You can plan and create technology-enhanced classroom projects and activities such as the ones that follow. Projects can involve the Internet, multimedia, communications, specific site projects, WebQuests, and software.

INTERNET PROJECTS

Use the Internet for collaborative and research projects.

Recognizing that all collaborative projects are not research projects and vice versa, we believe that the Internet and the Web give students access both to people and information. Encourage students to use these tools to engage in both collaborative and research projects.

Collaborative Projects

You can plan collaborative Internet learning experiences using activities that Judi Harris (1997–1998) identified and grouped into three categories. The categories are interpersonal exchanges, information collection and analysis, and problem solving (p. 17).

- **Interpersonal exchanges** include connecting your students to keypals, participating in global classroom activities in which two or more classes study the same topic, inviting someone to make an "electronic appearance" (through e-mail or a chat room) so your students can interact with that person, and engaging in question-and-answer exchanges between classrooms (What is your town like?) or with experts (e.g., The "Ask An Expert Sites" page of the Center for Improved Engineering and Science Education offers links to many sites, including literature and language arts sites, at **http://njnie.dl.stevens-tech.edu/askanexpert.html**). A more creative use of the interpersonal exchange involves enabling impersonations in which a person pretends to be a character from a book and as such corresponds with students.
- Students engaged in **information collection and analysis** can exchange information between classrooms, participate in the creation of databases using exchanged information, electronically publish works provided by students in other classrooms, take telefieldtrips, and analyze data provided by students in other classrooms.
- **Problem solving** offers students opportunities to work collaboratively to engage in information searches (i.e., use references to answer questions posed by students at another location), provide feedback to one another as part of the

writing process (see chapter 6), solve problems jointly (e.g., the classes work to solve the same problem at the same time and then share their findings), and solve problems sequentially (e.g., one class starts writing a poem, short story, play, etc., and students in another classroom finish it (Harris, 1997–1998).

Your efforts to help students develop literacy skills usually occur in the classroom, but school librarians can help you and students locate information efficiently. The technology resource people in a school can not only help you keep equipment running, but they can also help students learn new uses of hardware and software. The buck stops with you, however, when it comes to melding literacy and technology to advance students' literacy development.

Research Projects

A growing number of teachers are helping students use the resources of the Internet to engage in research. Through such projects, students learn to locate people (e.g., authors' web sites) and information (e.g., primary sources) that, in the past, would not have been possible. An examination of seventy-nine Internet projects (Oliver, 1997) revealed that there are several common elements in such research projects.

- ◆ Prior to a project, students typically engage in making hypotheses and brainstorming, getting together in teams, gathering the equipment they need to work on their project, and creating partnerships or finding mentors from universities or corporations.
- ◆ Students gather information online by using sources either they or their teachers find or by communicating with experts, by searching for information during field trips and observations, or through in-class or library research.
- ◆ After collecting data, students integrate the information by compiling, analyzing, and discussing it.
- ◆ Students share their results with others using online databases or by exchanging information through other collaborative efforts.
- ◆ Sharing sometimes involves constructing web pages that summarize the data gathered or feature student writings.
- ◆ There is usually an evaluation of student work by the teacher or mentor and a presentation of findings to peers or parents. (p. 34)

As you prepare students to engage in Internet research projects, consider conducting a metasearch of the chosen topic to determine if there are enough worthwhile and relevant web sites available to make the project successful. As you survey the sites, keep in mind both language arts and technology standards to decide which standards you will emphasize throughout the project as a whole. Be clear about what understandings, skills, and attitudes you want students to address as they work on the research project. You will also want to determine whether or not the sites you find will support or enhance the print and electronic materials (CD-ROMs) available in the classroom or school library.

Sites That Suggest Projects

The Web contains sites where you can create activities that are just right for your students. Take advantage of such sites by (1) identifying appropriate activities for your students, (2) sending students to a site for specific purposes such as reporting what it contains, or (3) asking students to show the class how to do something they learned while visiting a web site. When you find a good web site, think of ways to help students create literacy activities using the information and features that you find at the site. You may wish to create a database of web sites that lend themselves to making presentations, conducting research, fostering writing activities, and other curricular matters. Here are just a few examples of sites that seem to suggest specific projects.

Some sites seem natural for specific literacy projects.

WEBLIOGRAPHY

- **American Memory**
  http://memory.loc.gov
  American Memory is the Library of Congress's entry point to more than one hundred government-maintained collections of primary materials. Topics range from collections of baseball cards, to Civil War maps, to former presidents' papers to African American sheet music from mid 19th to early 20th century. This is a fine source of original materials that students can use to write formal reports.
- **HistoryChannel.com**
  http://www.historychannel.com/
  The web site of the History Channel cable television station offers many useful features, including "This Day in History." Students can read about important historical events of the day and then search for more information about those events that they can share with the class.

WEBLIOGRAPHY (continued)

- **Hobbies and Games**
  http://home.about.com/hobbies
  This site contains information about many hobbies that students can learn about and discuss. Ask students to see if their hobby is listed. If not, help them create a project about their hobby—perhaps a presentation or web site.

- **Scope Systems**
  http://www.scopesystems.com/anyday/
  Students can read about the historical events described at this site, keyboard a quick report, then put the printout on the bulletin board or read the information to the class (Scolari, Bedient, & Randolph, 2000). The Library of Congress's American Memory site, described above, has a similar site.

MULTIMEDIA PROJECTS

Multimedia projects are becoming increasingly popular. Some multimedia projects involve the Web, while others do not. Regardless, Agnew, Kellerman, and Meyer (1996, p. 120) note, "The first key to helping students create a well-organized multimedia project is for a teacher to articulate a well-thought assignment." They suggest several ways to frame assignments:

- Ask students to answer questions that you create.
- Have students find and describe the pros and cons of an issue.
- Give students words to define, or have students explain how groups of words are related.
- Give students a text and have them create links to audio, graphics or photos, animations, other texts, or definitions to increase understanding of the text.
- Have groups of students create one-page templates into which other students can place information. See the Tech Tip "A Slide Show Template."
- Have students create a multimedia slide show of text and other features that will make a concept clear (e.g., the water cycle).
- Remind students to carefully consider which aspects of a concept they want to highlight.

Your well-introduced multimedia activities will help students become engaged in active learning. As they work cooperatively, students need to

TECH TIPS: A SLIDE SHOW TEMPLATE

You or students can create a template that, when each student completes one, turns into a HyperStudio presentation for all to enjoy. The pictured template lets students type in information about pets. They can draw a picture or scan in a picture of the pet to place in the box. All of the students' templates merge into the final presentation.

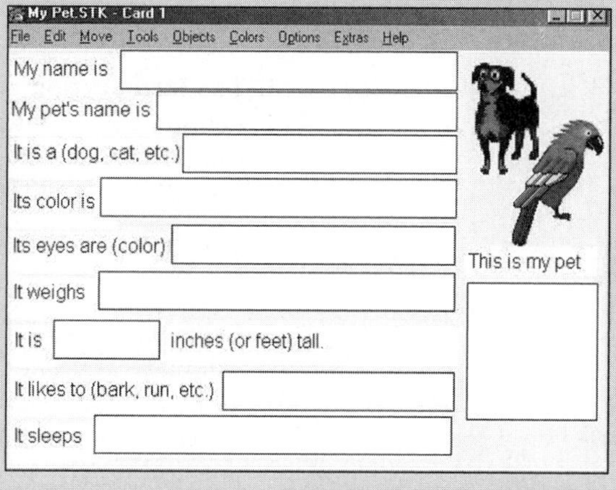

Source: Screenshot reprinted by permission of Brian Grove and HyperStudio. HyperStudio is a registered trademark of Knowledge Adventure Inc. All rights reserved.

decide how and with whom they will share their projects (audience), and they need to consider whether there are ways to extend their projects. Depending on their prior experiences creating multimedia projects, you can teach students how to break down projects into easier steps, such as first dealing with the text, then selecting link words or buttons, and then creating secondary pages. Encourage students to share their ideas and technology skills with others so that everyone learns to create excellent projects.

WEBQUESTS

The WWW makes WebQuests viable learning experiences.

The Quest Channel at **http://quest.classroom.com** lets you know about forthcoming quests and provides information about previous quests undertaken by Dan Buettner, biking enthusiast, and his group of world travelers. The Amazon, the American Southwest, Africa, Asia, Australia, the Galapagos Islands, several Japanese islands, and the Yucatan Peninsula are all locations of former quests. The team of explorers engages in bicycling adventures on their trips. Expedition members send frequent reports, ask questions, tell tales, and ask for advice. Students get to vote on important matters, and you and students get lots of information about the trip and the location. While not free, quests have excited students for years and have helped them learn about past and present cultures. You can use this type of adventure as a model to plan a local quest, perhaps with the cooperation of a local museum or anthropologist.

WebQuests include certain stages you will wish to consider when you create your own WebQuest. According to Yoder (1999), the five parts of a WebQuest are:

1. **The Introduction and the Task: Writing Compelling Scenarios.** Scenarios, said Yoder, "tend to fall into categories, including: Bringing contemporary world problems into the classroom, evaluating history, creating products, dealing with life's realities, and sparking students' imaginations" (p. 9).
2. **The Process.** Teachers guide students through the activity, perhaps using step-by-step guides.
3. **Resources: Gathering Relevant Materials and Links.** Locate resources you will make available for students to use. Resources can be print, electronic, or human. A school librarian can be particularly helpful as you search for relevant materials. Be certain to include local museums and similar resources when practical.
4. **Evaluation.** "Many WebQuests result in products—paper or oral reports, multimedia presentations, dramatic performances, artwork, or musical compositions," said Yoder (p. 53). She recommends using rubrics that include specific criteria and benchmarks as part of evaluation.
5. **The Conclusion.** When the WebQuest is completed, you and students can reflect on what students learned and then sum up the major findings of the project. Use students' feedback to help you plan the next WebQuest.

You can learn more about WebQuest development at a site maintained by Bernie Dodge, one of the originators of WebQuests at **http://edweb.sdsu.edu/webquest**. And visit **http://www.ozline.com** for information and ideas by Tom March, the other originator of WebQuests.

Recommended Learning Activities That Merge Literacy and Technology

Technology-proficient educators have created model projects you can use.

The following learning experiences integrate literacy and technology with classroom work, and they are recommended by technology-using educators. We offer them here to suggest effective ways you can integrate literacy and technology in your own classroom. As you read them, imagine how they might work in your classroom.

BOOK REPORTS

Students can make a different kind of book report using a database, according to Simonson and Thompson (1997). Students can enter information about the books they are reading into a database. Each student creates a record for each book he or she has read. "The record can include items such as topic of the book, number of pages, and student ratings of different aspects of the book. This type of book report is much more usable than the traditional book report, because other students can easily access and use the recorded information" (p. 197). With students, create the database by brainstorming the categories of information you would like to find in a book report database. Start with the characters and the setting and add other categories you all agree would be worth knowing about (e.g., plot elements, the book's genre). A book database, according to Kahn (1996–1997),

> can be used as an assessment tool, to document that a student has read the book. The more data fields the database has, the more a student is required to tell about the book. But that also makes the database more helpful to a student looking for something good to read. (p. 16)

TRADING CARDS

Students can create trading cards by scanning in pictures for the front of the card and writing the "vital statistics" of a relative or unsung hero on the back (Reissman, 1998). Encourage students to record relatives' oral histories while they are gathering information. Students can also make trading cards about facts or major points they are studying and swap them with other students to use as study aids (McNally & Etchison, 2000).

CREATE A "SAID WEB"

The "Said Web" is a word-study technique that starts with a "tired," overused word—such as *said*—for which students suggest synonyms, antonyms, or other related words (Laframboise, 2000). This brainstorming activity can easily involve the use of a graphic-organizer program. While developing the graph, students learn to group together those words that can be used instead of the tired words, and they can show relationships by drawing lines to connect words. After creating Said Webs, students can visit the Visual Thesaurus at **http://www.visualthesaurus.com/** and compare their webs with the three-dimensional one there.

CREATE ALTERNATIVE-HISTORY STORIES

One technology standard that is fairly common is to help students understand how technology impacts society over time. You can help students think about this topic through these activities based on ideas suggested by Moursund (1997, pp. 4–5):

1. Talk to students about things their parents did not know about, have, or use when they were the students' age.
2. Encourage students to write an alternative-history story that "explains" how today would be different if something had not been invented.
3. *A Connecticut Yankee in King Arthur's Court* (Mark Twain), *Timeline* (Michael Crichton), and similar stories involve characters finding themselves transported back in time. Have students brainstorm and then write about the things they could tell teachers or other people if they were transported back in time at least fifty years. For this and the previous activity, students can conduct research about when things were invented.
4. Ask students to interview a parent or grandparent (or someone from a previous generation) about what school was like when that person was in elementary or middle school. Have each student write or make a presentation about his or her findings, and encourage students to pool data (in a database) to see if any trends emerge.
5. Have students predict what schools might be like twenty years from now.

REVIEW SOFTWARE

Reissman (1999) collects software reviews, groups them by age, grade, and interest levels and has students read them. Students think of possible uses for the software and report to Reissman, who notes, "The students began to see how they might personally benefit by reviewing programs designed for them, even if it only helped them decide what should not be purchased" (p. 22). Students can also learn about software by creating original reviews of software they find online or through printed catalogs or advertisements.

CELEBRATE STUDENTS' FAMOUS BIRTHDAYS

Fun4Birthdays.com at **http://www.fun4birthdays.com/birthday/index.html** is useful for finding the names of famous people who were born on the same days as students in the class. After adding the student's name to a list of famous people, you can print it and place it in a prominent place for the day (Scolari et al., 2000). After you model this activity, you can have individuals or groups of students take over the reporting duties.

READ ALONG WITH CD-ROMs OR ONLINE STORIES

You can enhance reading behaviors by having students read online or CD-ROM stories and directing students to look for and discuss certain words or elements in the stories (Labbo, 2000). Students can listen to the story first and then read it, or vice versa; either strategy helps the student attend more closely to the story. Provide opportunities for students to have multiple encounters with the text (thereby encouraging literacy) by using such strategies as echo reading (students repeat words or phrases), reading along while a recorded voice reads the story, or letting students select and read the words as story characters in a Readers' Theatre presentation. These strategies give valid purposes for rereading stories. Extend the literature by inviting students to create new, original stories about characters (e.g., create a new adventure for *Arthur*) or to read the print version of a CD-ROM story (Labbo, 2000).

ACTIVITIES AT A NON-NETWORKED COMPUTER

Engaging in round robins (or write-arounds), making bookmarks, and designing business cards or magnets are creative language arts activities students can participate in using a non-networked computer (Lee, 2000). Place a list of five or six items at several computers and ask students to choose one of the items to include when they write the opening part of a creative story. Students write for five minutes or so, and then they move to the next computer. There, they read what has been written so far and choose one of the remaining items from the list at that computer. They write the next part of the story that the first person started. This rotation continues until students are out of time or objects to write about. Lee notes that you need to give students more and more time to read as they move through the lengthening stories at the various computers. She suggests that at the end of the process, either students can share the stories or the person who started the story can become the editor for the complete story (Lee, 2000). Have fun choosing items you can use to encourage creative stories. The same kind of writing activity can take place with networked computers when students in one school start a story and pass it on for students in another school to continue. Students can work individually or in groups to do their writing at the various schools. Be certain to track the story so that all participating schools get copies of the story when it ends. Include your e-mail address with a request to receive the finished story.

In the bookmark activity mentioned above, Lee uses a word-processing program and sets up two or three columns on a page in **landscape mode** (a horizontal page layout, as opposed to the vertical **portrait mode**). The limited space helps students learn to summarize while writing book reviews. After showing a few sample bookmarks, Lee tells students what she wants them to include. On the front of the bookmark, students include "the title, author, a summary, and at least one clip art illustration that is pertinent to the book. . . . The back of the bookmark has a character list with a short description, as well as a review of the book" (p. 28). Students include a symbol (e.g., 1–5 stars) to show how high they rate the book. Lee laminates the finished bookmarks, printing extra copies for students to share with other students, and she gives each student's bookmark to the librarian to display.

Lee also has students design a business card for a book character. Many stores—office suppliers, copy centers, computer retailers—sell card stock. She has students type the character's name and place directly beneath it three adjectives that relate to or show a trait of the character. Students can experiment with fonts, clip art, and size as they paste a symbol at each

FIGURE 2.1

A Story Character Business Card

Source: William Valmont. Based on an idea by Gretchen Lee. Used by permission.

corner of the business card. Use peel-and-stick magnetic sheets, cut them to fit the cards, and attach the cards to make refrigerator magnets (Lee, 2000). See Figure 2.1.

Real-Life Projects That Integrate Literacy and Technology

Teachers around the world are merging technology and literacy activities in effective ways The following are brief descriptions of a dozen activities practicing teachers are using today, many of which you can see for yourself at their web sites. These are model strategies you can use, too.

MISSING WORD BOOKS

Creative teachers use technology to help students learn language and visual arts.

Dyanna Brent (kindergarten, Gaithersburg, MD) uses Microsoft Word to create Missing Word Books for her kindergarten students. She uses the cloze technique to leave high-frequency words (e.g., "is," "and," "see") and other predictable words out of short sentences, and she uses clip art or digital photos to illustrate the books, thereby providing picture clues for the children. After students discuss the pictures and ask questions, they write in the missing words while hearing all words—except the missing word—spoken by the teacher. Students can discuss among themselves all of the possible word choices for the missing words. See Figure 2.2.

A COMMUNICATION WEB SITE

Jonathan Yorck (kindergarten, Honolulu, HI) created a classroom web site that serves many purposes. He documents weekly activities, posts monthly newsletters and calendars online, provides curriculum information, and much more. One exceptional feature of this site is the listing of international web sites. This feature helps his students learn words and phrases from several languages. Students' work appears on the site, and parents can learn about the kindergarten students' activities. The site is Wilcox F HomePage (Punahou School) at **http://www.punahou.edu/js/gradek/f/index.html.**

FIGURE 2.2

A Missing Word Book

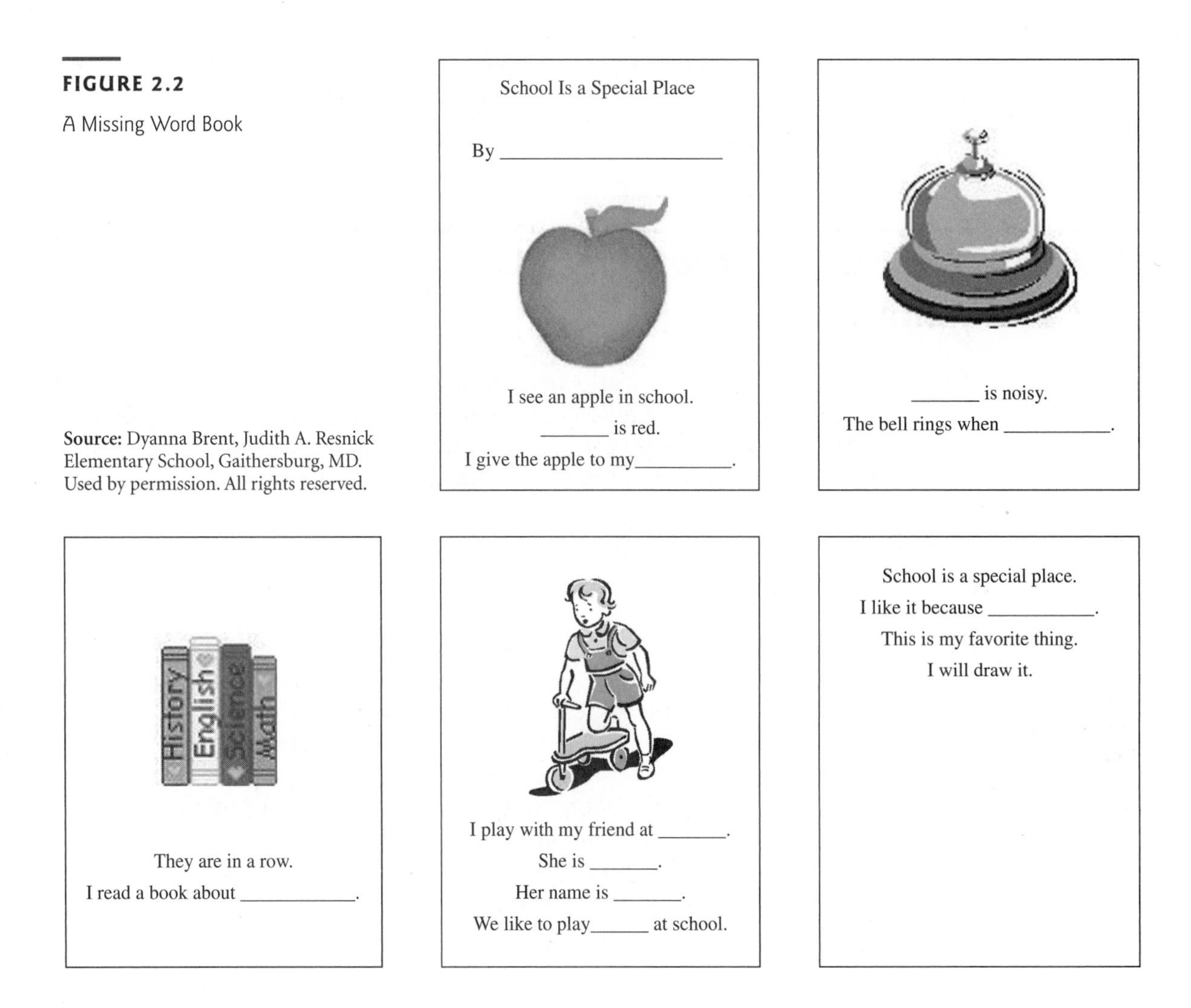

Source: Dyanna Brent, Judith A. Resnick Elementary School, Gaithersburg, MD. Used by permission.

PANDACAM

Rhonda Boggs (first grade, Olive Hill, KY) discovered the San Diego Zoo's Panda Cam (see it at **http://www.sandiegozoo.org/special/pandas/pandacam/index.html**). Her students became fascinated with watching the pandas in real time, so she turned the Internet experience into a major thematic unit. Students discussed their observations as they watched the zoo's pandas, wrote about them, read the book *The Year of the Panda* by Miriam Schlein, made panda masks (see Figure 2.3), and learned new vocabulary words (e.g., *species, habitat*). They even made Chinese hats. There are numerous online video cameras that you can use to pique your

FIGURE 2.3

Olive Hill First Grade Students with Panda Masks

Source: Reprinted by permission of Rhonda Boggs, Olive Hill Elementary School, KY, and students' parents.

students' interest in observing the world they live in. Find a "web cam" and develop activities around a theme that is appropriate to what you and students observe.

WRITING AND ILLUSTRATING SENTENCES AND BOOKS

Denise Bonczek (first-grade teacher and reading specialist, East Orange, NJ) teaches students to work with Kid Pix Studio Deluxe to create sentences and books. After introducing students to the program, Denise has students write original sentences using the high-frequency words that they are learning. Next, the students illustrate the story using crayons. For their first independent computer activity, students type their sentences into Kid Pix Studio Deluxe and use the drawing program to recreate their original art. This activity lets students learn similarities and differences when drawing in two media. (See Figure 2.4.) From this basic beginning, students move on to writing short stories.

USING A TALKING SOFTWARE PROGRAM FOR LANGUAGE EXPERIENCE AND OTHER ACTIVITIES

Pattie Meyer (first grade, Powhatan Point, OH) uses Write:OutLoud, developed for students with disabilities, to engage students in a variety of language experience approach (LEA) activities. The program "speaks" as

FIGURE 2.4

Hand-Drawn and Computer-Drawn Art

Source: Reprinted by permission of Denise Bonczek, East Orange, NJ, and students' parents. All rights reserved.

letters and words are typed, then repeats the entire sentence. Ms. Meyer's computer is connected to a TV monitor so the whole class can participate and hear "Fred" speak. In the traditional LEA, students see correct punctuation modeled, and Ms. Meyer models it using Write:OutLoud as well. She also targets high-frequency words and creates questions for the students. Ms. Meyer and her students have fun with the software and learn a great deal in a short period of time. See the Teaching Tip "How I Use a Talking Word Processor."

WEB SITE PROJECTS THAT GROW FROM READING BOOKS

Patricia Taverna (second grade, Sleepy Hollow, NY) and Terry Hongell (computer teacher, both teachers at Pocantico Hills School) collaborate to help students work on major projects. Sometimes they plan the projects well in advance (Rockefeller), and sometimes they stem from student interest in the subject (Vietnam). The projects, usually based on a book students have read, involve creating a web site. Students do online and print searches to gather information for their project. Eventually, students place their web site on the school's web server. Ms. Taverna's students are motivated to do good work, especially when high school and other students compliment them on their projects. See the projects at **http://www2.lhric.org/pocantico/taverna/taverna.htm.**

TEACHING TIPS How I Use a Talking Word Processor

As a first-grade teacher in rural Appalachia, I have thought that technology would allow me to offer my students the same advantages as children from more affluent school districts. I have used technology in my classroom for the past eighteen years, ranging from simply recording, with a camcorder, my first graders' reading of stories to creating multimedia presentations of thematic units. But I must say that the way I incorporate a talking word processor into the curriculum has had the greatest impact on their learning.

I use a program called Write:OutLoud by Don Johnston, Inc., but I assume any talking word processor would work. I call the voice that is talking from the computer "Fred," and he has actually become an entity in our classroom. We do a variety of activities with Fred. Among them is show-and-tell. Every day one child places an item in our show-and-tell bag. I ask parents to help write down three clues concerning the secret item in the bag. I type the clues on Write:OutLoud and then Fred reads them aloud. A typical show-and-tell text may look like the following:

Write:OutLoud - [UNTITLED1.WOL]
File Edit Text Options Speech Utilities Help

Joey's Show and Tell
1. It is white and black.
2. It has keys.
3. It makes music.
David said, "Is it a keyboard?"
Joey said, "Yes."

After the clues are read, the child who brought in the item asks a volunteer to guess what it is. After several readings by Fred, I mute the TV and volunteers read the clues. The child's show-and-tell is then printed and taken home to successfully read to parents.

From this simple everyday activity, a whole learning process evolves throughout the year. In the beginning of the year, when Fred tracks by highlighting the text, children learn left-to-right transition, word spacing, and capitalization of titles. As time progresses, Fred can target sight words. I have seen a dramatic change in the number of children who spell *said* correctly in independent writing after I started using the talking word processor. *Said* is a difficult word for most first graders, but most of my students consistently spell it correctly because of the repetition.

I also saw a big change in students' ability to use punctuation. They see quotation marks, commas, and question marks used from the second day of school on. In turn, they use punctuation more correctly in their own writing. When we work on quote marks I highlight the words that come out of a student's mouth, and the children better understand quote marks.

Perhaps the most useful reading strategy I teach is simply the power of rereading. Fred displays this every time he says something to us. At first I was concerned about the slow unnatural language in Write:OutLoud, but I soon realized what a great advantage this is. Most first graders read in a slow, choppy way the first time they read a sentence, but because Fred goes back and automatically rereads every sentence faster and smoother, my first graders mimic this powerful reading strategy.

A talking word processor is based on phonetic rules, so sometimes Fred doesn't pronounce words correctly, especially names. An important point is made with this. We don't laugh when Fred makes a mistake! After phonics instruction, my children go to recess, and as they come back, I have Fred talk to them using the targeted sight words for the week. As Fred talks, almost all of the students watch the screen. If I am targeting the word *want*, Fred might say the following:

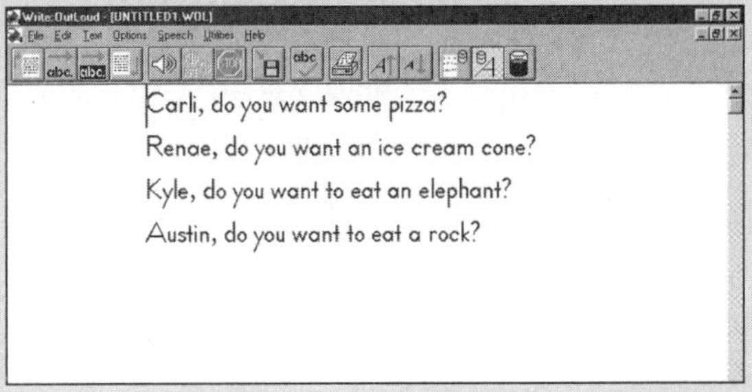

Write:OutLoud - [UNTITLED1.WOL]
File Edit Text Options Speech Utilities Help

Carli, do you want some pizza?
Renae, do you want an ice cream cone?
Kyle, do you want to eat an elephant?
Austin, do you want to eat a rock?

TEACHING TIPS
(continued)

(I shift into the first-grade sense of humor if the children start to become inattentive, and they instantly perk up again.)

I incorporate the talking word processor into my "Working with Words" lessons. To show initial consonant substitution, I make Fred say "Bill," "fill," and "hill." The children learn how to highlight just the first sound and then type the new beginning sound. We do this with endings, too. I might type, "Yesterday, I want to go home." I say, "Fred is a little tired today. Who could help him say this in a better way?" I also use Fred while doing "Language Experience" stories. For example, after making peanut butter, we gather around Fred, and I say, "Fred was asleep when we were making the peanut butter. Let's tell him what we did."

In order to keep the children's attention after several readings of a language experience story, I change Write:OutLoud to a woman's voice and say, "Fred's cousin Shirley wants to read your story now." First graders love to hear the different voices! Like most first-grade classrooms, we do many retellings of stories. I use Fred to model initial retellings in the "once upon a time" mode. I make the first retelling extremely short and boring, then Fred asks the children to help him think of better, more exciting words.

This simple use of a talking word processor has had a dramatic effect on my first graders' mastery of sight words, punctuation, word parts, comprehension, and respect for the reader. It is a way to tie children's love of the screen into their learning to read.

Source: Reprinted by permission of Pattie Meyer, Powhatan Elementary School, Powhatan Point, OH, and Don Johnston Inc.

PARENT OPEN HOUSE AND OTHER PROJECTS

Adele Thompson (second grade, Flagstaff, AZ) recommends having students prepare a presentation for a parent open house in which students write four sentences about themselves and type them into the computer. These sentences are then wrapped around each student's picture. She likes to start the open house with the presentation, effectively introducing all of the students to all of the parents. She also has students engage in these language arts activities:

- Writing and illustrating bat poems for a Halloween collection.
- Creating a "Holiday Goodies Cookbook" of students' favorite recipes in which the students type their own versions of the recipes.
- Making a weather book by asking students to define and illustrate their favorite weather word.

ILLUSTRATING FABLES

WWW

Dodie Ainslie and Kimberly Haney (third and fourth grades, Spencer, NY) have students write and illustrate fables as part of their children's literature genre studies. See several students' fables at **http://sites.netscape.net/dainslieainslie/fables.html.** See the Teaching Tip "Fables and Legends and Other Genre Studies" and the Student Project "How Raccoon Got His Markings." You will find additional genre studies by Ainslie and Haney on this book's web site.

DOWNLOADABLE POWERPOINT PRESENTATIONS

Danya Jaworsky (fifth grade, Winnipeg, Manitoba) has students create PowerPoint presentations you can download and play on your own computer. See these projects, which incorporate history and geography as well as original writings and poetry, at **http://www.wsd1.org/nnl/l_nelson/hp.htm.** Be certain to look at the "Prairie Arts Quilt" for which eight schools contributed research, art, and poetry. Ms. Jaworsky is not only helping students learn about their community, she is helping them share it with the world.

TEACHING TIPS — Fables and Legends and Other Genre Studies

In our school, we chose genre studies to focus on at each grade level. Third-grade students study fables, and fourth-grade students study legends. During both genre studies we immerse students into the chosen genre, reading many different fables or legends to them and with them. Once the students understand the components of the genre they are studying, we start writing. We use process writing. Students use a storyboard to create their story, then write a rough copy, have peer and teacher conferences for revising and editing, and work on their final copy. What makes these genre studies work well is that the publishing step incorporates technology that really excites the students. They know from the beginning that their final story and illustration will be published on the Internet. Students use Paint to illustrate their stories, then they type them in Microsoft Word and insert their picture. These documents are then put into a class book, *A Collection of Legends Written by Mrs. Haney's Fourth-Grade Class.* This book is bound and shared with other students in the school. After that, we get parental permission to have the stories published on the Internet, and the students learn how to use an HTML editor. We use Netscape Composer because it's easy! Students copy and paste their stories into this program; change the background, font colors and styles; and reread the stories to make sure they are ready for publication. After that, it's just a simple step to the "Internet Publishing Station," our laptop where we create active links to their pictures and upload the pages to the Internet. It's that easy! If you want to see this year's proud publishers, log on at: **http://sites.netscape.net/dainslieainslie/fables.html.**

Source: Used by permission of Dodie Ainslie and Kimberly Haney, Spencer Elementary School, Spencer, NY.

HOW RACCOON GOT HIS MARKINGS

By Heather Poole

Long, long ago, deep in the woods, raccoons were not known to have good sharing abilities. Raccoon would go deep in the woods, so no person or animal could find him. This would allow Raccoon to hoard all of the nuts and berries for himself and never leave any for the other animals.

Fox finally lost his patience with Raccoon and complained. "Raccoon thinks he can take all of the food for the winter. That's not fair! We need to teach Raccoon a lesson that he will never forget!"

When Raccoon was hibernating, Fox climbed to the tallest mountain to tell Creator about his problem with Raccoon. The Creator said, "I think we're going to have to do something about that." The Creator and Fox started brainstorming ideas while Raccoon was still sleeping. Fox was very intelligent and came up with an idea first. He said, "I have a great idea, Creator. Why don't you make it stormy one night, so Raccoon will be shocked by lightning. This would cause his tail to get so bushy and heavy that he would slow down. Raccoon wouldn't be fast enough to take all of the food for himself anymore."

The Creator liked this idea and made it all happen. He sent a powerful storm and lightning struck Raccoon. Not only did Raccoon's tail get bushy, but parts of his fur burned black. And from that day on all raccoons have bushy tails to keep them from stealing all of the food for themselves. Now all animals have a chance to save food for the winter and Raccoon has burglar markings so all the animals remember how he used to steal their food.

Source: Used by permission of Heather Poole, fourth grade, Spencer Elementary School, Spencer, NY, and her parents.

IDENTITY QUILTS AND OTHER PROJECTS

Lola Mae De Smith (K–6 gifted teacher, Thoreau, NM) recommends making identity quilts, creating virtual tour collages, and giving photojournalism assignments. Students make identity quilts by using digital cameras, drawing programs, or clip art as well as manipulating font sizes and styles to make a quilt of images. They transfer the images onto T-shirts or other pieces of cloth. For their "Virtual Tours Around the World" project, Ms. De Smith has each student select a country or famous landmark and then use electronic resources to find text, photos, or illustrations and create a PowerPoint presentation that is a collage of images and text. For the photojournalism assignments, she has students become photojournalists through taking digital photos, editing them, and offering the photos to other teachers to use in school projects.

POWERPOINT WORKSHEET

Mary Kayser (seventh and eighth grades) and Shelby Fannin (media center specialist, Dayton, OH) have students vote for the annual winner of the Stivers Tiger Award. (Author Note: They teach at the Stivers School for the Arts.) Students create presentations after reading novels from the school library. Ms. Kayser helps students prepare their presentations using a "PowerPoint worksheet." Specifications for the worksheet are:

Slide 1: Name the title and author and scan a picture of the book.
Slide 2: List five statements about the author.
Slide 3: Write five statements that describe the plot.
Slide 4: Relate the part you liked best.
Slide 5: List examples of vivid language.
Slide 6: Give 4–5 reasons why you think the book should be nominated.
Slide 7: Give some information about yourself.

Not only do students have an opportunity to use a presentation program, the structure of the worksheet helps them think about presenting information effectively, so that other students can vote intelligently based on information in their presentation. See a sample PowerPoint worksheet on this book's web site.

WWW

KIDS ASSESSING WEB SITES

Dawn Morden (seventh and eighth grades, Altoona, PA) encourages students to find, evaluate, and write recommendations about web sites and then post them on the Internet. Her students have contributed reports about the Civil War, award-winning books and authors, and heroes for the twenty-first century. For a similar kind of project, see Student Recommended Sites at **http://www.madison.k12.wi.us/tnl/detectives/main.htm.** Ms. Morden also created a simulation lesson for students about inviting authors to their school; it can be viewed at **http://trackstar.hprtec.org:80/main/display.php3?track_id=658.**

Lesson Web Sites

Countless lessons that integrate literacy and technology are available for you to use or adapt, and they in turn can suggest lessons for you to create. Most online lesson resources are free if used for educational purposes, but remember that some of the lessons or materials might be copyrighted. You will wish to judge the value of the activities and verify facts because some materials are "homegrown" and not reviewed by others. More sites appear on this book's web site, but here are a few sources of lessons and activities.

WEBLIOGRAPHY

- **Dr. Susan Tancock's Literacy Web Page**
  http://web.bsu.edu/00smtancock/
  This site contains information for several reading education classes that Dr. Tancock teaches at Ball State University. You will find many ideas that can be adapted to your own classes.
- **Florida Center for Instructional Technology**
  http://fcit.coedu.usf.edu/
  This site contains basic information about the Internet, networking schools, and telecommunications. The site also is a source of lessons (e.g., on the Holocaust) utilizing technology and free Internet simulations.

- **The Library in the Sky**
  http://www.nwrel.org/sky/index.asp?ID=3
  Lesson plans and links for a variety of language arts activities are included at this site, which is maintained by the Northwest Regional Educational Laboratory.
- **Teachers.Net Lesson Bank**
  http://www.teachers.net/cgi-bin/lessons
  Hundreds of lessons submitted by teachers from everywhere are presented at this site.

SUMMARY

- You can use familiar literacy strategies and enhance them with technology.
- Ample technology in the classroom is critical to students' literacy learning.
- The Internet enables valuable communication opportunities for students.
- The Internet has spawned a variety of excellent literacy projects.
- WebQuests are a recent instructional technique for fostering literacy growth.
- Creative educators are linking literacy and technology in inventive ways.
- Use the Web's resources to design technology enhanced literacy lessons.

ACTIVITIES

1. Talk to a school technology person to learn what technology capabilities the school has.
2. Evaluate software programs using Buckleitner's questions from this book's web site.
3. Prepare a WebQuest.
4. Visit several of the teachers' web sites to see their web pages. Plan your own site.

CHAPTER 3 Managing Technology in Your Classroom

INTRODUCTION

You may still work in a one-computer classroom and take students to a computer lab once or twice a week, or you may be fortunate enough to have six or more computers in a classroom where students can easily use technology throughout the days and weeks of school. By now, most classrooms in the United States have at least one Internet connection, but 100 percent classroom connectivity is not yet the case for most schools. Whatever your circumstances, students can participate in many activities involving literacy and technology before they get to a computer. That is, students can engage in a great deal of creative and disciplined thinking, preproduction planning, researching, and organizing before they actually sit down to work at a computer. This lets students make efficient use of their time when they are working with software or the Internet.

The shift from taking students to computer labs and turning things over to the lab teacher to having students work on computers in classrooms is causing teachers to scramble for new ways to integrate technology into classroom learning experiences. Fortunately, melding technology and literacy activities is not hard to do. There are many great ideas you can use in the classroom daily, as you discovered in chapter 2. If you are a longstanding computer user, share your knowledge of literacy activities with both students and other teachers. If you are new to the use of computers, find experienced users and ask them to teach you some of their strategies. Here are some important things to consider as you integrate literacy and technology in the classroom:

- Maximize students' time at computers. Prepare clear instructions so students know exactly what they are expected to do at the computer. On the Internet, preselect sites to get them started. As students gain more research capabilities, you can encourage them to be more independent. See "Research Reporting and Writing to Produce Electronic Reports" on this book's web site.

- Convey to students that working with a computer is an *essential* part of literacy learning—not an add-on activity.
- Learn the assets and liabilities of software and learn to use the unique features of electronic media that contribute to developing new or different literacy capabilities.
- Place students in appropriate software or other learning situations to develop literacy capabilities. (Drill programs are not necessary for everyone. Games can be very engaging, but many are without adequate educational value.)
- Understand the objectives or purposes of software applications, then determine if they are appropriate for the students with whom you work.
- Ensure that state and district literacy and technology standards are working together in the classroom.
- Work with other school or district teachers to create a sequence of understandings, skills, and attitudes across the various grade levels to ensure that important standards are sequenced and reinforced in order to acquire mastery.

You do not need to be an expert in understanding technology and software to start using it for teaching and learning. It takes a long time and continuing attention to learn new hardware and software. Gloria Antifaiff, technology coordinator of Qu'Appelle Valley Shared Services in Regina, Saskatchewan, recommends using "'just-in-time' training for some situations—having teachers learn enough to introduce something to students and then letting them take the information and run with it, using their curiosity" (Personal communication, May 2001). Some of the students you teach today will be tech wizards, so be open to learning from them. See the Teaching Tip "The Jagwire Project: TechCats in Action," which can be found at this book's web site, to learn how sophisticated some students become by high school.

See also the Teaching Tip "Library Technology Helpers" on this book's web site to learn how librarians can be helpful to you and students in promoting effective use of technology.

It is helpful to learn what practicing teachers have to say about integrating technology into classrooms. Teachers at the Amphitheater School District in Tucson, Arizona, developed practical suggestions to deal with frequently asked questions. This chapter has four sets of these suggestions, each directed at a particular issue that might arise when integrating technology and the Internet. Peggy Steffens, instructional technology coordinator for the district, provided the lists and updates them. See **http://www.amphi.com/~psteffen/index.html.**

District and School Considerations

You work within the context of district and school policies that relate to the language and visual arts curricula as well as technology. Helping students make the most of their time at computers calls for districts or schools to ensure that important decisions are made about (1) having a well-constructed technology plan for the district or school, (2) defining acceptable use policies (AUPs), and (3) determining if and when Internet filtering software will be used. The presence or absence of these three conditions affects your daily work with students and may provide specific guidelines for your classroom.

TECHNOLOGY PLANS

A technology plan gives direction, over time, to technology infusion in schools.

It is beyond the scope of this book to provide teachers and administrators with enough information to create a school or district technology plan. If your district already has a technology plan, you should become very familiar with it. If your school lacks such a plan, encourage the administration to create one. You may wish to check with your state's department of education or with other districts to determine what plans other schools have created. If you have never seen a technology plan, see "Critical Issue: Developing a School or District Technology Plan" at **http://www.ncrel.org/sdrs/areas/issues/methods/technlgy/te300.htm.** This page on the North Central Regional Educational Laboratory's web site deals with creating school technology plans. It contains an excellent discussion of the topic and gives state and district examples.

ACCEPTABLE USE POLICIES

If it does not have one, your district or school will want to create an **acceptable use policy** (AUP) so students, parents, and you know what rights and responsibilities everyone has, and understand, as Grabe and Grabe (2000, p. 280) note, the "consequences when expectations and procedures are violated." If the district or school has an AUP, you need to know it well. An AUP should explicitly specify behavior that can get students into trouble, including:

- Placing unlawful information on the Internet.
- Using abusive or objectionable language in public or private messages.

- Sending messages that are likely to result in the loss of the recipient's work or systems.
- Sending "broadcast" or "chain-letter" messages to lists or individuals, or any other use that congests the networks or otherwise interferes with the work of others (Truett, Scherlen, Tashner, & Lowe, 1997, p. 54).

An AUP can address a variety of subjects such as plagiarism, freedom of expression, online etiquette or netiquette (see **http://www.fau.edu/netiquette/netiquette.html**), harassment, and privacy of e-mail. You, students, and guardians should sign printed AUP forms that can be kept on file, ensuring that there is no question about everyone's knowing the rules. If you have not seen an AUP, you can read the Houston Independent School District's, as well as link to related sites, at **http://dept.houstonisd.org/technology/aupmain.htm.**

INTERNET FILTERING SOFTWARE

You and administrators need to cooperate about the use of Internet filters that attempt to keep students away from certain web sites. See the Teaching Tip "Policies and Resources to Monitor Internet Use." If the district or

TEACHING TIPS — Policies and Resources to Monitor Internet Use

Try as you may to prevent it, some students will accidentally or intentionally access web sites that you or the school or district do not believe are appropriate for them to visit. Clear policies and consequences can help, and software that attempts to limit access to sites with certain content is used by a growing number of schools. A "three strike policy," according to Summerville (2000, p. 33), can help you deal with students who access unacceptable web sites. She says,

1. If a student is found on an "unapproved" site, the student is told that he or she has a first strike. An unapproved site is one that is either not on an approved list of sites to search or one that is not related to the search topic (e.g., latest sports team scores).
2. On a student's second offense, a note is sent home to the student's parents explaining the offense, mentioning that the student has been warned verbally on one other occasion, and stating the consequences of the next offense.
3. On the third strike, another letter is sent home to the parents and the student loses Internet privileges for a predetermined amount of time. It is important that the duration of time is specifically stated in a written policy. I recommend that institutions adopt a single policy regarding Internet use and post this policy in any room with access to the Internet.

Source: Summerville, J. (2000). WebQuests: An aspect of technology integration for training preservice teachers. *TechTrends, 44*(2), 31–34.

Internet filters are helpful, but they are not foolproof.

school uses a filtering system, you need to know exactly how it works. If a web filter is not required, you will definitely need to discuss your Internet use policies *thoroughly* with students. Filters do *not* guarantee that students are completely protected, so you need to let students know they should quickly get out of any web site that you do not want them to access or that is clearly inappropriate. See the Teaching Tip "An Accident on the Information Highway" and Figure 3.1.

You will want to examine various Internet filtering applications to learn about their features. Here are sources of information about several popular and well-known Internet filtering software applications:

- **N2H2** (N2H2, Inc.): **http://www.n2h2.com/**
- **Cyber Sentinel** (Security Software Systems, Inc.): **http://www.securitysoft.com/**
- **Cyber Snoop** (Pearl Software): **http://www.pearlsw.com/home/index.html**
- **CyberPatrol** (Surf Control): **http://www.cyberpatrol.com/**
- **CYBERsitter** (Solid Oak Software): **http://www.solidoak.com**
- **Net Nanny** (Net Nanny Software Int. Inc.): **http://www.netnanny.com/**
- **SurfWatch** (Surf Control): **http://www1.surfwatch.com/**

TEACHING TIPS An Accident on the Information Highway

Jennifer Rosenboom was the 1999 southeast regional winner of the IRA's Presidential Award for Reading and Technology. Every year she has sixth- and eighth-grade student buddies work on a six-week project about hurricanes—often a timely topic for students at the Carlos E. Haile Middle School in Bradenton, Florida. The first year she undertook the project, students tracked what turned out to be the disastrous Hurricane Georges. Below, Jennifer describes one little research-on-the-Internet "disaster" in a brief anecdote.

While researching hurricanes on the Internet, one little gal typed in "hurricanes" under SEARCH and somehow ended up on a web site for men's underwear actually called Hurricanes. (I think this happened because she put an "s" on "hurricane.") Anyway, the most interesting advertisements were displayed, and, bless her heart, she was just scrolling away trying to find the information she was looking for in amongst these ads! She really was innocently looking for storm info. Of course, another student noticed her screen and announced, "Hey! Look at that!" We quickly removed the site.

It really hit me how easy it is for kids to get where they should *not* be and quite by *accident!* Even with experienced teachers, Internet-trained students, and careful monitoring, it can happen.

FIGURE 3.1

Amphi Teachers Respond: How Do We Ensure That Students Stay on Appropriate Web Sites?

Source: Used by permission of Peggy Steffans, Instructional Technology Coordinator, Amphitheater School District, Tucson, AZ.

- Watch the students. Be within line of sight of the students at the computers.
- Check their "Go Menu," "History," and "Cache" periodically.
- Present clear guidelines for what students are supposed to be accomplishing while on the Internet.
- Create guidelines for consequences of improper use. Guidelines need to be in place before punitive measures are administered.
- Present structured activities with specific tasks in an amount of time that will allow them to accomplish the task and not allow time for surfing or going to inappropriate sites.
- Insist on student responsibility. Teach students the realities of the Internet and to be responsible for their actions and decisions.
- Create a short cut on the desktop to the site you want students to visit and allow them to go only to that site.
- Bookmark the sites you want students to visit and allow them to go to those sites only.
- Visit sites and check the links to see if they are all appropriate prior to students' using the Internet.
- Allow students to perform searches only on Yahooligans!
- Group your students so that each group has a trustworthy student who will report inappropriate activities.

PARENTAL PERMISSIONS

Some schools have policies prohibiting the placing of children's names, faces, or any other personal information on the Internet. They fear that unscrupulous people could track down a child and cause harm. Others permit first names and photos, but not last names. Some schools permit long shots of children but not close-ups. Decisions such as these need to be made at local, district, or state levels because they guide you in determining which parental permissions you must seek before placing any student information on the Internet. You will need to know this information thoroughly!

SAFETY ON THE INTERNET

Internet safety is a major concern.

You will want to discuss Internet safety with students. The first discussion is likely to involve a determination of who is and who is not a stranger. For instance, if a student talks to a worker at a well-known fast-food restaurant, the fact that the student knows the *restaurant* does not make the employee any less of a stranger.

The National Center for Missing and Exploited Children (NCMEC) publishes two brochures dealing with safety issues. They are *Teen Safety on the Information Highway* (1998) and *Child Safety on the Information Highway* (1994). The NCMEC's mailing address is Department 201, 16th Floor, 747 3rd Avenue, New York, NY, 10017. The web site, **http://www.missingkids.com/**, contains much information about the organization and its services. Some NCMEC publications are downloadable using Adobe Acrobat Reader, which is free. You and students can find much to discuss at the web site. If you or students happen upon child pornography on the Internet, call the National Center for Missing and Exploited Children at 1–800-843-5678.

Be certain to discuss with students the following points, as well as any others you believe relate to their safety:

- Never give personal information to someone you meet on the Internet but do not know personally.
- Never give information about your school, including the name of the school or its street address.
- Never give personal information about others, including friends.
- Never give your own street address or telephone number to a stranger on the Internet.
- Never tell strangers anything about your parents, particularly when and where they work.
- Never send a picture of yourself to a stranger.
- Never continue to correspond with someone who talks about things your parents or teachers would object to. Report such e-mail or chat material to your teacher.
- **Never** agree to meet a stranger.

To reiterate, district and school considerations are important. They set the parameters of how you can use technology in your classroom. The school board and school administrators need to support your efforts to integrate technology and literacy instruction by providing sufficient amounts of hardware and software to help you do an effective job. You and other teachers must be involved at the district level in evaluating and recommending for purchase suitable equipment and instructional materials, and you will want to enlighten the administration about effective ways to use technology with students to develop their literacy capabilities. Portfolios of excellent student work can make graphic many of the instructional learning experiences involving technology that you have students engage in every day. Let administrators see how technology is helping students prepare for higher education and eventual employment.

Classroom Considerations

Within a classroom, you have many decisions to make. You have to set the tone so students see that using technology for literacy development is a beneficial thing, decide how and when students can use classroom computers, help students learn online and offline strategies, and plan their time wisely. You need to make hundreds of other decisions, not the least of which is how to coordinate your use of computer resources to build on what students now know and what they will need in their future school years. You must also be cognizant of those local, state, and national standards that may have high-risk consequences for teachers and students alike. Some classroom considerations are easy for you to deal with, but others are more complex and hard to implement.

CLASSROOM ENVIRONMENT AND MANAGEMENT

A positive attitude about technology will convey its importance to developing literacy.

Having satisfactory technology resources in your classroom is necessary for you to use technology in educationally valid ways, but your overall classroom climate will be greatly influenced by your positive attitudes and actions regarding using technology for instruction. A positive attitude conveys to students the idea that although technology may be imperfect and troublesome to use at times, the hardware and software students use create greater opportunities for learning than their parents or grandparents had prior to the information explosion and the networking of computers. Most youngsters already understand this, but you must convey it as well because you set the tone for technology usage. Another tone you set is that of encouraging students to use technology resources *independently* to help them in their studies. Once tasks are defined and interests are identified, you should provide ample opportunities for students to use your technology resources with minimum guidance to help them define their quests, expand or narrow tasks, locate appropriate information to use, and create effective ways to share their findings. Another action on your part that influences the climate for learning is the way you enable students to have *equity of access* to the learning tools in your room and your school. Assigning daily or at least frequent amounts of computer time, perhaps in a classroom "computer center," will help solve some of the barriers to using hardware, software, or the Internet. See Figure 3.2.

You can provide equity through individual or small-group instruction and by creating assignments that permit thoughtful uses of information, as opposed to regurgitation of facts. If you work with special-needs students, you will need to take steps to meet their technology needs. See the Tech Tip "Assistive Technologies" on this book's web site. Ensuring that all

FIGURE 3.2

Amphi Teachers Respond: How Do You Keep One Computer in Your Classroom Used Effectively Most of the School Day?

Source: Used by permission of Peggy Steffans, Instructional Technology Coordinator, Amphitheater School District, Tucson, AZ.

- Rotate students through centers.
- Schedule blocks of time so each child gets two 20-minute time blocks on the computer during a week.
- Each week locate the "Site of the Week," which pertains to the main topic of learning for that week. Everyone must go to the site by the end of the week and write a synopsis. Students sign up for times during the week. Have a time limit so that all students will have an opportunity to work on the computer.
- Every few weeks, teach students a new skill on the computer. Give them two weeks to complete the task, with each child having a scheduled time. Have open times available to all students.
- Leave the computer on with a word processor running. Allow students to come and type documents. Keep student disks next to the computer so that they can save their work to the disks.
- Have expectations that your students will use the technology.
- Have PowerPoint presentations running that teach something.
- Design "Fun Brain" activities such as math games, puzzles, and so forth, that are related to what the students are learning.
- Have students learn new programs, or design puzzles or math games for the rest of the class.

students use technology frequently in their schoolwork will enable them to become comfortable and more confident about using technology tools.

INTERNET INTERACTIONS

Student use of the Internet to locate correct and age-appropriate information is, and will continue to remain, problematic because anyone can place just about anything online, much of which may be extremely unsuitable for students. You will want to discuss several matters with each student's parents or guardians.

Teach students to respect hardware and software as valuable learning aids.

1. Assure all parents and guardians that students will be supervised in their use of the Web, either directly by you or through the use of products that filter out those web sites that students should not access.
2. If you wish students to communicate with family members through e-mail, be certain you receive, in writing, a list of those family members with whom students may correspond.
3. Online communication activities students undertake involving other students or adults will be monitored.
4. Students will be helped to understand the kinds of information they can (e.g., first names) or cannot (e.g., last names, home phone numbers, etc.) divulge to others.

Whether created by you, the school, or the district, policy guidelines will ensure that students gain an understanding of responsibility and good citizenship as they pertain to using the Internet for literacy learning.

SOFTWARE INTERACTIONS

Computers and their software are expensive, somewhat delicate tools that need to be treated with care. Most students will not mistreat them. You will want to discuss proper handling of CD-ROMs, laserdiscs, data on disks, and applications programs with students, and you will want to create, post, and discuss classroom policies you deem necessary. Typically, experts recommend software, district or school personnel evaluate it, and you preview it to determine how you can best use it to meet your instructional objectives. These procedures ensure fairly well that you will not have those problems you might encounter with unfiltered materials on the Internet.

There are a few things you can do to set a good tone for using computer software in your classroom. One is to avoid sending students to a computer center or giving them a piece of software as a *reward* for finishing their "real" work. Such actions show a low opinion of the effectiveness of technology in the teaching and learning environment. The actions also undermine the value of computers as important, even critical, tools for developing literacy in its broadest sense. You will not want to convey the idea that computers are add-ons to the literacy curriculum instead of being a central part of it.

Another practice you may wish to avoid is placing students in "games" that have little or no direct relation to their needs in developing new capabilities in the language and visual arts. Often such games are a waste of valuable educational time. For instance, having a student who thoroughly knows phonics play a phonics-based game is probably not an efficient use of that student's time. The student could and should be learning something new. Ensure that students actually need to develop specific skills by assessing their capabilities before placing them in such programs. (See chapter 10). Carefully matching tasks to software that will help students grow will help you create a classroom environment that demonstrates the beneficial uses of technology in literacy learning.

You can model effective use of software by creating lessons using programs such as Microsoft PowerPoint. See the Tech Tip "Making Interactive Lessons Using PowerPoint" on this book's web site. Students will want to use features in programs that they see you use.

TEACHER ROUTINES

Technological developments make possible a worldwide community of learners. You can access a potpourri of ideas, languages, and cultures from all over the world, and these form the basis for studying a multitude of visual and language arts. Having so much to choose from, however, can overwhelm some students—and teachers! Therefore, you can perform an excellent service to students by learning how to create themes, use efficient search strategies to "mine" the Internet's resources, and locate both online (CD-ROMs, for instance) and offline resources of value to students in their research. You can create and bookmark webliographies, which are lists containing the URLs of suitable web sites that relate to a given topic. As students polish their Internet search strategies, they can assume more and more responsibility for locating additional sources of information, but you will help them a great deal by providing initial scaffolding for them.

PLACEMENT AND CARE OF COMPUTERS

The location of computers in a classroom influences their use and student interactions.

Many schools were built long before anyone imagined that so many computers would someday be placed in labs and classrooms. Just getting telephone and Internet lines into some classrooms has been a major task, but new wireless access to the Internet is growing in popularity and is making access easier. Electricity has been a problem also because there may not be enough electrical outlets in classrooms, and the ones available are placed around the perimeter of the rooms. It follows, then, that computers tend to be placed against the outside walls of classrooms. I have said elsewhere (Valmont, 2000) that "although efficient in terms of installing electricity and network connectivity, these placements are the least teaching and learning friendly, especially for literacy development where interacting and sharing are common" (p. 171). If you can do so, place computers in "pods" of three or four computers with the backs of the monitors facing inside the triangle or square that is formed. Place at least two chairs at each table. Students will be able to work together more easily and collaboratively when computers are configured this way. If computers are placed in long lines, communication is curtailed—or loud—but some teachers prefer short rows or computers along the walls because they can monitor several screens at the same time. Your decisions and circumstances will dictate the placement of computers and peripherals.

Most students respect computer equipment and treat it with care—especially when they enjoy working on projects and see that they are learning and creating things of interest. Be sure that all students know how to boot up a computer and shut it down properly. You can garner respect and cooperation by assigning students, on a rotating basis, to turn on computers and their peripherals (e.g., printers, scanners) in the morning and shut them down correctly at the end of the day. In addition, you can have students use a computer to check and report the day's weather, read online newspaper headlines, or tell a joke of the day from web sites you have bookmarked for such uses (Scolari et al., 2000, p. 30). These kinds of activities help students appreciate how computers are important to their learning and information gathering.

LIMITING WASTED TIME

Most teachers say insufficient time hinders them from learning more about using technology in their classrooms. You and students have much to accomplish during a school day, and students cannot afford to waste time. It usually takes a while to feel comfortable working with computers, software applications, and the Internet. However, you and students will soon learn the common features of applications, and the learning curve becomes less burdensome. You can learn much about the Internet by exploring your own interests or engaging in professional development activities online. You can help students work efficiently by having them work with partners, scheduling students' computer time, and incorporating a variety of other strategies.

Be sure that students have ample and equal time at computers. There are various ways to schedule students to work at computers, and if you work with learning centers you already know how to rotate students through them. Keep a log at each computer so students can keep track of the time they spend there. This gives you a record of who worked at each machine and how much time they spent. You can change the form daily or weekly and review it to ensure that students are sharing properly.

It is a good idea to have each student create a computer journal to record not only when they work at a computer, but also what they did while they were working. They can jot down URLs, the software names, descriptions of their projects, and other information in such journals. Students can also keep track of new vocabulary words they encounter and write down questions that come up in their work. See Figure 3.3.

One of the first things you should learn about the Internet is how to conduct efficient searches. Combine learning about a few powerful metasearch engines with exploring one of your hobbies. It will not take you long to learn to leave off plural endings, think of several pertinent keywords, narrow or broaden your search terms, and use **Boolean logic,** commands that limit searches. Soon you will learn to conduct a search and then use a *second* keyword to search through the original search results. For example, you could use the search engine Google, to get results from a search of the keyword *phonics.* Then, you could use the "Find in Page" feature of the web browser to search through the original results for the word *worksheet.* This second search takes you to a place on the original search listing where both *phonics* and *worksheet* are mentioned. This results in real efficiency!

Save students time by sharing what you learn about conducting metasearches. In addition, bookmark sites to help them get started on projects.

FIGURE 3.3

Amphi Teachers Respond: How Can We Get All Students Through a One-Computer Center or Mini Lab?

Source: Used by permission of Peggy Steffans, Instructional Technology Coordinator, Amphitheater School District, Tucson, AZ.

- Create groups in which partners switch roles. One person types, one person reads, and one person uses the mouse.
- Create sequential activities.
- Have a student of the day demonstrate a site to the entire class.
- In a ten-computer lab with a class of about thirty students engage in a three-day rotation process. Each student is on for one day. The two days that the students are off, they engage in other activities. This is especially useful if the computers are near the library. The students can use the library for research on the two days that they are not on the computers.
- Make a center with a schedule that all students rotate through.
- Schedule the time so students know their time for the week (i.e., Maria's time is Tuesday from 10:20–10:40; Joseph's time is from 10:40–11:00).
- When one student or group finishes, have them tell the next group what to do. In this manner you do not have to explain as much.
- Create efficient groups. Have at least one student who can read the material, have one student who is a confident technology user, and so forth.
- Encourage peer tutoring.
- Follow a "learn-teach-learn" process in which the first group learns from the teacher. That group teaches the next group. Continue this until everyone has learned the new task. We know that we learn things better when we have to teach about them, so make students part of this process.
- Use a projection device to show an entire class what they will be doing on the computer before the students begin.
- Have one group start an activity, and then have another group finish the activity.
- In a group of six people, have three people engage in a role-playing activity. The other three students stand behind watching. The trios switch half way through the activity. Students watching during the first phase are attentive because they realize they must know what is going on. The second group is attentive because the activity was meaningful, and they bought into it during their time. They want to learn what happens.

FIGURE 3.3
(continued)

- Have students share what they accomplished on the computer with the entire class.
- Use a storyboard or other preorganizer so that prethinking occurs before the child is on the computer. Key ideas or concepts can be outlined beforehand, allowing most efficient use of time.
- Encourage active participation of all students in the group, so they know what they are supposed to accomplish and how they will demonstrate learning.
- Have students develop questions for the teacher or quizzes or puzzles for other students.
- Show the "student of the week" key things that might happen with the computer activities for the week. Tell the other students that they will need to ask the "student of the week" if they have problems.
- Post schedules, responsibilities, and assignments.

Sometimes, you should locate sites for students, but at other times they should search for their own sites. Consider these points:

- If the purpose of the activity is *to use the content* at web sites, locate sites for students.
- If *time* is a factor (i.e., limited lab time or few computers in the classroom for lots of students), locate sites for students.
- If the purpose of the activity is *for students to learn and use online search strategies,* let students find pertinent sites after you teach them how to conduct searches.
- If students are working alone or in small groups and are *expected to be independent researchers,* let them find their own sites after you teach them how to conduct searches.

See the Teaching Tip "Create an HTML Document to Access Specific Web Sites."

TEACHING TIPS Create an HTML Document to Access Specific Web Sites

Students can use word-processing programs such as Microsoft Word, Corel WordPerfect, or web page creation programs such as SiteCentral or Web Workshop to create an HTML document that can serve as their own personal "Internet library" (D'Ignazio, 1996–1997). The computer on which they make such a document does not need to be connected to the Internet. It can be created entirely offline for use later on a computer with Internet access.

Help students decide what to include in their personal Internet libraries. Students might want to include sites that report the local weather or the latest news, that can track airplanes when someone is coming for a visit, or that have information about their pets or hobbies. You can build decision-making opportunities into the planning of personal Internet libraries. Students can decide how to organize their bookmarks, what text they want to include about the sites they list in the document, and how they want the HTML document to look. Students may wish to add animations, decorations, or icons to it.

Students must take two critical steps so their HTML document will work correctly when they use a computer with Internet access:

1. Every time they type in a URL, *it must be 100 percent correct before they press the enter key.* If they later discover that the link does not work because they made an error, they need to completely erase the URL that has the mistake and type the entire URL again correctly.
2. When they have everything typed correctly, students must use the "Save As" option and save the file as an HTML file.

To use their personal Internet libraries online, students open Netscape and pull down the "File" menu, click on the "Open Page" option, and then either type in the location of the file (e.g., A:\My-Library) or locate the file on the "A:\" disk drive using the "Choose File" option. (Microsoft Internet Explorer uses similar steps.) The browser will open the pages as web pages because they were previously turned into HTML files. If students click on a link, the browser will treat the link just as it does any other hypertext link, quickly showing the linked web site. Pressing the "Back" button takes a student back to the Internet library HTML document, and he or she can then click on another link.

Although students' documents are used for accessing web sites, they are not web pages that others can access (i.e., they have no URL of their own and are not being "broadcast"). That means the documents you and students create this way can contain information (e.g., students' whole names) that someone on the Internet cannot access (D'Ignazio, 1996–1997, p. 60).

You, as a teacher, can use this strategy to create disks for students that contain specific sites you want students to visit. For instance, if you want to create an online scavenger hunt that takes students to specific web sites, you can type each question you want them to seek answers for and follow it with the link to the URL of the web site they need to visit. Save this as an HTML file, and make as many copies of the file as you need to, depending on how many students can access the Internet at the same time in your classroom. If you are operating in a classroom with only one Internet-capable computer, you could create the document once, open it in the computer's browser, and use the "Save As" command to make a separate file for each student in the class.

Your browser lets you make new folders, so you can make a folder into which each student can enter their own bookmark choices (Grabe & Grabe, 2000, pp. 116–118). If, for instance, students find many web sites they wish to use in a report, they can bookmark them into their own folders, cutting and pasting only those really useful web sites into a document or web page creation program for use later in the final report.

Source: William J. Valmont, based on D'Ignazio, F. (1996–1997). Build a virtual library on disk. *Learning & Leading with Technology, 24*(4), 60–62.

PRETHINKING BEFORE COMPUTER USE

Offline planning enables efficient use of computers if students have limited access.

When you prepare a thematic unit of study, you will spend some time pondering what resources, activities, and methods will fit well into the unit. A natural step is for you to create assignments that will involve computer and other technologies as part of the unit. Once you know your overall plan, you can go a step farther to identify applicable web resources and software for students. In other words, you will engage in much prethinking and planning. In a similar fashion, teach students to be prepared to make efficient use of computer time by prethinking what they want to accomplish in the time allotted to them. Just as creating a storyboard is effective in planning a video production, prethinking and planning help focus work at a computer. Students need to understand what they want to accomplish and how the computer will help them achieve their goals. Be aware, however, that even preplanning and prethinking will not always help students finish their projects in a timely fashion. See Figure 3.4.

When students work together cooperatively, they should be thinking not only about the content of their projects, but also considering effective strategies to complete their tasks efficiently. Encourage students to spend some time thinking about how they can make the best use of print and electronic materials during their work.

REFERENCE SKILLS

In dealing with the vast amount of information readily available today, it is extremely important to foster students' respect for copyright laws. It is also important to maintain high standards in conveying to students fair-use laws, which govern what teachers and students can use in educational settings. Basic discussions about plagiarism—stealing and using other people's ideas as if they are yours—will help you establish a no-tolerance policy toward students' use of other people's work without permission or attribution, or in any way that implies it was a student's original thinking. A creative approach to assignments that is gaining popularity with teachers is to have students *act on* information they find rather than merely repeat it. That way, the emphasis is on thinking, not copying. For instance, instead of simply asking students to gather facts about the planet Mars, have students take information they find and write a one-act play about two astronauts who have just landed on that planet. Would there be gravity? Would it be hot or cold? Are there mountains? Students can blend the facts they learn about Mars with fiction to create a dialogue that tells a story. There is no easy way to plagiarize originality!

FIGURE 3.4

Amphi Teachers Respond: What Do You Do When Students Don't Finish a Task That Requires a Computer?

Source: Used by permission of Peggy Steffans, Instructional Technology Coordinator, Amphitheater School District, Tucson, AZ.

- Permit students to stay after school and finish the work.
- Have computers available during lunchtime for students to complete their work.
- Allow students to finish their work during recess.
- Let students sit behind others who are completing the task to observe and help finish the assignment.
- Let technology "Whiz Kids" assist students. Whiz Kids are students who attend after-school meetings to become the technology experts at the school. They assist in troubleshooting hardware and software problems, and they teach other students and teachers how to use technology.
- Encourage students to attend homework help nights.
- Provide alternative assignments that don't require a computer.
- Adjust the assignment's timelines.
- Print information from the Internet and allow students to take it home and read.
- Get more computers! : -)
- Depending on the reason the student didn't complete the task (lack of responsibility, illness), give the student a grade of 0 or choose to ignore the assignment and don't average it into his or her grade.
- Provide buffer activities. Build extra time into the schedule so students who didn't finish will have more time to finish and those who finished can do an enrichment activity like creating a picture or slide show in Kid Pix Deluxe. Make the activity one that students will want to do so that they work hard to finish the assignment on time.
- If students finish early, partner them with someone who hasn't yet finished.
- If you know that a student or group of students will not be able to finish an entire assignment, target the most important parts and tell them what you expect them to accomplish.
- Provide follow-up discussions with the entire class so that all students will learn the information even if they didn't accomplish it on the computer.
- Suggest that students finish the assignment on computers at the local public library.
- Schedule computer time during an elective period.

FIGURE 3.4
(continued)

- Use techniques to motivate students to want to finish. Most students like to work on the computer, and you might tell them that if they don't finish in the provided time, they will have to take it home and complete it with paper and pencil.
- Design activities with the possibility that students might require additional time or that assignments could be finished without the computer.

COORDINATING WITH OTHER LANGUAGE ARTS TEACHERS

Knowing the scope and sequence of both literacy and technology development is vital.

You may, for example, be working with fourth-grade students, but those students possibly have been learning to integrate technology with literacy activities since kindergarten or even before starting school. Also, they will have four more years of elementary and middle school to engage in activities that link technology and literacy. It behooves you to coordinate your efforts with other language arts teachers so you can ensure that your students are learning appropriate technology skills as they develop language and visual arts capabilities. You and other teachers will want to discuss together not only required language arts standards, materials, and teaching-learning activities in general, but also how each of you is currently using technology to help develop literacy capabilities. There is no right or wrong way to coordinate technology use throughout elementary and middle school years, but you definitely need to know what your students have learned before coming to you and what they will likely encounter at higher grade levels.

The Internet Pyramid (Johnston, 1997–1998) is just one example of a possible progression of Internet instruction that moves from teacher-directed to student-centered activities in grades one through five. Students learn about the Internet in first grade by visiting web sites for which the teacher creates questions for students to answer. In second grade, students and their teacher routinely search the Internet for information and pictures dealing with specific topics (e.g., birds). Third-grade students, under close teacher supervision, participate in a variety of group and individual Internet searches. Fourth-grade students engage in research and create projects using information found on the Internet, and they use e-mail to communicate with students and adults in other locales. Independent research by fifth-grade students involves getting information from Internet resources, bookmarking sites, taking notes, and asking an author's permission to use graphics. Students also discuss copyright issues (Johnston, 1997–1998).

You and other teachers may wish to develop an *overall progression* in order to create a broad sense of direction throughout the grade levels. In reality, however, students' abilities to use technology and your opportunities to integrate technology and literacy activities may vary greatly, so flexibility is important. You will need flexibility during the year as you work with students, and you will need to vary technology usage in your classroom based on what students already know and will need to know in their remaining years of school. More and more students are already computer savvy, and you will not want to restrict their ability to use technology as they engage in language and visual arts activities.

STANDARDS

IRA and ISTE standards can help you develop effective learning experiences.

The International Society for Technology in Education (ISTE) has developed *National Educational Technology Standards for Students* (1998), often referred to as NETS. See Figure 3.5. It later produced a follow-up to that work titled *National Educational Technology Standards for Students: Connecting Curriculum and Technology* (2000). For this latter work, teams of writers created English language arts learning activities, essentially thematic units, across the grade levels, as well as multidisciplinary resource units for pre-K–2 to 9–12 grade levels. This valuable reference models how teachers working within a curriculum area such as language arts (or blending several content disciplines together) can easily integrate technology into a daily teaching routine. You can learn about the thematic units created by ISTE at **http://www.iste.org.** The joint standards of the IRA and the National Council of Teachers of English (NCTE) are keyed to activities in the NETS units. See Figure 3.6. As you saw in chapter 1, these excellent model thematic units can help you develop similar units for use in your own classroom. (You might like to review the ALA's "Nine Information Literacy Standards for Student Learning" as well. View them at **http://www.ala.org/aasl/ip_nine.html.**)

ENSURING TECHNOLOGY IS THE MEANS (NOT THE END) FOR LEARNING

As noted in chapter 1, broad themes afford opportunities for you to build in essential knowledge bases while permitting students flexibility and choice in identifying parts of the theme that interest them the most. You can determine and sequence literacy skills and influence the content to be

FIGURE 3.5

ISTE NETS for Students

1. Basic operations and concepts
   - Students demonstrate a sound understanding of the nature and operation of technology systems.
   - Students are proficient in the use of technology.
2. Social, ethical, and human issues
   - Students understand the ethical, cultural, and societal issues related to technology.
   - Students practice responsible use of technology systems, information, and software.
   - Students develop positive attitudes toward technology uses that support lifelong learning, collaboration, personal pursuits, and productivity.
3. Technology productivity tools
   - Students use technology tools to enhance learning, increase productivity, and promote creativity.
   - Students use productivity tools to collaborate in constructing technology-enhanced models, preparing publications, and producing other creative works.
4. Technology communications tools
   - Students use telecommunications to collaborate, publish, and interact with peers, experts, and other audiences.
   - Students use a variety of media and formats to communicate information and ideas effectively to multiple audiences.
5. Technology research tools
   - Students use technology to locate, evaluate, and collect information from a variety of sources.
   - Students use technology tools to process data and report results.
   - Students evaluate and select new information resources and technological innovations based on the appropriateness to specific tasks.
6. Technology problem-solving and decision-making tools
   - Students use technology resources for solving problems and making informed decisions.
   - Students employ technology in the development of strategies for solving problems in the real world.

Source: Reprinted with permission from *National Educational Technology Standards for Students—Connecting Curriculum and Technology,* © 2000, ISTE (International Society for Technology in Education), 800-336-5191 (U.S. and Canada) or 541-302-3777 (International), iste@iste.org, www.iste.org. Permission does not constitute an endorsement by ISTE. For more information about the NETS Project, contact Lajeane Thomas, Director, NETS Project, 318-257-3923, lthomas@latech.edu.

learned. Incorporating various kinds of media, including computers and other electronic materials, helps you integrate literacy and technology naturally. Technology is not used for the sake of learning the technology. Rather, it is the means students use to locate, arrange, analyze, and present their knowledge as they develop literacy capabilities.

FIGURE 3.6

Standards for the English Language Arts (1996)

The vision guiding these standards is that all students must have the opportunities and resources to develop the language skills they need to pursue life's goals and to participate as informed, productive members of society. These standards assume that literacy growth begins before children enter school as they experience and experiment with literacy activities—reading and writing, and associating spoken words with their graphic representations. Recognizing this fact, these standards encourage the development of curriculum and instruction that make productive use of the emerging literacy abilities that children bring to school. Furthermore, the standards provide ample room for the innovation and creativity essential to teaching and learning. They are not prescriptions for particular curriculum or instruction.

Although we present these standards as a list, we want to emphasize that they are not distinct and separable; they are, in fact, interrelated and should be considered as a whole.

1. Students read a wide range of print and nonprint texts to build an understanding of texts, of themselves, and of the cultures of the United States and the world; to acquire new information; to respond to the needs and demands of society and the workplace; and for personal fulfillment. Among these texts are fiction and nonfiction, classic and contemporary works.
2. Students read a wide range of literature from many periods in many genres to build an understanding of the many dimensions (e.g., philosophical, ethical, aesthetic) of human experience.
3. Students apply a wide range of strategies to comprehend, interpret, evaluate, and appreciate texts. They draw upon their prior experience, their interactions with other readers and writers, their knowledge of word meaning and of other texts, their word identification strategies, and their understanding of textual features (e.g., sound-letter correspondence, sentence structure, context, graphics).
4. Students adjust their use of spoken, written, and visual language (e.g., conventions, style, vocabulary) to communicate effectively with a variety of audiences for different purposes.
5. Students employ a wide range of strategies as they write and use different writing process elements appropriately to communicate with different audiences for a variety of purposes.
6. Students apply knowledge of language structure, language conventions (e.g., spelling and punctuation), media techniques, figurative language, and genre to create, critique, and discuss print and nonprint texts.
7. Students conduct research on issues and interests by generating ideas and questions, and by posing problems. They gather, evaluate, and synthesize data from a variety of sources (e.g., print and nonprint texts, artifacts, people) to communicate their discoveries in ways that suit their purpose and audience.
8. Student use a variety of technological and informational resources (e.g., libraries, databases, computer networks, video) to gather and synthesize information and to create and communicate knowledge.

9. Students develop an understanding of and respect for diversity in language use, patterns, and dialects across cultures, ethnic groups, geographic regions, and social roles.
10. Students whose first language is not English make use of their first language to develop competency in the English language arts and to develop an understanding of content across the curriculum.
11. Students participate as knowledgeable, reflective, creative, and critical members of a variety of literacy communities.
12. Students use spoken, written, and visual language to accomplish their own purposes (e.g., for learning, enjoyment, persuasion, and the exchange of information).

Source: *Standards for the English Language Arts,* p. 24. Copyright 1996 by the International Reading Association and National Council of Teachers of English. Used by permission. All rights reserved.

You probably created (or will create) thematic unit plans during student teaching. An in-depth discussion about creating such units is outside the scope of this book, but Heinich et al., who write extensively about using instructional media as part of teaching, mention these five important points to consider (1999, p. 21):

- Select a theme that involves a variety of areas.
- Provide content and skills learning in each unit.
- Incorporate a variety of media and methods.
- Include meaningful learner activities.
- Make your thematic unit the proper size for your students and the topic.

Heinich et al. (1999, pp. 32–33) also emphasize the importance of effectively using media for instruction. They developed a model that may be helpful to you in planning instruction. They call the model ASSURE.

A — Analyze Learners
S — State Objectives
S — Select Methods, Media, and Materials
U — Utilize Media and Materials
R — Require Learner Participation
E — Evaluate and Revise

ASSURE can remind you to be selective in the use of media and all types of technology. Just because you have a software program does not mean you should automatically use it. To carry this idea a little further, just because an application has a particular feature does not mean that all students should use it. For instance, with clip art it is easy to cut and paste, but sometimes students get a better effect by drawing objects that differ from one another. A barnyard full of identical chickens facing the same way just does not look as natural or creative as assorted chickens of different sizes and colors.

In the early stages of planning how to use technology in your classroom, you will want to decide which hardware, software, and other media will help students best engage in their various learning experiences. There are computer applications of various types, and you will want to determine which kinds you might recommend for purchase or have students use for specific purposes.

- Some programs help students organize ideas and information and are useful in developing concepts visually.
- Some programs are drill and practice software (also known by some as "drill and kill" because they are often limited and boring).
- Tutorial software is designed to teach content. You can find online tutorials, for instance, that teach how to use features of a given program.
- Recreational games and instructional games are plentiful. Recreational games are better used at home or, at most, to help students develop mouse skills. Students who need to learn—or reinforce their knowledge of—the content or actions called for in the games profit most from using instructional games.
- Simulations permit students to deal with real-life decisions without suffering real-life consequences.

Think about the qualities of various types of software as you plan thematic units and ask yourself these questions: "Will the nature of the software add to or distract from my overall teaching and learning goals?" and "Do I have the right types of software for my selected activities?" Thinking and acting on the issues raised in this chapter should help in your efforts to effectively integrate technology and literacy in your classroom.

SUMMARY

- Schools need to have technology plans and acceptable use policies.
- Decisions must be made about using Internet filters and obtaining parental permissions.
- Stress the importance of safety when students deal with people on the Internet.
- Be proactive in obtaining necessary equipment and software for your classroom use.
- You set the tone for valuing technology as an aid to improving literacy capabilities.
- Advance offline preparation can help students make efficient use of technology.
- You should determine which literacy and technology abilities students already possess and will need to acquire in later grades in order to coordinate system-wide technology and literacy growth.
- Literacy and technology standards can help you create beneficial literacy experiences.

ACTIVITIES

1. Locate and discuss a school or district's technology plan and acceptable use policy.
2. Visit several web sites for Internet filtering products to determine how the filters work.
3. Visit some classrooms to see how other teachers have arranged computers in technology centers.
4. Discuss with teachers how they integrate literacy and technology standards.

SOFTWARE

Camp Frog Hollow (MAC), Don Johnston Incorporated, Pre-K–3
These are activities for students with special needs.

Chronicle (MAC), Sunburst Technology, K and up
This program creates timelines with videos, graphics, and sounds.

Co:Writer 4000, Don Johnston Incorporated, Pre-K–Adult
This is a grammar-smart word-prediction program. The software prompts students with word choices.

Factory Deluxe, The, Sunburst Technology, 4–8
This program offers practice in sequencing, ordering skills, spatial perception, and visual discrimination.

Get Up and Go, Sunburst Technology, 2–3
Students can make and interpret timelines.

IntelliKeys, IntelliTools, Inc., K–3
This software has a special keyboard and basic activities for students who have difficulty using a standard keyboard.

IntelliPics®, IntelliTools, Inc., K and up
Using graphics from any source, you can create multimedia activities. You can record messages up to seven minutes and animate graphics.

IntelliTalk II, IntelliTools, Inc., K–2
This is a word-processing program that combines speech, text, and graphics for students with special needs. It, as well as other programs designed for students with special needs, can be used by students who respond well to information delivered in multimedia formats.

IntelliTools Reading, IntelliTools, Inc., SpEd
IntelliTools Reading is a balanced literacy program. There are story kits to use with this product.

K. C. & Clyde in Fly Ball, Don Johnston Incorporated, 1–6
Students decide which direction to take the story. The program is designed for special education students.

Rosie's Walk, Texas School for the Deaf, 1–6
The story is animated and signed with American Sign Language. It is designed to build signing and reading vocabulary.

TimeLiner, Tom Snyder Productions, K and up
Students can make, illustrate, and print timelines in English or Spanish.

WebHEARit, The Productivity Works/is Sound, All
This is an ActiveX component that allows any Internet Explorer application to "speak" a web page's content and navigational links.

FOR FURTHER READING

D' Ignazio, F., & Davis, J. (1997). "What I did last summer" 21st century style. *Learning and Leading with Technology, 24*(8), 44–48.

Dockstader, J. (1999). Teachers of the 21st century know the what, why, and how of technology integration. *T.H.E. Journal, 26*(6), 73–74.

Kahn, J. (1996–97). Help! I only have one computer. *Learning & Leading with Technology, 24*(4), 16.

Wood, J. M. (2000, January/February). 10 ways to take charge of the web. *Scholastic Instructor,* 69–72.

Using Technology to Develop Reading and Thinking Strategies

INTRODUCTION

There are several kinds of reading. **Literal reading** involves a basic understanding of what a writer is trying to convey. **Interpretive reading** occurs when the reader understands what is implied "between the lines," often making numerous inferences and intuitive leaps. Today, when anyone can place anything on the Internet, a third type of reading has become more important than ever. It is **critical reading.** According to Burns, Roe, and Ross (1999), "Critical reading is evaluating written material—comparing the ideas discovered in the material with known standards and drawing conclusions about their accuracy, appropriateness, and timeliness" (p. 242). Being a critical reader involves:

1. knowing one's own beliefs and prejudices;
2. knowing standards set by the community, state, and country; and
3. knowing strategies people use in verbal and nonverbal electronic materials to persuade you to do or not do something (or to think a certain way).

The Internet holds a large amount of material that you and students can use to develop critical thinking abilities. From first grade on, students can learn to think critically about things they see, read, and hear. We will discuss how technology and a more inclusive definition of literacy are affecting comprehension instruction. An important point to keep in mind as you read this chapter is that many of the things you and students have done in the past can still be done, only now you can use technology as a valuable new teaching and learning tool. You can use a variety of traditional strategies to help students read and interpret as well as write and construct print and electronic texts. Over time, said Kathy Jongsma (1999–2000), a former board member of the International Reading Association,

> I've learned that DRTAs (Directed Reading-Thinking Activities), Reciprocal Questioning and Reciprocal Teaching, QARs (Question Answer Relationships), E-T-Rs (Experience-Text-Relationships), Story Maps, Story Webs, Plot Relationship Charts, K-W-L (What I know–What I want to learn–What I learned), and K-W-L-Q charts (adding a category for new questions I've generated) work well to help students comprehend texts. (p. 310)

We will explain how you can use the Directed Reading-Thinking Activity (DRTA) as a major, overarching strategy to help students become independent, more thoughtful readers, and we will introduce you to excellent electronic materials you can use to help students become literate. In addition, we will present basic ways to help students learn DRTAs, sometimes using K-W-L as a way to track students' predictions. For many years, authorities in the field of literacy have described and recommended a variety of strategies for developing comprehension capabilities, and they are just as pertinent when you use electronic materials for instruction as they are when you use print materials. You will certainly want to continue to use all of the effective strategies you already know, while adding other strategies to enhance online comprehension.

As you read, search for answers to these questions:

- How do evolving definitions of literacy affect how you create learning experiences?
- What are the major values of the DRTA strategy?
- What other strategies can I use to help students become independent learners?
- How can I encourage effective student interactions with electronic materials?

The Importance of Critical Thinking and Critical Reading

In a wonderful Mark Twain story, "The Man That Corrupted Hadleyburg," the residents of a town were so protected from reality that when the first evil person came to town, they were easily bamboozled.* People had

*A radio play of the Hadleyburg story can be accessed at **http://www.freeyellow.com/members6/jpdoran/hadley.htm.**

not learned to protect themselves. The alternative to *you* protecting students from harm is to help *them* acquire the tools to protect themselves. There is a great deal of distrust of much of the information that resides on the Internet. Not only are people concerned that students might gain access to pornography or fall prey to unscrupulous criminals, they are also concerned that students will read inaccurate or misleading information online. Indeed, there are web sites that try to rewrite history or that make nasty people appear to be the ones who were maligned. Some people who have their own agendas put materials online. Because much of the information on the Internet is "unfiltered" by churches, governments, experts, publishers, librarians, and other trusted people, some individuals want to censor the Internet. Of course, they forget that even highly reliable publishers have, on occasion, let factual inaccuracies and misleading or just plain fabricated information get past them. Historians also note that throughout human history, people in power sometimes act with malice aforethought when "filtering" information. Societies and cultures are shaped and preserved by the information people access. Today, anyone with a modern computer and access to the Internet can locate materials from anywhere in the world. Some of the traditional gatekeepers of knowledge will suffer because they may become ignored. However, voices that never would have been heard through traditional publishing channels can now be heard.

What can you do to help students use information on the Internet wisely? First, you can emphasize strongly that a healthy skepticism is needed no matter what an individual reads, whether the material has been filtered or not. Elementary school teachers are the first teachers to help students learn to think logically and critically. Teachers have traditionally asked students to be wary of an author's purpose, to investigate an author's credentials, to suspend judgment until other sources are examined to verify information, to learn the propaganda tricks that people use, and to engage in a variety of other critical-thinking behaviors. You need to continue to stress such reading and thinking skills *precisely* because students will likely encounter misinformation on the Internet.

Sadly, too many people believe that the information they read in newspapers, magazines, or books is completely valid. They take things at face value. Unfortunately, some individuals also believe that the information they obtain over the Internet is fully reliable. There is no guarantee that this is the case, so we must help students learn to develop a questioning attitude, to guard themselves against propaganda, to distinguish between facts and opinions, and to verify information using reliable sources.

AUTHOR'S MOTIVES AND CREDENTIALS

You can help students think about why a web site exists by questioning its purpose. Ask students: Why do you think this web site is online? Is it there to sell something? Is it there because it is public information paid for by a government agency? Is it there because someone is trying to help other people? Does someone have a big ego? These are the kinds of questions you can raise with students, alerting them to possible motives for placing things online.

Help students question an author's authority to present information. Here are more questions for students to raise: Who is the author and what are his or her credentials? Can you find the author in *Who's Who* or some other reference? Does a reputable organization or government agency sponsor the site? Does the author have a résumé you can access online or request by mail? Is contact information (e-mail address, mailing address, phone and fax numbers) provided? Are other references or people available to confirm information found at the site? Are there print materials you can request? Is the web site sponsored by a particular organization? What product is being promoted, if any? Are there advertisements on the pages? How does the advertising relate to the information?

Another area you can help students consider is the tone of the author's message. Is the information presented logically? Are there emotionally loaded words in the text? Is there an attempt to persuade through propaganda strategies? Are you being pressured to buy something—either ideas or products? Are there subtle appeals to your senses?

Still other things to consider are: Is the information current? (Check the "this page last updated" information.) Has the site received any awards? (If so, by whom?) Is there a counter to tell you how often people have visited this site? (What might that information mean?) How did you get to the site? (Referral, search, directed by the teacher, by accident?)

PROPAGANDA

Propaganda techniques have been taught in schools for decades. The Institute for Propaganda Analysis in 1937 described the major types of propaganda that are widely used to sway people. Included are: name calling, glittering generalities, transfer, testimonial, plain folks, card stacking, and bandwagon. The institute's "Propaganda" page at **http://carmen.artsci.washington.edu/propaganda/contents.htm** has a table of contents that links to in-depth information about each of the common techniques, as well as other information about propaganda. Use web sites to show students examples of both World War II propaganda and that used today in several countries. See also the article "Reading and Propaganda: How To Believe It or Not!" at **http://wphs.ohio.k12.wv.us/warwood/skills9.htm.** This site contains a short discussion of propaganda techniques and ends with a short quiz to see if you can identify the techniques used in the given examples.

ADVERTISEMENTS

Another area for critical thinking and analysis is advertising. Ask students: How can ads distract you from scholarly interests? One method of analysis is to determine to which of your senses an ad is attempting to appeal. Ads can appeal to sight (animations, color, novelty), sound (music, sounds of horns), touch (the softness of tissues), smell (homemade bread), or taste (chocolate with almonds), or some combination thereof.

Online ads are new iterations of the kinds of ads found in newspapers, magazines, and your mailbox, but their purpose generally remains the same—to gain your attention in hopes that you will buy something (a product or maybe an idea). Therefore, you and students can study online ads to see how they are trying to lure you. Particularly, be on the lookout for the following:

- **Using keywords:** "free" (to the first 100 people), "you," "money," "save"
- **Using attention grabbers:** Appeal of "getting something for nothing"
- **Encouraging action on your part:** "Click here for . . ."

Online newspapers are excellent sources of advertisements. Students can monitor an online newspaper over time to see whose ads appear, and they can make a database of the *kinds* of ads that appear. They can study the ages or occupations of the potential ad users. Students also can keep track of how ads are placed on the web site to either blend in with other texts or stand out from them. Web sites are a rich source of advertising that you and students can scrutinize for ads aimed specifically at school-age students. Your work with ads can help students become critical readers of materials meant to manipulate them. The Flying Inkpot, an online magazine based in Singapore has a list of links to major newspapers throughout the world; see **http://inkpot.com/news/majint.html.** You can also find links to local, state, or regional newspapers at this site.

SYSTEMS THINKING

Some critical thinking results from working with systems thinking. A system, according to Kauffman (1980), "is a collection of parts which interact with each other to function as a whole" (p. 1). Systems thinking involves looking at patterns in an organization that indicate how the various parts work together. I once observed students dealing with systems thinking in a middle school. Students varied the amounts of insulin in a computer simulation program in order to determine the resulting change in glucose levels in diabetics. In another example of systems thinking, I watched as students "designed" two dinosaurs, determining such characteristics as what they ate, how aggressive they were, how fast they reproduced, the number of offspring they produced, and other factors. When they ran the computer program, students discovered how long the animals they created survived. STELLA is a major educational program used to build simulations. Download a demonstration of STELLA from **http://www.hps-inc.com/STELLAdemo.htm.** Also helpful is the "Systems Thinking & Practice" page at the Oregon State University web site, located at **http://www.orst.edu/instruct/stp/systhnk.htm.** This site includes materials about systems thinking concepts, habits, models, and exercises.

The Changing Nature of Literacy

NEW DEFINITIONS OF LITERACY

Astonishing amounts of materials are being produced today that will be available only in electronic formats. According to Moore (2001), "Over 80 percent of the world's data are born digital, not on paper, fiche, charts, films, or maps, meaning that . . . [their] first occurrence is in a computer-generated format" (p. 28). It is absolutely necessary that you help students learn to deal with electronic formats and to make intelligent use of the information they contain. Outside schools, you see heavily interconnected digital communication systems becoming central to governments, businesses, industries, the entertainment world, and personal agencies. Technology has heavily influenced culture; these cultural forces are not only affecting literacy education (Leu & Kinzer, 2000) but, according to

McNabb (2001), "are compelling enough to validate use of the Internet for educational purposes" (p. 48). The Internet continues to dominate the digital communications world, but other digital materials (e.g., CD-ROMs and DVDs) also contain important fiction and nonfiction resources that students must learn to use thoughtfully.

Current definitions of literacy include verbal and nonverbal components.

As we discussed in chapter 1, literacy in a polysymbolic environment includes much more than a knowledge of the traditional language arts; it also involves interpreting and constructing in visual and other symbolic worlds. Literacy requires active listening to and active reading of both paper and electronic language-based verbal messages. Literacy additionally includes the active interpretation of nonverbal symbolic systems that authors include in electronic messages. It includes the writing and speaking of verbal messages as well as the construction of sounds, images, graphics, photos, videos, animations, and movements to add nonverbal components to electronic messages. It behooves you to think carefully about what you must do with electronic materials to help students as they become both verbally and nonverbally literate.

Today, students can read electronic texts, view beautiful artwork and photographs, hear clear audio, see live action or videos, and click on animations—perhaps in 3-D—with considerable ease. Verbal texts do not evoke meaning alone. Rather, all of the auditory and visual features of CD-ROMs and the World Wide Web are used to illuminate, or provide additional meanings to, verbal texts. Literacy has moved well beyond the basic ability to "gain or arrive at meaning" as a result of interacting with print and illustrations on paper.

IMPACT OF ELECTRONIC FEATURES ON COMPREHENSION

Comprehension of verbal and nonverbal digitized symbols is being affected by access to digitized learning materials, as well as manipulation and use of digital information.

Access

Access, manipulation, and use of electronic materials affect comprehension.

With Internet-enabled computers and CD-ROM or DVD capabilities, today's students can instantaneously access more information delivered in multiple formats than at any other time in the history of education. Central to how this affects comprehension is the fact that students can choose what *they* want to access and learn about at school and at home. This appeals to their intrinsic motivation.

Manipulation

Once they access a given source of information (fiction or nonfiction), students can make a number of choices. What will they focus on (e.g., texts, animations)? When or in what order will they access various components of the information (e.g., buttons)? What will they ignore or dismiss (e.g., advertisements)? What resources will they follow or not (e.g., links)? What features will they use or not (e.g., audio, video; annotations)? Students must make intelligent choices when manipulating features in today's polysymbolic digital environment, and their comprehension is affected both by their choices and their application of strategic verbal and nonverbal literacy capabilities. See the Tech Tip "Unique Electronic Capabilities."

Use

After interacting with verbal and nonverbal symbols at a web site or from a digitized disk, students have choices about how to use the information they have found. Will they save all or some of the information for further analysis or use (e.g., cut and paste into a document; take notes)? Will they simply think about the materials while they are interacting with the site (i.e., "fix" a few key ideas in their minds)? Will they act upon materials found on a web site (e.g., fill out a form) or afterward (send an e-mail to an author)? Will they use reference skills (e.g., record the URL; search for author information)? Comprehension is affected by the purposes students set for accessing, retrieving, and using information they obtain through electronic media as well as by their navigational and organizational abilities.

IMPACT OF ELECTRONIC FEATURES ON WRITING AND CONSTRUCTING

Chapters 6 and 8 discuss these topics in detail, but at this point we will briefly consider how electronic features affect writing and the constructing of verbal and nonverbal symbols through access to digitized learning materials, as well as manipulation and use of digital information.

Access

You write about what you know, and so do students. The accessibility of digital information for the purpose of writing and constructing messages

TECH TIPS — UNIQUE ELECTRONIC CAPABILITIES

Hypertext

One feature of electronic media has emerged that is helping to redefine what "reading" means. That feature is hypertext. Hypertext is produced when an author or authoring program places a code into an electronic text field that when clicked on by a mouse, moves the reader to another field of view. For instance, click on a word and you might see or hear its definition—or both. Click on a name and a picture of a person, accompanied by a biographical sketch, might appear. Click on the picture of a car's engine and you might see an animation of the pistons moving. When hypertext is used, readers have choices about which, if any, links they want—or feel a need—to access. Making choices in whether to click or not, clicking in whatever order they might wish, and deciding whether or not to return to the original text they were dealing with affect readers' roles in constructing meaning. Readers become "authors" when they have control over reading materials. The nonlinear nature of hypertext challenges traditional ideas about reading.

Search Engines

Specific electronic text can be found on the Internet through the use of search engines. As noted in chapter 1, Profusion (**http://www.profusion.com**) is an example of a metasearch engine that can search other search engines and report back a compilation of results. Search tips found on the Profusion web site explain how to use Boolean language and suggest other ways to conduct searches efficiently. You, perhaps working with a librarian, can help students learn to conduct electronic Internet searches by teaching them about Boolean logic. Some search engines are designed to help students visit safe places on the Internet. Examples of these are Surf Monkey (**http://www.surfmonkey.com/**), Yahooligans! (**http://www.yahooligans.com/**), and Ask Jeeves for Kids (**http://www.ajkids.com/**).

Search Features

Readers who are proficient at using search features in electronic documents can locate specific words, phrases, sentences, and so forth quickly, making the speed of acquiring specific text a factor that influences comprehension. For example, I have a copy of the complete works of Shakespeare in an old, unwieldy printed edition. To find a specific quote from *As You Like It*, I would need to skim or scan the text, perhaps for a long period of time. Let's say I like the quote "Thou speakest wiser than thou art ware of." Online, within an electronic text, I can find keywords such as "speakest wiser" in an instant. The ability to efficiently and quickly locate a specific word or phrase allows me to get on with the reading or writing tasks at hand, and this affects comprehension by eliminating long distractions that impede or delay thinking.

You can also search Internet text files by keywords. In Netscape Communicator you can use the "Find in Page" function in the edit pull-down menu to search through lengthy fields of text. The same feature on Microsoft Internet Explorer's edit pull-down menu is called "Find (on This Page)." The ability to skip to instances of a keyword can lead you quickly and efficiently to a particular topic. You can also search your bookmarks in Netscape Communicator (but not Internet Explorer) using keywords in the "Edit Bookmarks" function "Find in Bookmarks." This can help you get to a site you previously bookmarked if you search part of the site's title.

Teach students to use the find and replace feature of Corel's WordPerfect or find in Microsoft Word to move directly to a part of a text they want to deal with. For instance, when I'm writing a long document in Microsoft Word and get to the end of it, but then I want to say more about a topic, I pull down the "Find" feature from the "Edit" menu, type in the keyword or phrase, and click on "Enter." I am taken to a place in the text where the keyword or phrase is found, and I can quickly resume my writing. Teach students to become proficient in moving to specific keywords. This skill will enable them to make productive use of their time at a computer. Efficiency of editing using search features is a unique benefit of using electronic tools.

Access, manipulation, and use of electronic materials affect writing and constructing messages.

influences a student's ability to create first drafts. Students, particularly in rural areas with Internet access, have more information to write about because of easy access to it through technology. They can locate digital information online and offline, transfer it to a computer, and access it as needed from files stored on a hard drive or disk. Technology now delivers ample raw materials for writing and constructing messages.

Manipulation

Using various word-processing programs and other software applications, students can use built-in features (e.g., cut and paste; insert graphics) to manipulate verbal and nonverbal texts and objects until they are satisfied with the clarity of their messages. Electronic materials are easy to manipulate because everything else in a document can remain nearly the same while you add, delete, or move verbal or nonverbal materials. Students are more willing to revise electronic print because revision does not mean starting all over on a clean piece of paper. Students use built-in features to manipulate fonts, point sizes, colors, images, and so forth, until materials convey the precise messages they want to convey. Through technology, writers are now multimedia producers, often distributing their ideas to others around the world.

Use

The amount of verbal text being produced through e-mail and other messaging applications is mind boggling. For instance, while about 300 million e-mail messages were sent on an average day in 1995, it is predicted that about 8 *billion* daily e-mail messages will be sent by the end of the year 2002 (Moore, 2001, p. 34). True, much of what is written is not worthy of being etched in stone, but the desire to communicate with others is indisputable. If technology helps students become motivated to be better spellers or writers, it is well worth using. Students can produce materials for their personal use (autobiographies; digital photo collections), for schoolwork (electronic portfolios that are easier to maintain and store than the actual artifacts), and for publication in digital form on CD-ROMs or web sites where authentic audiences read them. Because of these and other uses for digitized writing, students are learning to keyboard, organize, and sort information in databases or spreadsheets; to create graphic organizers to structure their writing; and to use writing processes effectively.

The Directed Reading-Thinking Activity

In this section, we describe and discuss the use of the Directed Reading-Thinking Activity (DRTA) as a major strategy to help students learn to be thoughtful readers. Dr. Russell G. Stauffer's two seminal works, *Teaching reading as a thinking process* (1969) and *Directing reading maturity as a cognitive process* (1969), fully describe the DRTA. An additional useful reference is *Reading strategies and practices* (Tierney, Readence, & Dishner, 1999). The following is based on Stauffer's work, as well as on my first-hand knowledge of the strategy, which I learned while his student and later used in my work as a reading clinic coordinator and professor of reading. The DRTA originated in the late 1950s and early 1960s, well before the impact of computers was felt, but the strategies Stauffer defined are critically important today in a polysymbolic world. (See Table 4.1: Teaching Materials Then and Now.)

DRTA strategies are important in today's polysymbolic literacy milieu.

You need to be able to differentiate between the DRTA and the Directed Reading Activity (DRA), the two major general frameworks employed by K–8 teachers who work with basal reader materials. The DRA was first described in the 1940s in an attempt to clarify various strategies that authors of basal readers were employing. The description became the standard for publishers and authors for creating instructional materials. There are five components of a DRA. First is the readiness phase, in which teachers link students' background knowledge to the subject at hand, try to create interest in the subject matter, introduce vocabulary, and set specific purposes for students to pursue while they read. Second is the guided silent reading phase, during which students search for answers to the purpose-setting questions. Third is the comprehension check and discussion of the story. At this time, students give answers to the teacher's purpose-setting questions. In addition, the teacher uses this time to discuss other details of the material or to deal with comprehension. Fourth is oral rereading. Often, teachers use this stage for round-robin reading, where one student after another reads portions of text aloud. Sometimes, teachers set new purposes for oral reading. Finally, teachers prescribe follow-up activities.

One major problem with the DRA, particularly in today's literacy milieu, is that it is heavily teacher dominated. "Teacher-pupil interactions," say Tierney, Readence, and Dishner (1999), "flow mainly from the questions and activities that the teacher prescribes" (p. 6). Teachers preintroduce vocabulary—often on the chalkboard—instead of letting students first attempt to use their decoding skills, and teachers direct students to read to find answers to questions that often are literal level questions and usually come out of teacher's manuals. Round-robin oral

TABLE 4.1

Teaching Materials Then and Now

TRADITIONAL LITERACY MATERIALS

These have been the most common print materials used by teachers to help students learn to read, their content being "locked in" at the time they are printed.

- Basal readers with controlled vocabulary words
- Trade books (not made-for-basal stories)
- Workbooks from the publishers of basal readers
- Photocopies of teacher-created worksheets
- Books from book clubs
- Pamphlets, newspapers, and magazines
- Store marquees and street signs; trading cards of any type
- Comic books and cartoons
- Dictionaries, encyclopedias, and other references

TODAY'S LITERACY MATERIALS

Most of the traditional materials above are still used, and some are available in electronic formats. These additional materials were made possible by the digital revolution, and most can be updated or altered easily.

- E-mail
- Electronic text (i.e., digitized print text with no embellishments)
- Electronic texts that integrate audio, video, graphics, photographs, and animations along with text on CD-ROMs and the World Wide Web
- Images generated on computer screens or through computer projection units
- E-books
- Teleconferencing; live or streaming video

reading has been condemned for decades as being boring to students and ineffective for much of anything other than correcting students in public (an often-painful experience) when they mispronounce words. Finally, follow-up activities are often author-or-editor-created, but students have few or no opportunities to pursue things that interest them.

In much of this chapter, we will describe the DRTA. We will look primarily at the group DRTA, which involves interactions among teacher and students, but we will also examine an important variation: the Independent DRTA. As the name implies, in this version students work together on their own, with your informed observations. Other chapters in this book (chapters 7 and 8) contain information about strategies that are based on DRTA practices. Here we discuss why the DRTA is an important overall instructional strategy for helping students to become independent, thinking users of print and electronic materials.

LINKS BETWEEN THE STRATEGY AND ELECTRONIC MATERIALS

DRTA strategies can be used with electronic materials.

The "T" in DRTA signals that this strategy encourages authentic thinking before, during, and after readers' interactions with print or electronic materials. Students set their purposes and ask their own questions about which they want to find answers. It is in the act of setting purposes that students engage in important critical thinking behaviors—behaviors they need today while using electronic resources. You become a facilitator, helping students learn to select and attend to all available evidence to use as the basis of predicting. Students must examine verbal and nonverbal evidence when dealing with electronic materials because most online materials are not explicitly designed as instructional materials. When using DRTA strategies, you do not set purposes for students, and you do not have already-prescribed answers to questions; therefore, DRTA instruction prepares students to learn to ask questions and find answers for themselves when using Internet or CD-ROM resources.

Constructivism and cooperative learning work well with DRTA instruction.

The DRTA is an ideal strategy for today's emphasis on constructivism, collaborative learning, and changes that the information explosion has brought about. Your role of facilitator during DRTAs coincides nicely with the constructivist stance of helping students learn for themselves. Students can work together as coinquirers during DRTA sessions. You and students can collaboratively work to use additional online and offline resources when seeking answers to questions that are not found in the current materials. The information explosion has made it impossible for teachers, schools, and publishers to be the gatekeepers of knowledge. Just as churches and governments lost a great deal of control when the printing press was invented, today's institutional gatekeepers are struggling to maintain authority in the face of a communications network that enables access to more and more unfiltered information. Once students internalize DRTA strategies, they are able to operate more independently and more thoughtfully with both fiction and nonfiction print and electronic materials.

A final thought: the DRTA is an overarching instructional strategy. Many comprehension strategies that work well in conjunction with DRTAs have been described over the years. The shared-reading routine and the fluency-reading routine described by Cooper (2000) as well as the reciprocal-teaching strategy (Palinscar & Brown, 1984) during which students predict, question, clarify, and summarize are just a few of the many comprehension strategies you can employ that are compatible with the DRTA. You should use a variety of age-appropriate comprehension strategies along with the DRTA to help students grow more literate.

ASSUMPTIONS UNDERLYING THE DRTA

Students bring many cognitive and other skills to the acts of reading, listening, and interpreting.

Throughout several periods of history, some people believed that young children were ignorant or incapable of understanding much until they were formally taught. Today, educators understand that when children are born, they are immediately ready to start interacting with the environment in order to make sense of the world. In the DRTA, students are asked to play important roles in examining evidence, making predictions (hypotheses), and actively thinking as they encounter and verify information and ideas while reading. The major assumptions upon which the DRTA is based appear here. Note that many of the ideas in this section first appeared in Stauffer's *Teaching reading as a thinking process* (1969). For instance, in the list that follows, the ideas in boldface are Stauffer's assumptions (pp. 19–20), but the accompanying comments are mine.

- **Children can think.** They may not be seasoned scholars, but they are able to deal with cause and effect ("I know why I didn't get my allowance!"), sequence ("Let me tell you about Casper. First, . . ."), and other aspects of thinking.
- **Children can examine.** Give students something they have not seen before and they will describe its attributes. (I showed students my Great Pyrenees dog, and they quickly discovered that she had double dewclaws (toenails) on her rear feet, and white eyelashes.)
- **Children can act purposefully.** They will do chores to earn money to go to the mall.
- **Children can use their experiences and knowledge.** They abandon "baby stuff" as their interests change and mature.
- **Children can weigh facts and make inferences.** ("I shouldn't play football with the older students because I'm too small and I might get hurt.")
- **Children can make judgments.** ("I like Batman better than Robin.")
- **Children become emotionally involved.** You know this is true if you have seen children viewing the video or reading Bambi.
- **Children have interests.** Have you ever tried to take a Harry Potter book from a fifth-grade student?
- **Children can learn.** They master oral language and learn complex concepts even before starting school.
- **Children can make generalizations.** Ask a seventh-grade student to describe someone of the opposite sex.
- **Children can understand.** Ask poor children why they do not go on cruises.

Together, these assumptions indicate that most students are able to deal with reading and interpreting when they are taught as thinking processes. Mature, skillful readers must think before, during, and after interacting with verbal texts and nonverbal symbols—whether they appear in paper-based or electronic-based material. You can help students toward mature reading and interpreting from the earliest grades onward by using DRTAs and related strategies.

ASPECTS OF THE READING-THINKING PROCESS

There are three major aspects of the reading-thinking process: (1) the reader establishes purposes for reading, (2) the reader reasons throughout the act of reading, and (3) the reader makes judgments throughout the act of reading and afterward. *Extending* and *refining* ideas, according to Stauffer, are additional aspects to consider (p. 14). The following explanations of the three major aspects should help clarify their importance.

Declaring Purposes for Reading

Declaring purposes, reasoning while reading, and judging are foundations of thoughtful reading.

The DRTA encourages students to set their *own* purposes for reading. In the DRA, the teacher's manual lists questions and their answers. In the DRTA, students use verbal or visual evidence to create questions that *they* want to answer. In asking questions, they set their own purposes for reading.

Purposes fix (determine, set, specify) the answers being sought. "The key step in the DRTA is developing purposes for reading," said Stauffer (p. 24). There is an astute saying, "A wise man's question contains half the answer" (Solomon Ibn Gabirol, reference unknown). Questions alert students to look for appropriate information that answers them. When a student says, "I think the story is about two kids that go to the circus," that student immediately will be on the lookout for words naming animals, clowns, amusement rides, and such to prove that the assumption is correct. Purposes can be expressed in the form of statements, as above, or in the form of questions (e.g., "Will there be an elephant in the circus?"). Both forms show *intent* to confirm predictions and find answers, which is central to setting purposes for reading.

Purposes regulate the scope of the reading-thinking process. Sometimes reading materials contain simple facts, and a reader might need to interact with a text just long enough to find a specific name, date, or word. That kind of reading is quite different from reading carefully in order to understand key ideas for a test or reading to discover the theme or major plot points in a fictional story. Setting clear purposes has an impact on *how* the reader approaches a given text.

Purposes regulate the *rate* of the reading-thinking process and influence the amount of time a reader needs to interact with a text. It would be poor judgment for a reader to spend the same amount of time and effort reading to find a name or date as he or she would spend to study the text thoroughly. You can teach students to vary their rate of reading to achieve different purposes. Teach them to **skim** print or electronic text for specific kinds of information (e.g., names or dates), **scan** texts (e.g., read lightly for the gist without an intent to memorize), or **study** texts (e.g., with intent to remember), depending on students' purposes.

Self-declared purposes are of special significance. Stauffer believed strongly that students' self-declared purposes increase their motivation. He said, "When pupils have become involved in the dynamics of a purpose-setting session, the self-commitment on an intellectual as well as an emotional level has tremendous motivating force" (p. 25). He further believed that self-declared purposes give direction to reading, adding, "The reading-thinking process begins in the mind of each reader as he experiences a state of doubt or curiosity about what he knows or does not know, and what he thinks will or will not happen" (p. 25). As noted earlier, today's students have many and varied interests, and they now, through technology, have access to more information than ever before. You can help students seek information related to their interests and learn to act with intention by helping them become expert in setting their own purposes for reading. This is particularly important when students deal with CD-ROM and WWW materials—where a simple mouse click can distract them from their original intent and carry them to another place in another text. Help students think with purpose *before* they click. See more about evoking motivation on this book's web site.

WWW

Reasoning While Reading

"As the reader proceeds," Stauffer said, "he balances what he finds against his purposes, experiences, and knowledge" (p. 13). While working through print or electronic texts, readers are constantly thinking. They make inferences, draw conclusions, make generalizations, and so forth. This leads to productive thinking that helps students achieve their goals (i.e., purposes) for reading. When dealing with nonfiction materials, encourage students to use thinking strategies, as well as study skills such as taking notes and summarizing, to help them meet their goals.

Making Judgments During and After Reading

Critical reading involves determining how well an idea, a fact, an example, etc., measures up to one's own or some generally accepted standard. "To judge," said Stauffer, "the reader must select and weigh the facts and make decisions that are pertinent and discriminate" (p. 14). You can help students grasp the concept of standards in several ways. First, talk about standards in current vogue in society, comparing, for instance, standards for a healthy diet nowadays with what was considered healthy at some previous time. This helps illustrate that standards change and that it is very important to understand what causes them to change. Second, you can help students think about their own standards. What do they think is funny? What do they consider to be appropriate behavior on the school bus? Such discussions help students understand that as they read, they need to judge ideas in terms of what *they* believe is appropriate and acceptable to society, their families, and themselves.

Declaring purposes, reasoning, and judging are central to thinking. These form a foundation for refining and extending ideas beyond specific polysymbolic texts. If you want students to engage in such behaviors, structure learning experiences that ensure students will use them during many literacy activities. Begin by maintaining a classroom atmosphere that encourages students to feel comfortable practicing DRTA behaviors.

THE TEACHER'S ROLE IN GROUP DRTAs

The teacher is an intellectual agitator, evoking more precise thinking by students.

"A teacher needs to . . . have a lively imagination; be willing to parry, agitate and convert ideas presented; and be convinced that reading is a process of active searching and inquiry," Stauffer said. "The teacher should ask questions that stimulate the students to tell why they inquire and interpret as they do" (p. 26). Stauffer wanted teachers to be "intellectual agitators" who constantly challenge students to think.

Asking Questions

According to Stauffer, you can agitate students to think by asking them three key questions:

1. What do you think?
2. Why do you think that?
3. What is your evidence?

Even though these three questions seem deceptively simple, they help students take ownership of their literacy and thinking skills in order to answer them.

You can help students improve their thinking by guiding them—not too much and not too little—to learn to use evidence as the basis of making predictions, fine-tuning their ideas while reading, and acting on the information they find. When working in groups, students learn to refine their ideas through interactions with other students. Therefore, at first students can profit from engaging in small-group DRTAs. Group DRTAs help students realize that others may have differing points of view. This helps them gain a broader perspective to use when working unassisted. As students gain greater ability to use evidence and improve their predicting and confirming skills, they can use DRTA strategies while working alone with print or electronic texts to engage in **Independent DRTAs,** discussed later in this chapter.

Leading Group DRTAs

For group DRTAs, you examine the material to select appropriate stopping places. Stops usually occur naturally just before or after a turn of events in the plot for fictional materials, or at a logical division (e.g., the end of a section or unit) in a nonfiction work. Online, brief discussions may be appropriate before clicking to more new screens. Your effective use of stopping places will allow you to ensure that students understand the text. If they are comprehending, students' predictions for the next section will be reasonable; if they have not comprehended, you will realize that fact quickly from their fuzzy or irrational comments. Your purpose is not to drill and grill about what students have already read. Unless students are hopelessly off-track (fiction) or have misunderstood key concepts (nonfiction), keep their attention focused mainly on the parts of the material that remain to be examined.

See the Teaching Tip "A DRTA Using Fiction," and notice the skillful way the teacher reveals evidence without telling students what they are seeing. Notice how she keeps them thinking ahead in the story, helps them relate the story to their own lives, and has students read sentences to prove their ideas. With fiction, attending to verbal and nonverbal evidence, reading, and thinking are the important literacy behaviors the teacher is trying to elicit—not the fixing of facts in their minds. Notice the students' very creative ideas and attention to the story.

TEACHING TIPS A DRTA Using Fiction

Ms. Tina Thompson is a reading teacher at the Homer Davis Elementary School in Tucson, Arizona. In the following dialogue, she and five of her third-grade students are discussing The Robber Child *by Sandra and Michael Rokoff.*

Ms. T. Today's story could actually happen to a person your age, even though it's fiction. Look at this picture of a story called "The Robber Child." What might happen?
Brandon. The child is a robber and the cops are chasing her.
Dana. The police are chasing her, and she looks kinda scared.
George. She's in bed.
Nathan. It's her dream.
Kendra. Because, it's in a cloud. *(The illustration shows a "dream cloud.")*
Ms. T. Why might a child be dreaming such a terrible dream?
Brandon. Maybe she took something once.
George. Maybe she's thinking what would happen if she gets caught by the police.
Nathan. Maybe she's thinking about stealing something?
Ms. T. What's another reason?
Brandon. She might have done it, and then the cops might have chased her the next day.
Nathan. It's probably déjà vu.
Ms. T. Déjà vu. What does déjà vu mean? That's a great phrase.
Nathan. You have a dream about it, and then the next day it'll happen.
Ms. T. All right. So, it's already happened, or she's thinking about it happening, or it could happen. Let's make some more predictions. If she's a thief, what do think she stole?
Students. Maybe something that she likes; toys; candy; bikes; yo-yos; expensive stuff like jewels. Maybe money; maybe stuff from her parents; other people's pets.
Ms. T. OK. What about from school?
Students. Pencils and notebooks; a teachers' marker; other people's erasers; notebooks.
Ms. T. Read pages 3 and 4 silently *(points to a K-W-L chart)* to see if your predictions are right. *(Students read silently.)*
Ms. T. Did she steal something?
Brandon. No.
Kendra. I think yes, 'cause she wants to know about the police and putting her in jail.
Ms. T. Where does it say that?
Kendra. *(Reading)* "Are robbers real, she asked her mother."
Ms. T. What else did she want to know?
Dana. *(Reading)* "Do policemen really put robbers in jail."
Ms. T. Which sentence says that?
George. *(Reading)* "Yes, sometimes, said her mother. But why do you want to know?"
Ms. T. What would your parents think if you asked them those questions?
Nathan. Did you steal something?
Ms. T. *(Laughing)* Good answer. Were you right about this being a bad dream? *(Students nod.)* Should she tell her parents she had a bad dream?
Nathan. She should tell her parents, and then they'll probably do something about it.
Kendra. If she stole something, she should tell the truth.
Dana. She could give it back to where she stole it.
Ms. T. Turn to the next page. What do you think is happening?
Kendra. Her face tells me she probably stole something. She's really, really scared to tell.
Brandon. *(Points)* She maybe stole that little doll over there.
George. Maybe she stole the book.
Ms. T. How can we find out? *(Students say, "Read!")* OK, Read pages 6 and 7. *(Students read silently.)*
Brandon. She stole the yellow book that was on the table.
Ms. T. What makes you think so?
Brandon. Because it says over here *(reading)*, "Jessica looked under it. A book was there. Jessica opened it. Then she closed it very fast and pushed the pillow back over it."

Ms. T. Say some words that tell how she is acting unusual.
Students. Strange; scared; weird; nervous.
Ms. T. Where do you think she got the book?
Students. Maybe a bookstore; from a friend's house; the library; maybe a market place.
Ms. T. How is she feeling? Someone read it to us.
Dana. *(Reading)* "Jessica got ready for school, but she felt just awful."
Ms. T. Any new predictions about what she should do?
Students. Tell the truth and take it back; leave a note in the book to tell the person; give it to her parents to take back; she could buy it; she could probably ask a friend to take it back.
Ms. T. Good ideas! Look at this picture on pages 8 and 9. Here's the teacher, Mr. Potter, and all the kids. Read from page 8 to page 13 to see if your predictions are right. *(Students read silently.)*
Ms. T. The students are at school, and Mr. Potter is going to read them a story. What's the problem?
Dana. They couldn't find the book.
Nathan. Jessica stole the book.
Ms. T. Why is there such a big deal about this book?
Dana. It said *(reading)*, "He wanted to hear the one about the seven magic giants. Everybody wanted to hear that story."
Ms. T. Does Mr. Potter know that Jessica has taken his book?
Students. No.
Ms. T. Find on page 11 exactly how he feels.
Dana. *(Reading)* "'That's too bad,' said Mr. Potter sadly. 'We all liked that book.'"
Brandon. When school was out, she daydreamed that she was put in jail.
Nathan. She said, "I hate it."
Ms. T. Why do you think she hates it?
George. Because everybody liked it, but now they can't read it.
Ms. T. What else about her day.
Kendra. She was weak, and she couldn't do anything.
Nathan. Because she took that book from the school.
Ms. T. And all her energy is being spent feeling guilty. Any new ideas?
Dana. I think she should tell Mr. Potter the truth and tell him why she did it.
George. Confess.
Ms. T. Look at this picture. What do you think will happen?
George. The book's gone from her room.
Kendra. I think her Mom found it and took it.
Ms. T. If Mom found the book, would she think Jessica stole it? *(Students say, "No.")*
George. She probably would think it's Jessica's book.
Ms. T. How do you think Jessica feels?
Students. Horrified; scared; worried; really scared; surprised.
Ms. T. All right. Read page 15 through page 17 to see if your predictions are right. *(Students read silently.)*
Ms. T. What's the problem?
George. The book is not there.
Ms. T. What does she think happened to the book?
Nathan. Her mom probably took it.
Ms. T. If your mother found a book under your pillow would she think you stole it?
Students. She'd think it's a library book or a friend lent it to her; it could have been her book before; it could be a special book or a diary or something.
Ms. T. She's afraid she's going to be in trouble. Any new ideas of anything else she could do?
Nathan. She could probably take it to the lost and found.
Dana. You could mail it.
Ms. T. Those are things you could do without Mr. Potter finding out who did it. It would return the book. Is it the best plan? *(Several say, "No.")* Let's find out what happens next. Read pages 19 through 21. *(Students read silently.)*
Ms. T. What happens?
Dana. She sees Mom with the book, and she's scared.
Kendra. Mom found it when she was cleaning.
George. Mom doesn't think there's a problem.
Ms. T. What did she ask that let you know what Mom thought?
Nathan. *(Reading)* "Did somebody leave it here?"
George. Jessica went to her room and started to read it.

TEACHING TIPS
(continued)

Nathan. Now she doesn't like the book.
Dana. She wishes she could just give it to someone.
Ms. T. Look on page 20. What is this cloud here for?
Kendra. It shows what the book is about.
Nathan. It's the castle.
Dana. And the seven magic giants.
Ms. T. Turn to the next page. When do think the next thing is happening?
Kendra. At dinnertime.
Ms. T. Read all the way to page 27. *(Students read silently.)*
Ms. T. What was alike about this conversation and the one at breakfast?
Kendra. She asked about the police stuff.
Nathan. She said *(reading)*, "If a child is a robber, will she go to jail?"
Ms. T. Yes, she asked that this morning. OK, what is different?
Brandon. She told the truth.
Ms. T. Where does Jennifer say there are three things she doesn't want to leave?
George. *(Reading)* "I don't want to leave you, and school, and my friends."
Ms. T. What did Mom and Dad do?
Dana. They just asked what was the problem.
Nathan. And they said, "We'll take care of you."
Ms. T. What was her reason for taking the book?
Brandon. 'Cause she really, really liked it.
Ms. T. What did Dad say when she told the truth?
Nathan. *(Reading)* "Hmmm, let's think. I wonder what to do?"
Ms. T. Did Dad really not know what to do? Did he have to think about it? *(Students say, "No.")*
Kendra. He said that so Jessica can try to get the idea herself.
Ms. T. All right, let's see if you are right. Read from here to page 28, the end of the book. *(Students read silently.)*
Ms. T. Did Jessica do what you thought she should do? *(All say, "Yes.")*
George. She tells Mr. Potter the truth and gives him the book.
Nathan. He was happy to get the book back.
Kendra. Her friends weren't mad because she brought the book back.
Ms. T. Is there a lesson that we could learn from this story?
George. Never steal.
Ms. T. Suppose you did steal something. What lesson would you learn from this story?
Dana. I would take it back and tell the truth.
Kendra. I learned not to steal anything or lie to your parents. If you lie when you are older, you'll get put in jail.
George. And, never cheat.
Ms. T. I think you really learned good lessons in this story. You are some of the best readers and predictors I have ever seen. I'm very proud of you. *(Discussion continues.)*

Source: Reprinted with permission from Tina Thompson, reading teacher, Homer Davis Elementary School, Tucson, AZ, and students' parents.

Next, examine the Teaching Tip "A DRTA Using Nonfiction" to see how the teacher elicits students' own background knowledge by adroitly asking *channeling* questions that cause students to predict about areas of the topic she thinks are important for the students to learn. The teacher used a K-W-L strategy chart to track predictions, but you can use the chalkboard or a program such as *Inspiration.* The K-W-L strategy, described by Ogle (1986), encourages students to describe what they know and what they want to learn, and, later, to reveal what they have learned. Notice how the teacher elicits information and helps students "fix ideas in their minds" after they have read the various parts of the selection.

TEACHING TIPS A Nonfiction DRTA

Ms. Tina Thompson is a reading teacher at the Homer Davis Elementary School in Tucson, Arizona. In the following dialogue, she and five of her fifth-grade students are discussing nonfiction selections from the CornerStone reader CrackerJacks.

Ms. T. If I said to you, "Babies in their pockets," what might I be talking about?
Raynette. A kangaroo.
Ms. T. Why do you think that?
Raynette. Because kangaroos hold their babies in their pouches.
Trevor. It could mean babies with different stuff in their pockets.
Mark. I think it's one of those backpacks that you have that babies sit in.
Ms. T. What do we know about a kangaroo?
Trevor. It's a mammal.
Ms. T. Kayla, do you agree? Is it a mammal?
Kayla. No, not at all.
Mark. It doesn't eat meat.
Leilani. And, it doesn't have fur or hair.
Trevor. Oh, marsupial!
Ms. T. What is a marsupial?
Trevor. It's a mammal that has a pouch.
Ms. T. How do we know mammals from birds, fish, reptiles, and amphibians?
Students. They give milk; they have hair; they breathe air; they are warm blooded.
Ms. T. Who knows one more thing that makes them a mammal?
Kayla. They give birth.
Ms. T. So, if a marsupial is a mammal, it does all of these things, plus has a pouch. Do you know any examples of a marsupial? Raynette says a kangaroo. Are there any other marsupials?
Trevor. A koala bear.
Mark. An elephant.
Leilani. I was going to say that, but I wasn't really sure.
Ms. T. You don't have to be sure. We are making predictions. What do we think they eat?
Kayla. Plants.
Ms. T. Do they eat meat?
Several. No.
Ms. T. What else might we ask about these animals?
Trevor. Where is their habitat?
Ms. T. That's a great word. Does anybody think they know what their habitat is?
Trevor. In a jungle.
Ms. T. Do you have a country or a continent in mind?
Raynette. Africa.
Ms. T. Anybody have a different idea about where they live?
Raynette. I just remembered—Australia.
Ms. T. All right, she wants to go with Australia instead of Africa. What else might we want to know about them?
Leilani. How long they can live.
Ms. T. Does anyone know how long marsupials live?
Mark. No, but I have another question. Do they live on the ground or in the treetops?
Ms. T. We not only want to know the country, but we want to know the specifics of where they live. Do they live in a tree, on the ground, in a hole in the ground?
Trevor. How big do they get before they can't be in the pouch any more?
Ms. T. That's a good question. Are they endangered or extinct? What does *extinct* mean?
Leilani. Extinct, like if they are all gone.
Trevor. I think koalas are endangered.
Ms. T. All right. Turn to page 18 to see if you can find out *(points to K-W-L chart):* Are they mammals? Do they have all the things that mammals have? Are any of these examples? Do we know any of these things about marsupials? *(Students read silently.)*
Ms. T. First, let's check your predictions. Are marsupials mammals?
Kayla. Yes.
Ms. T. Prove it.
Kayla. *(Reading)* "The animals that carry their young in a pocket are called marsupials."
Ms. T. Good. Did you find out if kangaroos have fur?
Several. Yes.
Leilani. But when they're first born, they have no hair, and they can't see.
Mark. They're smaller than me.

TEACHING TIPS
(continued)

Ms. T. Isn't that an interesting thing? Were there any other things you were surprised to see?
Kayla. A possum.
Ms. T. Where does it say that?
Kayla. *(Reading)* "Only the opossum lives in North America."
Ms. T. So, you learned that opossums and kangaroos are. Koalas are, too. Are elephants?
Mark. No. Because elephants don't have a pouch.
Ms. T. Elephants have no pouch, although they are mammals. Do they all eat plants?
Leilani. Some of them eat meat.
Ms. T. Where does it say that?
Leilani. *(Reading)* "Some marsupials are meat-eating. Others eat only grass and plants."
Ms. T. You were right. Good job. Do they live in Australia?
Several. Yes.
Ms. T. Yes, you are absolutely right—their habitat is Australia. Did we find out the specifics like on the ground, in the ground, in the tree? *(Several indicate "No.")*
Raynette. Yes we did. *(Reading)* "Some marsupials live in the forest and climb trees."
Ms. T. *Some* live in trees. So the rest probably live on the ground. Do we know how long they can stay in the pouch or how big they get before they can get out?
Trevor. They have to stay inside the pouch for a few weeks.
Ms. T. Once they get out, do they stay out forever?
Kayla. They can go in if they feel they're in danger or if they just want a ride.
Ms. T. What's the other reason they keep going back to the pouch?
Mark. So they can drink milk.
Ms. T. Good. How is the opossum different from the other marsupials?
Leilani. Only the possums live in North America.
Ms. T. Now, we're going to read about just the opossum. We know he's a marsupial. Do we know whether he's a plant or an animal eater? What would you guess?
Trevor. Plants.
Ms. T. How big is he compared with other animals?
Leilani. Medium size.
Kayla. I think he's a bit bigger than a mouse.
Ms. T. Do they have fur?
Mark. I disagree on the size. I think he's about as big as a four-week-old cat.
Ms. T. We have two votes for small. Are they endangered or extinct? *(Students say, "No.")* There's something odd about an opossum that he does that's different from most other animals.
Trevor. He hangs upside down by his tail.
Ms. T. That's kind of odd. There's something very strange that an opossum does that's funny, and we're going to find out what he does. Turn to page 31 and find out about all those things you predicted about opossums. *(Students read silently.)*
Ms. T. I kept hearing you say, "Oh, wow!" "Oh, man, I didn't know that!" "That's cool!" And all these little comments, so I think you've learned a lot about opossums. What did you find out?
Mark. His favorite food is fruit and eggs.
Kayla. They are omnivores.
Ms. T. Good job. They eat both, but they mostly eat plants. They eat eggs, too.
Leilani. Can I say two things? They have fifty teeth, and they like to sleep in the day.
Ms. T. What else?
Raynette. A mother may have from five to eighteen babies. The babies stay in the pouch for two months.
Leilani. They're endangered, because people hunt them.
Ms. T. Where does it tell you that they are endangered?
Leilani. *(Reading)* "Opossums have many enemies. Other animals and man hunt them."
Ms. T. Even man hunts opossums. Why?
Leilani. To eat them.
Ms. T. Yes. Have you ever seen bumper stickers that say, "Eat more possum"? I think it's just a joke. Does it say that they are endangered?
Leilani. No.
Ms. T. They're all over the place, because they have so many babies. Mark, did you find out what size they are?
Mark. Yes. They are three feet.
Trevor. Half of them is their tail.

Ms. T. So their body is this long, and the rest of it is just tail. What do they use it for?
Raynette. For hanging upside down.
Ms. T. He has to have plenty of tail to wind around the branch, and then he hangs by the rest of his tail. What does he look like when he is young?
Mark. A rat.
Trevor. He has no fur.
Kayla. He has big ears.
Ms. T. So, you know, this guy's not very cute. Once he comes out of the pouch and is too big to ride, he still gets a free ride. How?
Kayla. He gets to ride on his mother's back.
Ms. T. Opossums do something very strange, and Trevor was very excited when he found this.
Trevor. When an enemy comes by, he plays dead.
Ms. T. Why does he do that?
Trevor. Because, there are way too many enemies.
Ms. T. And they are bigger than he is, because most of him is tail. So, he plays dead.
Leilani. He lays down on the ground and starts acting like he's dead.
Ms. T. Animals think they are dead, and they just walk off. Who else plays dead like an opossum?
Kayla. People.
Ms. T. When my dad came in the morning to wake me up, I would pretend I was sound asleep. He would say, "You're playing possum." He knew I was awake.
Mark. What kind of snake will play dead? It will play dead, and when a rat is looking around, it will jump up and get it.
Ms. T. I don't know. Animals have lots of neat ways of protecting themselves.
Brandon. Mom protects me.
Ms. T. That's it! Moms protect us kids. *(Discussion continues.)*

Source: Reprinted with permission from Tina Thompson, reading teacher, Homer Davis Elementary School, Tucson, AZ, and students' parents.

Facilitating Independent DRTAs

Eventually, you can help students learn to practice DRTA strategies on their own. During Independent DRTAs, students must keep track of their ideas and stop from time to time to think and make new predictions. Every so often, you will want to meet with them to discuss their understanding of the materials they are using. Even when you have not dealt with the materials the students are working with independently, your habit of asking "What do you think will happen next?" and "Why do you think that?" will let you know how well students are comprehending as they guide their own learning. Their explanations of the evidence they have used, the predictions they have made, and their new predictions will help you assess their comprehension. You will learn more about Independent DRTAs later in this chapter, but you might like to read a transcript of an Independent DRTA on this book's web site.

THE STUDENT'S ROLE IN GROUP DRTAs

Students examine evidence and make predictions to interact with print and electronic materials.

During a group DRTA, you do not use a teacher's manual with its questions and right answers. Students' predictions are often very creative, and students sometimes think of things that publishers would not include in a teacher's manual. The student's role in a DRTA involves *active* thinking and the examining of evidence, which require much more than simply finding answers to "canned" questions. Following are the cornerstones of students' reading-thinking behaviors.

Examining Evidence

There are dozens of ways to conduct DRTAs. You can show a picture to form the basis of predicting, or students can read a sentence, paragraph, page, section, or chapter. Tell students how a story starts or ends and let them predict from that information. The point is that students need something to think about to get the DRTA started, as well as during stopping places throughout the DRTA. You decide what the first evidence will be; it is then up to students to consider that evidence and make predictions and logical inferences.

Making Hypotheses and Predictions

Once students examine evidence, certain possibilities will occur to them. They form hypotheses and phrase predictions that seem—at this point in their pursuit—to be reasonable. Once they fix their predictions either mentally or in text, they are ready to read to determine if their ideas are correct or need to be changed. You may place students' ideas on a chalkboard, a whiteboard, or a chart; you can project the ideas using a computer projector. It is up to students to create clear hypotheses or predictions, so you may need to encourage refinements at times. Divergent thinking is normal at the beginning of a DRTA when there are many possibilities. Convergent thinking occurs once students know more about the materials with which they are working.

Finding Proof

Sometimes answers are stated in the text, and students can point to the answers or read aloud sentences that contain answers. In some cases, even if the answer to a prediction is not directly stated in the text it can be inferred. In other cases, the predictions or hypotheses are not answered and additional print or electronic materials must be consulted to resolve issues of fact. Encourage students to examine other print or electronic sources when the need arises. Authentic follow-up activities can grow out of unresolved ideas.

Suspending Judgment

Students must learn to interact with a given text long enough to determine answers to their inquiries because, ultimately, it is the text (not the teacher) that determines whether they have answered their questions or predictions. Particularly during group DRTAs, students learn not to be too hasty about drawing conclusions when others find information that challenges their predictions.

Making Decisions

Students constantly make decisions as part of the DRTA process. They decide, in some cases, what to use for evidence, what that evidence means, whether or not they really have found answers to their questions, and so forth. While teachers and other students can help with some decisions, mature readers must ultimately learn to make decisions independently.

The actions identified above are based on the reader's experiences, knowledge of print or electronic texts, and life in general. Teachers must recognize that students have a wide range of life experiences, verbal and nonverbal experiences, computer experiences, and language capabilities that they bring to the acts of listening, reading, and interpreting. Therefore, teachers' guidance and encouragement are needed to help all students become productive users of DRTA and similar strategies.

THE ROLE OF INTERACTION IN GROUP DRTAs

An ideal size for DRTA group interactions is from 5 to 10 students. This permits each student to have many opportunities to contribute to predicting and discussing the reading materials. This group size also allows you to monitor each student's contributions and to give individual help as needed. Stauffer noted that "all members of the group are involved in the act of creating hypotheses, conjectures, [and] purposes, using them to guide their reading. . . . The group sits as auditors, authorized to examine the evidence, verify the questions and answers, and state the results" (p. 27). Being a member of a DRTA group is important because students must listen to everyone's predictions, perhaps agreeing with some and disagreeing with others, given the evidence presented. This means that each group member must thoroughly examine evidence and follow discussions thoughtfully. Each group member helps in verifying or disputing findings reported by others.

THE ROLE OF READING MATERIALS

Materials, not the teacher, determine if students' ideas are supported or not.

Text may contain an answer to a prediction, imply an answer, or it may not have any information that bears on the prediction. Text, then, rather than the teacher (or manual), is the arbitrator of "right" and "wrong." With fictional materials, if the text does not answer a question, that is usually the end of the matter, although a student might e-mail an author for clarification. With nonfiction materials, however, you or students must decide whether to clear up unresolved matters through research, using both print and electronic sources.

INDEPENDENT DRTAs

Group DRTAs are valuable for introducing pupils to beneficial ways of thinking before, during, and after listening, reading, and interpreting. Students learn, through group interactions, to test and refine their thinking. When they are correct, they have support from other group members. When they are incorrect, others help them understand why their thinking is incorrect. There are, however, many benefits to Independent DRTAs as well, as we examine below.

Benefits of Independent DRTAs

Independent DRTAs help students (1) develop habits of self-sufficiency in creating and attaining purposes, (2) pursue personal needs and interests when freed from group constraints, and (3) deal with electronic or print materials that are not available to more than one person at a time. Students must take increasing responsibility for selecting electronic and print materials that appeal to their interests and educational needs. They must show growing independence in surveying, or previewing, their selected materials in order to set purposes using verbal and nonverbal materials. They must learn to state or record their purposes and listen, read, and interpret to meet those purposes. They must evaluate, independently, their success or lack of success in meeting their purposes. They must learn to resolve perplexities that were raised—but unanswered—by electronic or print materials they have encountered.

There are major benefits from students' learning to self-regulate their listening, reading, and interpreting. Your goal is to help students apply DRTA strategies routinely to their own literacy activities. Pupils who are instructed in DRTAs from the earliest grades onward should have little difficulty internalizing the routines of setting, confirming or rejecting, and resetting purposes from time to time. You can provide a smooth transition from group to Independent DRTA experiences by weaning students from group interactions.

Weaning Students from Group Instruction

If students have been practicing group DRTA activities using print stories in basal readers or working together in small groups with electronic materials, you might have them deal independently with such materials and then get together to compare ideas. We recommend that you do this only a few times, however, because your prime objective is to help students operate completely independently with electronic as well as print materials. The main benefit of a weaning step is that it gives students opportunities to compare their *personal* efforts with the efforts of other students.

Purposeful Use of the DRTA and Other Strategies with Electronic Materials

Students engaged in **independent reading** work without assistance from you. They are on their own in terms of applying strategies to effectively comprehend the material (Cooper, 2000). When students deal with electronic materials on CD-ROMs or the Internet, you may have fewer opportunities to interact with them. Often, students work alone, with just one other student, or in small groups, and you may be unable to monitor their comprehension. Therefore, it is crucial to help students become independent, critical consumers of electronic materials through practicing and internalizing the DRTA and other self-regulating reading strategies. The DRTA strategy is particularly important for use with electronic materials because you can help students learn to set their own—not yours, an author's, or a publisher's—purposes for being online. DRTA strategies help students learn to search for and use verbal and nonverbal evidence as the basis for predicting, studying, and confirming or rejecting ideas. Using DRTA-based strategies with multimedia materials, students observe and listen to evidence and engage in critical and purposeful reading. You can help students be independent, successful listeners, readers, and interpreters of electronic materials. To help students efficiently locate and use electronic information, you can emphasize the strategy of making important decisions *before* they boot up a CD-ROM or go on the Internet.

MODELING THE USE OF ELECTRONIC DRTAs

You can create DRTAs using electronic materials from the WWW or CD-ROMs.

Just as you help students internalize effective reading strategies with print materials, you can model such strategies and engage students in thoughtful interactions online. Help them see that with practice, they will be able to use these strategies independently. You can be a model using both fiction and nonfiction.

Fiction

Select an online fiction story and plan a DRTA similar to the way you conduct one with print materials but using all of the features available in an online story. Whether you choose material from the WWW or a CD-ROM, examine each story's navigation features, audio options, video options, photos, and other graphics to determine how students can use them in making predictions. For instance, are there automatic animations, or will you or students need to activate them?

To help you present evidence easily when dealing with a web story, create a new bookmark folder and save, in the order you want to show them, the URLs of the pages from the online story that contain evidence you want students to first see. Throughout the predicting process, you can show any web page you place in the folder as evidence you want students to consider before they read. Also place the first page of the story in the folder so you can click on it when students are ready to begin listening, reading, and interpreting. CD-ROM stories vary considerably in their navigation features, so you should rehearse how to present evidence and begin stories on specific CD-ROMs. You might select an interesting screen somewhere in the story and start there, then go back to the beginning of the story and navigate through it.

If there is narration, decide whether or not you will use it. You may want to wait until after the DRTA and let interested students listen to the story on their own. If you do use audio, determine whether it can be started and stopped easily and, if so, whether you can stop it exactly where you want to stop it. (Note that RealPlayer opens a box that has "start" and "stop" buttons. Drag the box to the bottom of the screen so just the on/off buttons show. If the RealPlayer box disappears, hold down the "Alt" key and toggle the "Tab" key until it shows.) For CD-ROMs, you will need to experiment to learn how to control sound.

If a web story has navigation buttons, determine if they allow you to stop the story so students can make predictions at appropriate places. Also, decide how you will handle scrolling through text. If the stories' individual web pages make good stopping places, let students handle the scrolling. If you need to keep part of a screen from being seen until after predicting, you will want to do the scrolling.

Consider the overall length of the story. You might work with it all at once, or you can carry it over to a second day. If you plan on continuing another day, find a good place to stop so students will have some material to consider between the first and second days. On the second day, review predictions for the next part before you pick up the DRTA from where you left off the day before.

In your planning, determine if there are other online materials (e.g., stories by the same author) to bookmark and identify as potential follow-up activities, remembering that students may want to pursue something of interest to them that the present story evoked. On the Web, you can place such bookmarks in the story folder you created. For CD-ROMs, you might consider printing out a listing of pertinent materials. Fiction often leads to writing, speaking, and constructing, so encourage students to engage in creative writing or to prepare electronic presentations using the features in programs such as PowerPoint or SiteCentral as part of the messages they want to convey. We discuss using technology for writing, speaking, and constructing messages elsewhere in this book.

Nonfiction

As you saw in Ms. Thompson's adroit questioning about the marsupial and opossum materials, the key to modeling nonfiction DRTAs is channeling students' thinking about the information you most want them to learn about. You evoke their background knowledge and their predictions by revealing evidence that starts them thinking about what the evidence means. You model asking the "who," "what," and "when" kinds of questions so that students, too, learn to ask these questions as they deal with nonfiction electronic materials. For many years, I used a nonfiction selection about the building of the Union Pacific Railroad. To direct students' thinking, I asked: "Who built it? When was it built? Why did they build it? Where did it start and end? How did they build it? What materials did they use?" After briefly obtaining and recording predictions, during which Promontory Point, Chinese workers, bankers, and a host of other things were mentioned, students read the entire selection silently. Heads bobbed as students checked the chalkboard as they read, and murmurs confirmed that they had facts either right or wrong. Today, you can use a database or graphic organizer to record predictions and use a computer projector to show them to a group of students.

As you prepare to model nonfiction DRTAs, select a web site or portion of a CD-ROM reference and determine the key concepts and ideas you want students to learn and, ideally, retain. Study the structure of the presentation to determine if sections offer natural stops for predicting and discussing. Once you decide what is important and how you want to conduct the session overall, create the appropriate channeling questions. For nonfiction materials, you will want to locate additional electronic references and to bookmark web sites for possible follow-up experiences, depending on students' interests. When studying nonfiction, students sometimes want to learn more about a topic and to share that information with others, so be ready to help students—as you do when they are reading fiction—prepare to make impressive presentations for others.

INDEPENDENT ELECTRONIC DRTAs

Students can develop strategies to regulate their own skillful interactions with electronic materials.

Students can use fiction and nonfiction electronic materials to conduct their own independent DRTAs. To do so, students must know clearly that they will:

- Examine some part of web sites or CD-ROMs and decide what evidence they will use as the basis of predicting. Perhaps reviewing the main menu will let students make predictions about a site's entire content; or, maybe they can predict after visiting one or two linking pages.
- Using a word-processing program, record their predictions about possible content (nonfiction) or plot and characters (fiction), as well as the questions they wish to answer.
- Record speculations about the outcomes of their predictions and their plausible answers to the questions they ask.
- Stop occasionally to think, review, and record ideas as well as make new predictions. *(This is a key behavior!)*

- Find statements in electronic text to describe or point to nonverbal symbols they used as evidence.
- Keep records of where they can prove their statements (e.g., URLs, CD-ROM menus, titles).

Students will find it helpful to use an Independent DRTA record such as the one in Figure 4.1. The record serves two important functions: (1) it helps students *attend* to the basic steps they need to take in order to work

FIGURE 4.1

Independent DRTA Record

Student's name ______________________ **Date** ______________

Title and URL of web site: ______________________________

Name of CD-ROM: ______________________________

Type of material used (fiction; nonfiction): ______________________________

Page number(s) or total number of print pages or electronic digital screens: __________

A. What I used for evidence when making predictions:

Title _____ Photo(s) _____ Graphic(s) _____ Animation(s) _____ Chart(s) _____

Database _____ Video clip _____ Sound clip _____ Print text _____

I examined these electronic pages: ______________________________

Other: ______________________________

____

____

B. My predictions (or questions):

1. ______________________________
2. ______________________________

C. What I found and where I found it.

1. ______________________________
2. ______________________________

independently, and (2) it helps students *organize* independent literacy strategies by themselves. The record is not "busywork." Students can use it to refine and self-evaluate their literacy behaviors. They can review a record beforehand and talk about it at pupil-teacher conferences, during which you can use the record as a major focus for discussion. Independent DRTA records are especially useful at the intermediate grade and middle school levels. You can modify the one presented here or create similar records to suit the capabilities and maturity of the students you teach.

Students can reveal their understanding and successful handling of electronic and print materials in various ways. Sharing and other reporting activities that you use (e.g., PowerPoint presentations) should quickly replace Independent DRTA records. Also, you can encourage students to *mentally* set purposes and *mentally* keep track of evidence and where they find proof of predictions. You can ask them to keep track of their thinking in electronic formats of their own design. Perhaps students can create a database to organize their ideas, findings, and proofs.

Independent DRTAs are different from free reading, using software unassisted, or surfing the Net—interactions with materials that students do not typically discuss with teachers. You *do* discuss Independent DRTAs with students. Interacting with students about their independent listening, reading, and interpreting may require your asking some questions about facts because you may not have read the particular electronic materials a student is working with and you want to probe to learn more about the topic. That is fine. But the main thrust of questioning should be directed toward discovering how well students predict and how well they are able to determine if their previous predictions or questions were accurate, based on the initial evidence they used and the evidence they found throughout the entire activity.

You might wonder how you can discuss and assess students' understanding of material you have never dealt with. Good readers, listeners, and interpreters usually think ahead and can tell logical possibilities about the materials they are interacting with. Ask students questions such as "What are you wondering about now as you use these materials?" or "What do expect you will learn using this CD-ROM?" Students' answers to such questions will help you assess their understanding of what they have already read, listened to, or interpreted. This kind of questioning lets you know how well students are comprehending electronic stories or nonfiction materials. The predicting, inference making, and critical thinking that the Independent DRTA process evokes are very important to students' growth in verbal and nonverbal literacy.

THINKING ABOUT BEHAVIORS FOSTERED BY DRTA STRATEGIES

Students should engage in the following thinking behaviors before, during, and after the DRTA strategies:

Before Listening, Reading, and Interpreting Online Materials

- Determine what they already know and frame questions or predictions as appropriate, perhaps using a graphic organizer program.
- Identify clearly what kinds of information they will seek, expanding or narrowing topics as needed.
- Identify keywords that may help with electronic searches.
- Conduct efficient Web searches or use electronic menus or tables of contents while employing the available electronic navigation tools.
- Quickly analyze the material for quality (e.g., author's motives; content) and the likelihood it will be valid and useful.

During Listening, Reading, and Interpreting Online Materials

- Keep accurate records of sites visited (bookmarking) or electronic references used.
- Judge what they find in terms of whether the material meets their purposes.
- Monitor their predictions, use of evidence, and their thinking and learning, resetting purposes as needed.
- Take notes, paraphrase, select quotes, organize, and summarize information, possibly by means of alternating ("Alt" and "Tab" keys) between the electronic reference material and a word-processing program and using the cut-and-paste features.

After Listening, Reading, and Interpreting Online Materials

- Evaluate the sufficiency of the information they have found, going back as needed to electronic references for more material.
- Think about and organize information for purposes of clarity and to plan ways to share it electronically with others through writing, speaking, and constructing nonverbal materials.
- Determine if they wish to deal with the topic further.

Specific Materials That Students Can Read Electronically

A voluminous amount of outstanding fiction and nonfiction electronic materials are useful in developing literacy.

Governments, universities, school districts, individuals, and people who want to sell products publish online fiction and nonfiction you can use to interest students in literacy experiences. Instead of relying on classroom or school libraries, students can use CD-ROMs, DVDs, and online resources as the basis of literacy activities.

First, we will share a few of the many entertaining fiction materials that can grab a student's attention. Then, we will note a few of the rapidly increasing nonfiction references available online. Space permits just a few examples, but many additional URLs and brief descriptions are available on the web site containing resources related to this book. An important thing for you to know here is that numerous sites exist, and you can use them daily with students in their pursuit of learning to be verbally and nonverbally literate.

FICTION MATERIALS

Many web sites contain fictional materials with graphics and sound, and these sites provide ample opportunities for students to read, listen to, and interpret such works. Classic and recently created stories, text, hypertext, graphically augmented text, and audio-enhanced materials are available. Individuals, organizations, and companies have created online fiction materials. Some are plain text, but others are beautifully illustrated. Some use sound and animation to further the mood and message of the stories. Some are well written by seasoned writers, while some are less carefully crafted. Adults and students alike have contributed original stories, poetry, and other materials to the WWW, and both formal and informal writing styles appear. Not everything online is perfect, because intrusions such as hard- or soft-sell advertisements are present, and some sites require downloading **plug-ins** (small computer applications) to make music or animations work. You may find some misspellings, but you can turn such incidents into teachable moments about striving to be accurate when placing materials online. Learn more about plug-ins on this book's web site. The following are just a few of the very good fiction sites online.

WEBLIOGRAPHY

- The Amazing Adventure Series
http://64.224.164.54/index_fl.html
Read and listen to "June the Prune" (**http://64.224.164.54/june/jp1.html**). This site has engaging activities. Figure 4.2 shows this delightful character, and the RealPlayer narration is excellent! See this book's web site for some thoughts from Tom Tosi, the story's author.

FIGURE 4.2
June the Prune

Source: Used by permission of Tom Tosi.

- Bedtime-Story
http://www.bedtime-story.com/bedtime-story/indexmain.htm
Dozens of delightful stories with a range of topics and artwork are presented. The Summerland Group, Inc., an engineering firm, maintains this site. Some of these stories are very pretty and are accompanied by music. See "The Rain Angel," "The Dolphin and the Shark," and "The House on the Hill." In "Dolphin," animations help advance the story, something the electronic story format can do that print cannot.

- FunBrain.com
http://www.funbrain.com/index.html
This site has many word activities, including spelling games, and much advice for parents and teachers. On the Wacky Tales link (from the FunBrain home page, select "Words," then scroll down to "Wacky Tales"), students can create "Mad Libs"® at **http://www4.funbrain.com/wacky/index.html.** (See Figure 4.3.) Wacky Web Tales at **http://www.eduplace.com/tales/** is a similar site.

FIGURE 4.3
Haunted House

Source: Used by permission of Mike Cirks, FunBrain.com.

WEBLIOGRAPHY (continued)

- **Online Children's Stories**
  http://www.acs.ucalgary.ca/~dkbrown/stories.html
  This site has story collections, folklore, myths and legends, songs and poetry, classics, stories for and by children and young adults, and Readers' Theatre.

Software based on fictional materials is plentiful. For instance, stories in the *Little Planet Literacy Series,* designed for ages Pre-K–4 (Sunburst Technology/Houghton Mifflin), deal with sequence, story retelling, and writing. Values are embedded in the stories. That's a Fact, Jack! Read (Tom Snyder Productions) is an interactive game show for grades 3–10 containing questions about 340 books, many of which are popular fiction titles, among them *Harriet the Spy* and *Stuart Little.* The questions measure some aspects of comprehending the stories.

Some available software products deal with thinking that is pertinent to nonfiction materials but may use games or fictional characters or settings. For example, Decisions, Decisions (Tom Snyder Productions) is designed for social studies work in grades 5–10. Students engage in five-step decision-making processes in areas such as the environment, violence in the media, and more. Edmark's Thinkin' Things Collection 1 contains Pre-K–3 activities that address students' differing learning styles to strengthen memory, logic, musical, spatial, and kinesthetic areas as well as critical thinking. The company produces similar collections for older grades.

NONFICTION MATERIALS

A variety of nonfiction online references will be discussed in chapter 5, but we would like to mention a few very special web sites here. These are the impressive sites being constructed by people who are making available information that has been hidden away in libraries, attics, and old boxes. People are finding and sharing primary (original) resources about famous people and events, and they are placing public information online.

Governments, state agencies, cities, universities, libraries, and other organizations have been digitizing books, personal papers, diaries, journals, historically important documents, and other materials to place on the Internet. For instance, in the year 2000, the U.S. government placed online more than 27 million government web pages. See First.Gov at **http://www.firstgov.gov.** You can find links to the major federal governmental offices, and you can read about subjects such as taxes, passports, and much more. These pages enable U.S. citizens to communicate more easily with their government.

An excellent example of a university's effort to place rare materials online is a site hosted by the University of Virginia and maintained by Edward L. Ayers. The site takes one Northern community and one Southern community through the Civil War years. It is a "hypermedia archive" of letters, records, diaries, and so forth. The site, The Valley of the Shadow, has received nearly twenty awards from various organizations and is available on CD-ROM. You can see it at **http://jefferson.village.virginia.edu/vshadow2/choosepart.html.**

You can check your state and local government agencies as well as your professional organizations to locate factual information that may be useful to you and students. When cities and towns place information about their localities online, students gain valuable resources that will help them understand their own communities. See All About Tucson at **http://www.allabout-tucson.com** for an example of what one city has done to let people know about their community.

The hundreds of web sites cited in this book and on the book's web site clearly demonstrate that there is an abundance of electronic materials online. As more and more students gain easier access to the WWW's wealth of primary and public resources, they will be able to investigate topics that their older siblings and parents never had the opportunity to examine.

WEBLIOGRAPHY

- **Ellis Island**
  http://www.ellisisland.org/
  This site is a searchable database of immigrants.

- **Web de Anza OnLine Learning Community**
  http://anza.uoregon.edu/TeachersWWW/helping_teachers.html
  This site is "designed to promote historical inquiry about Juan Bautista de Anza and his two 18th century expeditions from northern Mexico to Northern California." This is a model site that demonstrates how web-based primary resources and original materials are being placed online by some university educators.

SUMMARY

- Computers delivering electronic verbal and nonverbal messages have affected all areas of society, and the definition of literacy is being reexamined and redefined in the polysymbolic world of electronic materials.
- The DRTA is an overarching instructional strategy that helps students learn to examine verbal and nonverbal messages and to use them as a basis for thinking about print and electronic messages. Students set their own purposes for interacting with texts, and they learn to monitor their comprehension. The DRTA and related strategies help students deal effectively and independently with literacy experiences.
- A wealth of fiction and nonfiction materials are available online. While some are unfiltered by agencies, many previously unavailable electronic materials are of good quality. You can help students become independent, critical users of both the information and the entertainment features of the WWW.

ACTIVITIES

1. At Reading Online (**http://www.readingonline.org/**), read and discuss with others one of the articles in the "New Literacies" section.
2. Select a fiction story, select stopping places, and conduct a DRTA with a few students.
3. Choose a web site with stories. Plan how you can use an online story as a DRTA.
4. Select one of the CD-ROM programs listed below and evaluate it.

SOFTWARE

Following are some of the software products designed to help students learn to listen, read, and interpret using electronic media. They are CD-ROMs useable by both PCs and Macintosh computers unless otherwise specified. You should always obtain evaluation copies of software programs and examine them carefully to determine if they provide a good fit with your instructional goals and the instructional standards you must help students meet.

Bailey's Book House, Edmark/Riverdeep Interactive Learning, Pre-K–2
This reading readiness and early reading skills program explores letters, sounds, words, rhyming, adjectives, prepositions, and storytelling.

Beginning Reading for the Real World, Wasatch Interactive Learning, K–3
This project-based interactive, comprehensive early literacy program is designed to promote reasoning, higher-order thinking, and decision making while building word recognition skills and comprehension.

CornerStone Reading Language Arts, Skillsbank/The Learning Company, 3–8
This comprehensive program builds language arts, comprehension, vocabulary, and mathematics in three levels of the program.

Cosmic Reading Journey, Sunburst Technology/Houghton Mifflin, 2–3
This reading comprehension program has activities for 100 classic and contemporary books and is similar to Sunburst's Island Reading Journey, but for younger students.

Decisions, Decisions: Lying, Cheating, Stealing, Tom Snyder Productions, All
This program deals with ethical concerns and critical thinking about those concerns.

Diascriptive Cloze & Writing Practice Activities, Educational Activities, 2–11
This program uses cloze passages to help students develop and master comprehension skills. There are four levels.

Dugout Collection (Little Planet Literacy Series), Sunburst Technology/Houghton Mifflin, 3–4
This series emphasizes reading comprehension and writing capabilities.

Elmo's Reading, Creative Wonders/The Learning Company, Pre-K–3
Students can learn early reading skills. The program adjusts to a child's performance.

Glowbird Collection (Little Planet Literacy Series), Sunburst Technology/Houghton Mifflin, 2–3
Designed to develop literacy and thinking skills, this program combines video, software, and print materials.

Inside Stories, Mimosa Technology, 1–3
The program has more than sixty interactive activities in eight modules of increasing skill level. It covers the areas of comprehension, sentence construction, punctuation, phonics, and word study.

Literacy Explorer, Sequoyah, 3 & up
This program contains reading passages from television and movies.

Literacy Place, Scholastic, K–6
This program uses both new and classic literature. It is also available in Spanish.

Multimedia Reading Activities, Orchard: Teacher's Choice Software, K–3
The programs contain beginning (K–1), intermediate (1–2), and advanced (2–3) sets of activities that students can complete in response to reading literature.

Rainbow Program, Curriculum Associates, 1, 2 & ESL
Literacy development is the goal of the program's activities, which are based on learning about world cultures and geography.

Reading Mansion, Instructional Fair Group, 1–3
The program offers opportunities for individualization of beginning through third-grade reading skills.

Ribbit Collection (Little Planet Literacy Series), Sunburst Technology/Houghton Mifflin, 1–2
This series is designed to develop listening, speaking, sequencing, reading, and writing skills.

Scholastic READ 180, Scholastic, 4 & up
This comprehensive reading program uses software, audio books, and print books. CD-ROM videos evoke background knowledge to assist comprehension.

Sequencing Fun, Sunburst Technology/Houghton Mifflin, K–2
More than fifty problems deal with sequencing, critical thinking, and problem solving.

Start-to-Finish Books, Don Johnston, 4 & up
These are high-interest (classics and biographies, etc.) materials you can use with ESL students and students with special needs. Materials include a CD, audiotapes, and print texts.

Strategy Challenges Collection 1 and Collection 2, Edmark/Riverdeep Interactive Learning, K & up
The program uses games to help students engage in problem-solving and strategic-thinking activities.

Student Writing and Research Center, The Learning Company, 4–12
This program integrates writing and research through access to a complete encyclopedia and other research materials.

Talking Walls Software Series, Edmark/Riverdeep Interactive Learning, 4–8
This software collection is about the world's great walls and includes activities designed to promote reading comprehension, note-taking, and report writing.

Waterford Institute Early Reading Program, Waterford Institute, All
This is a comprehensive reading program in three levels (emergent, beginning, and fluent readers). In all, there are 225 hours of individualized instruction available.

FOR FURTHER READING

Burns, P. C., Roe, B. D., & Ross, E. P. (1999). *Teaching reading in today's elementary schools* (7th ed.). Boston: Houghton Mifflin.

Jongsma, K. (2001). Using CD-ROMs to support the development of literacy processes. *The Reading Teacher, 54*(6), 592–595.

Labbo, L. D., & Kuhn, M. (2000). Weaving chains of affect and cognition: A young child's understanding CD-ROM talking books. *Journal of Literacy Research, 32*(2), 187–210.

Lenski, S. D., Wham, M. A., & Johns, J. L. (1999). *Reading and learning strategies for middle & high school students.* Dubuque, IA: Kendall/Hunt Publishing.

Vacca, R. T., & Vacca, J. L. (1999). *Content area reading* (6th ed.). Needham Heights, MA: Longman Publishing.

CHAPTER 5

Using Technology to Develop Word Recognition, Vocabulary, Reference, and Study Skills

INTRODUCTION

Chapter 4 explored the importance of comprehension. This chapter starts with the important area of word recognition. Some children learn to read with little assistance from their parents or teachers; others require intensive instruction. It is important to know how much support to give each student and how to keep students' word recognition and comprehension capabilities in balance. Too much phonics instruction causes some students to become overanalytic—overly dependent on sounding out words—while too little instruction leaves students with insufficient knowledge of phoneme-grapheme relationships to help them decode words. An overall teaching emphasis on word recognition instruction can delay growth in reading for meaning, while an overemphasis on comprehension development can cause students to flounder when trying to decode words. Balanced programs are vital to effective classroom instruction.

Words evoke conceptual understandings, and you should encourage students to use online and offline resources to learn about words and their meanings. You can find opportunities for vocabulary development online and through the use of CD-ROM materials. You can create and use a variety of electronic cloze activities to emphasize word meanings. Technology can help you work with strategies such as the language experience approach (LEA) to record and sort words, a process that once was very time consuming.

At the end of this chapter, we will look at a number of electronic reference materials and briefly examine some features of word-processing programs students can use to develop study skill strategies. Some are ideal for tracking quotes and organizing significant parts of electronic materials. Technology, then, can help you teach older strategies more efficiently, and it can help you and students in new ways. This chapter suggests ways to take advantage of these teaching and learning strategies.

Developing Word Recognition Skills

Learning to associate sounds and graphic letters is an important aspect of beginning literacy. You will learn about three different teaching approaches—synthetic, analytic, and analogy. Along with phonics skills, students need to develop **sight words,** or words they recognize instantly without using any decoding skills to analyze them. We will discuss strategies that have a whole-word emphasis, including the language experience approach. In addition, we will demonstrate cloze strategies to help students learn to use context and graphic information together as they read.

PHONEMIC AWARENESS AND PHONICS

Phonemic awareness is basic to learning to read.

It is widely believed that one of the earliest literacy behaviors students must develop is **phonemic awareness.** Phonemic awareness, according to Fox and Mitchell (2000),

> is the understanding that spoken language consists of words, rhymes, syllables, and sounds. Children who are phonemically aware are skilled at recognizing rhyme, identifying sounds in words, and blending sounds into words. Good phonemic awareness has repeatedly been correlated with success in reading and spelling, whereas poor awareness has been found to be one of the underlying causes of reading failure. (pp. 46–47)

Phonemes are the smallest units of sound in oral language that distinguish one word from another. The words *cat* and *hat* are each composed of three phonemes. They differ in initial phonemes only. According to most authorities, the English language contains forty-four phonemes. The number of phonemes in other languages varies, depending on the complexity of the spoken language. Unless children have hearing problems or are deprived of language interactions with others, most learn and use the sounds that people around them use: this happens quite early in life, well before they come to school. The task in the early grades is to ensure that students learn which sounds to produce when they see graphic letters and combinations of letters that are used in English **orthography,** the representation by letters of sounds in the English language. Letters on a page or computer screen, **graphemes,** do not make sounds; rather, *people* produce sounds based on the graphic evidence (letters or combinations of letters) that they see.

You produce sounds that graphic symbols cue you to produce.

Young readers learn to blend sounds together in order to produce an oral representation of the printed word they wish to say. If they know the word from oral or aural (i.e., speaking or hearing) experiences, they will recognize the word and, if necessary, make fine adjustments in order to pronounce the word as they know it. If they do not recognize the word as one they know, they may need to seek confirmation from some source (e.g., glossary, dictionary, person) that they are pronouncing the word correctly. One task, then, is to help students identify the twenty-six letters of the alphabet used in the English language in both their uppercase and lowercase forms. Other tasks are to help students deal with special combinations of letters (e.g., *sh, ch, wh, th, ng*), other common combinations of letters (e.g., *cl, dr, sw*), long and short vowels, and hard and soft *c* and *g* sounds.

You can use a computer to help students find words that contain specific phonic elements. For instance, you can use CD-ROM stories to have students electronically search for phonic elements or rhyming words (Labbo, 2000). You can have students use the "Find" feature to locate all of the words in a text that begin with *br, cl,* or some other phonic element you wish them to learn. Similarly, to search for words that rhyme with *hat,* students could use the "Find" feature by typing in the phonogram *at.*

Phonics refers to any system for teaching students to link the sounds of a language with the graphic symbols used to represent those sounds. To help students deal with grapheme-phoneme relationships, people have created hundreds of different phonics programs and systems. Some programs of the past used **diacritical markings** with letters (i.e., marks added to letters to specify specific phonetic values) to help students pronounce words, others used specifically created symbols (e.g., the Initial Teaching Alphabet) or colors (e.g., Words in Color) to teach grapheme-phoneme associations, and still another strategy had students read only consonants, leaving vowels to be learned later. Linguistic programs (e.g., *Miami Linguistic Readers*) capitalized on phonetic regularities (predictability of patterns) in English orthography but often resulted in stilted stories (*mat, rat, sat, cat*) (Aukerman, 1971). You can read about the ITA at **http://www.itafoundation.org/.**

Synthetic, analytic, and analogy are major phonics approaches.

Phonics strategies can be divided into three approaches: synthetic, analytic, and analogy. Each will be discussed here briefly because multitudinous software lessons and lessons on the Internet are based on these approaches.

Synthetic Approach

Synthetic approaches are what most people think of when they think of phonics. These are the programs that start with an individual sound such as /b/ and pair that sound with its graphic representation *b*. The teaching strategy used is a **deductive strategy** because the teacher shows the grapheme and tells students what sound to make. ("The sound of the letter *b* is /buh/.") After learning a few grapheme-phoneme relationships, students learn to produce the sound that each letter evokes (i.e., "sound out each letter") and then to blend the sounds together to make a word. A major criticism of this approach is that when they are segmented and blended (buh-a-tuh), phonemes are distorted from the way they occur in the real world. In fact, many people who create such programs advise teachers to be careful not to distort sounds, but that is impossible. Anyone who has seen a sound spectrograph recording of an entire sentence being uttered can attest to the fact that it is virtually impossible to see where individual words start and end, let alone to see individual sounds within words.

Analytic Approach

Analytic approaches keep phonemes in the context of words and are based on an **inductive strategy**. Often one word, for example *ball*, is used as a keyword. Then students listen to other words that start like the keyword (e.g., *bat, baby, bear*) to try to recognize other words that begin with the sound at the beginning of the word *ball*. Students later learn to produce the appropriate sound when they see words that begin with the letter *b*. The advantage of this strategy is that sounds are not isolated and distorted, making it easier for students to understand grapheme-phoneme relationships as they really exist in the context of words. The strategy is inductive in that students come to *discover* and understand (induce) the grapheme-phoneme relationship from the examples given.

Analogy (Word Family) Approach

The third phonics approach is an **analogy approach.** If you know the word *hat*, you know most of the words *bat, sat, mat*, and so forth. Therefore, by *inference*, you should be able to pronounce the additional words easily if you know their initial phoneme-grapheme correspondences. The analogy approach can be used in combination with either the synthetic or analytic approaches. Students often discover that they really know many more words than they thought they knew once they realize how to use an analogy—often called a word family—approach.

Determining Which Approach Is Best

All three of the above strategies have weak points. Some students learning with the synthetic approach become overdependent on breaking words into their individual sounds and continue to sound out words long after they should know them as sight words. For them, automaticity, quickly pronouncing words, does not occur. Some students learning with the analytic approach do not clearly internalize grapheme-phoneme relationships and get confused. Some using the analogy approach tend to overapply the strategy and end up finding *moth* in *mother* and *fat* in *father.* Regardless of their flaws, all of these approaches are commonly used to help students learn phoneme-grapheme correspondences. With an understanding of these basic approaches, you will be able to select or create appropriate computer and Internet materials for use in your classroom, and you will be able to adapt electronic materials to your specific ways of helping students learn. *We think the approach that works best with a given student is the proper one to use with that student.*

Use the approach that helps a given student learn best.

Phonics software programs designed for preschool children and up are listed at the end of this chapter. It is important for you to evaluate these programs to determine whether or not they are compatible with your preferred instructional strategies and whether or not they are flexible enough that students can be placed into such programs *in only those parts they need to learn.* That is, there should be a way to get to the phonics or other program elements individual students need, and students should be able to work *only* with those phonic elements and activities they do not know—not every element the program presents (Fox & Mitchell, 2000). The following web sites may be useful to you in locating online sources of information about phoneme awareness, phonics, and other strategies.

WEBLIOGRAPHY

- **Houghton Mifflin Education Place**
  http://www.eduplace.com/index.html
  This site provides free K–8 resources.

- **Phonics Page**
  http://www.teachers.net/lessons/posts/751.html
  The teacher gives students sheets of bulletin board paper on which letters are written. Students then cut out of newspapers and magazines pictures of objects that begin with those letter sounds. You can scan the sheets and make an electronic picture dictionary. (This idea was contributed to the Teachers.Net Lesson Bank by Sheri Eaton.)

WEBLIOGRAPHY
(continued)

- **Reading Environmental Print**
  http://www.sasked.gov.sk.ca/docs/ela/ela_envi.html
  Suggestions for dealing with environmental print are given at the site created by Saskatchewan Education.
- **Sounds of the Day**
  http://readmeabook.com/sounds/sotd.htm
  The sounds evoked by letters of the alphabet are produced and then spoken in context of words. Two sounds are presented. You can make similar sound activities yourself, using HyperStudio or other presentation programs.
- **Welcome to the Phonics Link**
  http://www.sdcoe.k12.ca.us/score/phonics%5Flink/phonics.html
  The San Diego County Office of Education's web site has a page that provides information about books and links to online materials about phonics instruction. Figure 5.1 shows the site's main web page.

FIGURE 5.1
Phonics Link

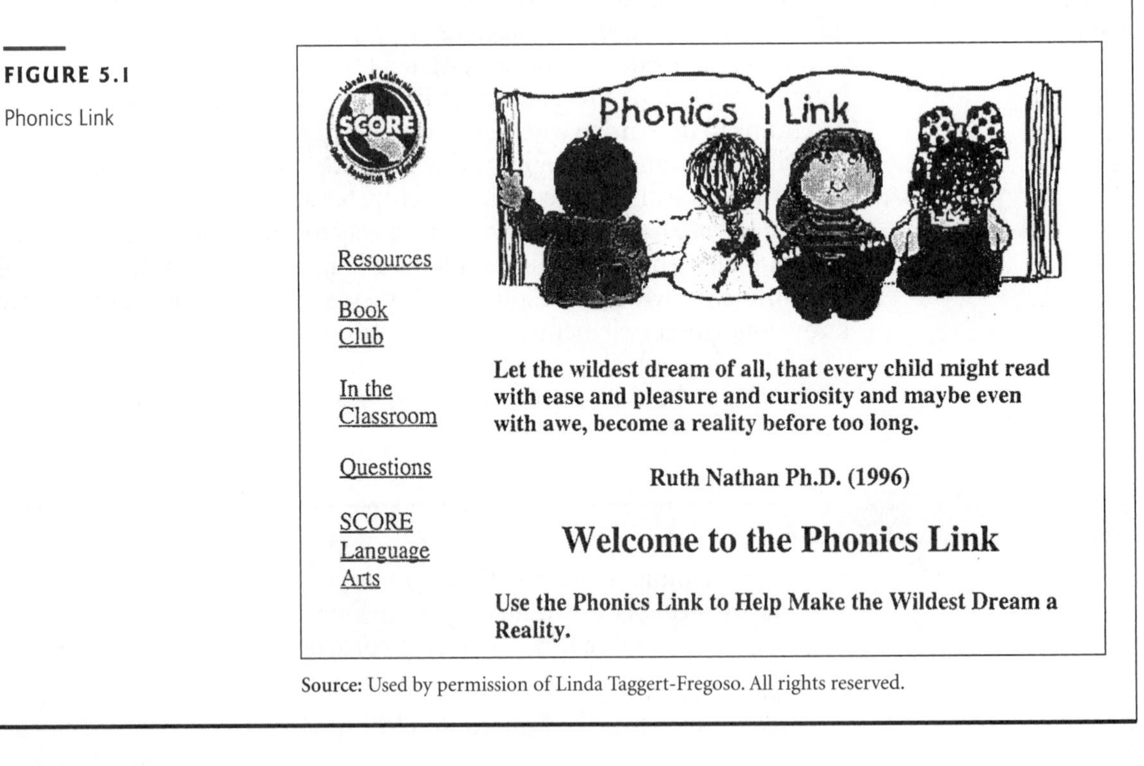

Source: Used by permission of Linda Taggert-Fregoso.

WHOLE-WORD EMPHASIS

Sounds spoken in words and words spoken in a sentence physically blend together, unless there is a specific effort made to pronounce one—word—at—a—time. But people do not speak one word at a time in daily conversation—that would sound clipped and awkward. Rather, because of our experiences with spoken language, we *mentally* know where to end one word and start the next. When children first encounter words in paper or electronic texts, they may need to learn what a word is if they have not gained this concept prior to coming to school. Teaching "wordness" is often accomplished when you label objects in the classroom, use flashcards, model the writing of words and sentences, and frame words individually with your hands.

You can use technology tools to help students learn whole words.

The word-processing program you use can help you teach the concept of "wordness." Experiment with font size, color, and typeface to your heart's content. Young children need to learn that regardless of its visual appearance, a printed or electronically generated word such as *dog* evokes the spoken word /dog/ and/or the mental construct of a "familiar barking animal." You can electronically create and print visual representations of words that grow out of classroom conversations, and you can gather students at a computer while they tell you individual words they want to learn to read and write. You can then print such words for students to keep in a folder.

Use programs such as HyperStudio, PowerPoint, or Kid Pix to add motion to texts and illustrations that can help students learn words or the concept of wordness. Two teachers from Texas, Marilyn Eisenwine and Diane Hunt, created a series of slides showing the action of sentences. They used the cursor (shaped like a hand) to point to each word. When they show the slides, the hand appears to point to each word as the sentence is being read. See the Teaching Tip "Making Original Stories for Reinforcing Words."

You can create rhymes, simple sentences, patterned language stories, and so forth with sound and animations using contemporary presentation software. Adding either your own voice or students' voices to accompany sight words, sentences, or stories can be helpful to students. Such activities introduce students to what a word is. This is an important concept that you cannot assume is automatically understood by all beginning readers.

TEACHING TIPS Making Original Stories for Reinforcing Words

The stories we created worked great with the kids! My colleague Diane Hunt and I had attended a district workshop during the summer to learn about the new computers we would be receiving soon for our classrooms. From our previous Reading Recovery training, we had learned to make up easy stories for our students at the first of the year when they needed success with known words. My friend's husband teaches at a small university in town, and he had his college students do projects on HyperStudio. He had a tutorial worksheet, and we basically self-taught ourselves to use the program while making the stories for our kids. At first we just made hard copies of stories with graphics, then we decided to have students also work on the computer to read them.

We had a type of competition going on where Diane would make one story, then I would make a different one. We created the stories to reinforce a certain fluency word [sight word] the students were learning during the week, such as *can* or *is*. First, one of us went through each story several times with a small group of

students. Then, we let the children view and read the story themselves during Computer Center time. They would eagerly wait for their turn at the computer to try out the stories for themselves.

We pictured them letting the computer read the stories to them, which they often did. However, they would also read the word or sentence themselves, then click the mouse to see if they were right. They also liked to repeatedly click on one word or sound to hear the computer do it over and over.

We liked the stories because they were similar to the talking books manufactured commercially, but they are more on the child's level using words we were teaching at the time. It is hard to find enough easy material to read early in the school year—especially for our literacy groups who were considered "at risk" from the individual testing that was done when they entered school.

Source: Used by permission from Marilyn J. Eisenwine, Diane Hunt, and HyperStudio. HyperStudio is a registered trademark of Knowledge Adventure, Inc.

Sight Vocabulary

Words become sight words when they have been encountered, identified, and then recognized immediately when they are encountered again. Some words become sight words after just one instance of identification. Others may require several exposures before a student recognizes them as sight words.

Many words are phonetically predictable and can be identified using phonemic knowledge or other word recognition strategies. Students can fairly easily help themselves learn such words as sight words. Other words are not phonetically predictable (e.g., *colonel*) and are best taught specifically as sight words. Often high-frequency words, words that are frequently used in the English language, are taught as sight words because educators believe students need to learn them quickly for both reading and writing. Unfortunately, many of the highest-frequency words (e.g., *is, in, it, two*) are easily confused and do not have the same richness of meaning of many longer words (e.g., *elephant, snake*), so it may take longer for students to learn them as sight words. One useful strategy for helping students learn and review sight words is to print words that students inquire about and let them file them in containers. These web sites are resources for locating ideas and materials to deal with sight vocabulary development.

WEBLIOGRAPHY

- Gemini Elementary Grade One: Dolch Word List
  http://www.geminischool.org/sheppard/reading/dolch.html
  This site is an example of how the Dolch 220 word list is used by some schools.

- Sight Word Soup
  http://www.teachers.net/lessons/posts/56.html
  This activity describes selecting sight vocabulary you want students to learn, having students practice reading the words in games such as memory, bingo, or go fish, then reading the words in the context of short sentences. (This idea was contributed to the Teachers.Net Lesson Bank by Dr. Candy Carlile.)

- Sight Word Vocabulary List
  http://web.mountain.net/~jndav/sight.htm
  This is an example of how one school created a list of sight words for students at the pre-primer through third-grade reading levels.

Language Experience Approach

The language experience approach is an effective strategy to help students acquire a basic sight vocabulary (Burns, Roe, & Ross, 1999). The approach, made popular in the 1970s by Roach Van Allen, Mary Anne Hall, and Russell G. Stauffer, involves having students, either in small groups or individually, discuss an actual experience with you or another adult. You then transcribe the statements and read them back to ensure the accuracy of your transcription, and you work with the story several times so students learn some of the words as sight words. For example, in a group-dictated story, you might ask six to eight students to examine an unfamiliar object (e.g., a bellows). Students might handle the object and talk about what they think it is made from, what its purpose might be, what they could do with it, and so forth. You might ask leading questions to draw attention to certain attributes of the object. After the experience, students tell a story about the experience, with each student encouraged to contribute a statement. Have students give the story a title and add the phrase "The End." Print the story and give students copies to place in their own "LEA Books." Encourage students to illustrate their own copies of the story as a visual reminder of what the story is about. In the following days, you and the group reconvene to read the story silently and aloud, with students first reading the sentences they have contributed and, later, reading the entire story. When you determine, through individual students' reading aloud of the story, that they know some of the words as sight words, you can place those words in word banks. *Only words that a student knows as sight words should be kept in a word bank.* Because sometimes students forget sight words and need to learn them again, students should review and sort these words in a variety of ways to ensure that these sight words remain as such.

Technology can support the LEA for developing sight words.

One major drawback of the LEA historically is that teachers, aides, or parents had to spend a great deal of time typing and retyping dictated stories and individual words for the word banks. Modern database and word-processing programs are valuable in reducing the typing and revising time of dictated stories. Instead of writing a dictated story on the chalkboard or chart paper, you can now have students gather around a computer to dictate their stories. With access to either a computer video projector or a connection to a large television set, you and students can easily watch the story as it is being typed. You can revise students' statements as necessary while typing, and you can revise the "master" dictated story as needed. (Note: While correct spelling is always required, it is best to use students' language patterns because that is how they will want to read the sentences when they "read back" their sentences. Grammar and syntactic considerations are best handled at another time.)

After students finish working with a story, you can make a simple database of all the words in the story as in Table 5.1. Create columns identifying each student and rows that list each story word in sequential order. It is easy for you to mark, after you work with the LEA story, those words each student learned as sight words. This tells you at a glance how well students have profited from working with a given story. (Note: You can determine a student's known sight words by having each student read the story aloud to you, marking words as the student reads. By the way the student reads, falters on specific words, or cannot recall words, you can determine which have become sight words.)

Some versions of the LEA encourage teachers to flash words of a story in sequential order using three-by-five-inch cards to uncover (expose) and recover (conceal) each word in turn. You uncover each word just long enough for the student to see—*but not study*—it. Flashing the words helps students begin to look at the story words as individual words and to learn to respond to words rapidly as sight words. Not all students need this step, but it is helpful to know that you can quickly generate a sequential list for students who need extra exposure to them. Use the Report feature in your database program or a word-processing program to print the story in sequential order in columns. Additionally, you can "scramble" the words by jumping around from place to place on the sequential list to determine whether or not students recognize the words out of their original story sequence.

Sorting the database by a particular student's column quickly reveals the words that student knows as sight words. We could have sorted Bobby's column, and his known words (designated with an *x*) would have

TABLE 5.1

Known Sight Words

Words	Bobby	Mary	Juan	Julietta	Andrea	Howard
The	x	x	x	x	x	
Bellows	x	x	x		x	
I	x	x				
saw		x		x	x	x
the	x	x	x	x	x	
brown		x	x		x	
thing		x	x	x		x
It	x	x	x	x	x	
was						
like	x	x	x	x	x	x
a						
balloon				x	x	
It	x	x	x	x	x	
blew		x		x		x
air						
The	x	x	x	x	x	
End	x	x	x	x	x	x

been grouped together. The sort feature lets you decide quickly whether or not to work with the *unknown* words further.

Using the Report feature, you can see a student's sight words listed and identified alphabetically. This makes it easy to discover duplicate entries as well as to identify words that can now be added to that student's word bank. You, an aide, a parent, or students can check the words marked with *X* to determine if they are already in a student's word bank. If they are, just line them out and ignore them. If they are not yet in the word bank, cut out those words and use them as word cards. (Note: Use a larger font and add space between words in the report if you want to make word cards from sequential lists.) Alternatively, you can type words into a word-processing label program and run off labels for students to place on heavy paper or card stock.

Individually dictated language experience stories follow many of the same procedures just described for creating group LEA stories. For these, students tell about their own—not shared—experiences. At first, students dictate such stories. Later, they may use **invented spelling** (their best attempt to make letters and put them in correct order) to write or keyboard their ideas. Have students read their story to you while you word-process it using standard spelling. On one side of a folder, tape a student's writing. Tape your version in standard spelling on the other side so they can compare the two. Students learn to self-correct the spelling of some words using this technique.

Teachers and students can use a computer effectively to keyboard LEA stories.

Whether dealing with group or individual dictated stories, there are a few important considerations:

- Not all students should be expected to learn each word of a dictated story. Some learn keywords; other students do not. That's just how it is.
- Overworking a story leads to boredom with that story. You will get tired of it, and so will students. Remember that high-frequency words will be repeated, so even if they are not learned in one story, they may be learned in the next.
- Repetition is important: read the story together, then have the student read it alone, then you read it while the student follows, and so forth.
- Calling attention to words or word elements helps students learn words. Ask students to reread a particular sentence—for example, "Read the sentence that tells where the cat landed" or "Read the sentence that has a word that rhymes with *cat*." A few minutes of this kind of focusing each time you work with a student can be quite valuable. When you use the LEA, you must impose a "scope and sequence" of word recognition strategies, since no sequence or hierarchy of skills occurs naturally.
- Print copies of stories for students to take home. This gives them something successful to share. In some cases, ask parents to listen as their child reads his or her stories. Or, ask parents to use various strategies for working with a story. In

still other instances, ask parents to transcribe additional stories if the child is amenable.

- Create a classroom or school library of students' stories. Students can read other students' books, and you can use the books to show parents a student's growth in quantity, quality, and variety of ideas throughout the year. At the end of the year, you can send books home or place them in the library.

You can use LEA strategies more easily now because of word processing. Of course, the LEA is not a total instructional program because students' experiences and vocabularies do not rival those found in literature or literacy programs, but for students who need a starting place—regardless of their age or grade level—the LEA is an effective strategy for developing sight vocabulary as well as basic word recognition and comprehension capabilities. These sites can help you create and expand LEA activities in your classroom.

WEBLIOGRAPHY

- **Developing a Language Experience (or Dictated) Story**
  http://bankstreet.edu/americareads/story.html
  This site explains the steps in creating an individually dictated LEA story. Bank Street activities are suggested as follow-up.
- **What Is the Language Experience Approach**
  http://sil.org/lingualinks/literacy/ReferenceMaterials/GlossaryOfLiteracyTerms/WhatIsTheLanguageExperienceApp.htm
  This site is part of the LinguaLinks library and provides basic information about the LEA.

Word Banks

Word banks are valuable for helping students work with sight words. You can make word banks from little cardboard boxes, metal file boxes, or anything that can hold small envelopes into which students place one-by-two-inch word cards. Students can print a capital and lowercase letter on one envelope for each letter of the alphabet. Buy or make alphabetical dividers, and place envelopes behind the appropriate divider in alphabetical order. Students are proud that they have words in their word banks, and this evokes intrinsic motivation to work with their words. You can help students engage in dozens of activities that stretch their knowledge of words based on their known words. For example, ask students to find words that are action words like *run* and *jump*, complete a sentence such as "I can __________," or name people, food, animals, and so forth. Have them find pictures for words to make a visual dictionary, create a sentence using all the words in the "B" envelope that start with the letters *br*, or find five words with two syllables. See the Teaching Tip "Suggestions for Using Words from Word Banks" on this book's web site for additional suggestions.

INSTRUCTIONAL CLOZE FOR WORD RECOGNITION

The cloze strategy helps students use context and graphic elements to identify words.

Originally, the **cloze strategy** was used as a method for *testing* students' comprehension. Words were deleted from passages (every *n*th word was deleted—such as every fifth, ninth, eleventh, etc.), and students used semantic, syntactic, and experiential knowledge to fill in the blanks. The more words students provided that were the *exact* words deleted, the better their comprehension was alleged to be. The cloze technique has some value for teaching both phoneme-grapheme associations and comprehension (Burns, Roe, & Ross, 1999; Sampson, Valmont & Allen, 1982). For learning grapheme-phoneme associations, students supply words in sentences that have selected graphic elements in the cloze blanks. For comprehension development, students supply either the exact missing information or equally acceptable alternative information. Depending on what is omitted, different thinking and performance behaviors are required. Cloze activities require students to practice hypothesis and confirmation strategies. Using available graphic or context evidence, students place logical words or thought units on the cloze blanks. Then, through discussion, students confirm predictions or discuss word or idea choices. Students learn to use context clues or context clues coupled with graphic information to make informed predictions—rather than wild guesses.

A typical cloze sentence looks like this: "The boy looked at the __________ that was next to the road." In this instance, the entire word is omitted, and since no other clues are available, the reader must use semantic, syntactic, and experiential knowledge to place a word on the blank. When several sentences are presented in longer passages, the extended context helps students determine which words to supply.

Cloze blanks can take several formats. The formats give clues and are helpful when you first introduce students to the cloze technique. Later, you can discontinue using these extra clues so students learn to use those clues that are available to them in real reading situations. Here are several basic formats:

1. _ _ _ _ _ Use one underline for each letter of the target word.

2. _____, or ____________________ Use short or long blanks depending on the length of words.

3. c____________ Use a standard size blank, but place the first graphic element of the word on it. (In the example sentence above, the word *car* logically could be placed on the blank, but *cat* or *cow* are equally plausible responses.) When a graphic element is supplied, *both the context and the graphic element must be used* as evidence for making a response. If either is ignored, the response is incorrect. Initial graphic elements are individual letters, blends, or digraphs in the initial position of a word. Part 1 of Figure 5.2 is an example of this strategy.

4. _____a_____ Use a standard blank, and place a vowel letter on the blank. Students must supply a word that makes sense in the sentence *and* contain, for example, the long "a" sound. Therefore, a word like *cake* would be possible, but a word such as *hat* would not, because it does not contain the long "a" sound. Part 2 of Figure 5.2 shows this strategy.

FIGURE 5.2

Using Both Graphic Elements and Context in Cloze Passages

PART 1: USING GRAPHIC ELEMENTS

Directions: Fill in the blanks with words that make sense and start with the sound of the letter *b* or the first sound you hear in the words *ball, belt,* and *big.*

The Toys

My little sister has many toys in her toy b_______. She has a b_______ with many pictures. She has a yellow b_______ that sings. She has a b_______ that she puts in the tub. She has a b_______ that rings. [The words, which would *not* be shown to the students, are *box, book, bird, boat,* and *bell*. Students may choose other logical words that start with the initial consonant "b," so do not hinder creative thinking by showing students "the right answers" in this activity or when using any of the other types of cloze activities described herein.]

PART 2: USING GRAPHIC ELEMENTS WITHIN A WORD

Directions: Fill in the blanks with words that make sense and contain the sound of the letter *i* in words such as *ice, pipe,* and *tile.*

My Brother

My little brother is a pest! I am thirteen years old, and he is ____i_____ years old. When we go swimming, he has to be the first one to ____i_____ off the board. When we go to the movies, he has to stand ahead of me in ____i_____. When we go for a ____i_____ with Mom and Dad, he jumps into the car first. [The words, which would *not* be shown to the students, are *nine* or *five, dive, line,* and *ride*.]

Source:

We never show or tell words before students make their predictions because that would rob them of opportunities to apply their knowledge of semantics, syntax and, when they have graphic clues, their phonics knowledge. For students who cannot read very well, you can read all the words of the sentences except the ones students are to supply. You might read the entire sentence or story first and then let students predict because sometimes context clues follow the blanks.

Create your own cloze instructional activities using a word processor or a presentation program such as Kid Pix, HyperStudio, or PowerPoint. Students can attempt to fill in the blanks by themselves online or using printed copies. Then, after dividing students into small groups so that each can actively participate, show them the cloze as a slide presentation. As they follow along, ask students to discuss and explain their choices to others. Discussing choices collaboratively is a valuable part of the cloze strategy. It is good for students to know when they have made logical choices. They learn that, given no additional constraints, sometimes several words logically fit.

When using cloze for word recognition instruction, you delete words for specific reasons (e.g., to highlight a phoneme-grapheme relationship). Figure 5.3 is a list of additional guidelines to help you create cloze activities.

FIGURE 5.3

Guidelines for Creating Effective Cloze Activities

The following guidelines will help you create effective instructional cloze activities:

- Generally, do not delete words in the first or last sentence of a passage.
- Do not delete two adjacent words, but rather vary the number of words between deletions. Choose which words to delete based on specific instructional purposes.
- Especially as students first learn the cloze technique, delete words that most students will be able to replace because of meaning.
- Delete words once they have already appeared in the passage. For instance, in patterned language books that contain repeated sentences, delete words from those sentences because of their repetition. Students will fill in the blanks easily once they have the pattern.
- Delete words only when pupils know the concept labeled by the word. If, for instance, students do not know what a "sluice" is, it would not be wise to ask them to provide that word. (You might want to use an online dictionary to define "sluice.")
- Delete words at the end third of sentences in order to provide a great deal of within-sentence context.
- Delete words near the beginning of sentences if you want students to use context clues after the deleted word.
- Always discuss words the students supply and their thinking because much learning occurs from such interactions.

Developing Meaningful Vocabulary

There are thousands and thousands of words in the English language, and it is impossible to teach all of them to students. Historically, 4,000 to 5,000 high-frequency words were carefully introduced in materials for elementary school students to learn to read and spell. Because these words appear frequently in print and electronic materials, some educators believe they must be mastered early in school. Beyond the highest-frequency words are thousands of additional words used by students in reading and writing activities. Each year, new words appear in the English language (e.g., *screenagers, e-zine*) and some current words get new meanings (e.g., "mouse," "enter"). Other words lose favor and are not used. It is necessary to help students learn the high-frequency, functional words of today. But it is equally important to help students learn to master unfamiliar words on their own. Further, we want students to be intrinsically motivated to learn new words and have fun with words. Helping students become aware of words in their environment, asking them to write about words in their journals, discussing words, and listing words on bulletin boards and word walls are some ways to interest students in words (Cooper, 2000). Sending students to fun sites on the Web or placing word activities on a class or school web site can also interest students in words. Students often like to hear words pronounced or explained while working with CD-ROM stories and other software.

Students must eventually learn vocabulary independently using print and electronic materials.

Students can learn words using online dictionaries. They can make their own databases of words they want to study and remember. You can create puzzles and other word games to help reinforce those words you and students believe are worth knowing and remembering. Using a program such as Inspiration, you can brainstorm about topics and words you might want to use to make puzzles. In this way, students can develop their vocabularies and have fun with words.

One useful site is Westlaw Campus's "Acronyms" at **http://www.libraryspot.com/acronyms.htm.** Type in an acronym and discover what the letters mean. You might also visit Ruth Filmi's "Vocabulary Help Page," which has links to dozens of online vocabulary resources, at **http://www.hut.fi/u/rvilmi/LangHelp/Vocabulary/.** Ms. Filmi lives in Finland, but her work is available everywhere.

PUZZLES

Dozens of web sites contain puzzles. Many online newspapers offer a daily puzzle, and some pages at specific kid sites are suitable for younger students. There are also sites where you can make your own puzzles.

WEBLIOGRAPHY

- **Crossword Puzzle**
  http://www.nytimes.com/learning/teachers/xwords/index.html
  Students can work the puzzle online or they can print it.
- **Discovery School's Puzzlemaker**
  http://puzzlemaker.school.discovery.com/
  You and students can make several types of puzzles and conduct word searches at this site.

WORD GAMES

Fostering an understanding of words and their nuances is a powerful reason to engage students in activities that help them interact with words in fun and interesting ways. Fortunately, there are many resources on the Internet you can use to engage students in vocabulary activities. These web sites provide ample opportunities to engage students in learning about words. See the Teaching Tip "Fun with Words and Symbols" for some clever ideas.

WEBLIOGRAPHY

- **Cool Word of the Day**
  http://www.edu.yorku.ca/wotd/
  You can visit this site and learn about interesting words.
- **Welcome to the Sniglets Page**
  http://www.idsi.net/~macten/ato/sniglets.html
  Learn what the definitions of Sniglets, or made-up words, would be if they were to appear in a dictionary—which they do not.
- **Word Play**
  http://www.wolinskyweb.com/word.htm
  This is a major source of references to sites that deal with words such as malapropisms, palindromes, homographs, and many more.

TEACHING TIPS Fun with Words and Symbols

Throughout the centuries, people have used graphics to convey meanings. Modern-day examples include international symbols seen on road signs, icons on web sites (e.g., forward and back arrows), and emoticons—for example, (;-)—in e-mail. It is not surprising, then, that graphics are intricately intertwined with electronic materials that students are now listening to, reading, and interpreting. Because of their use on the WWW, in software applications, and in the creation of electronic text for presentations, graphic symbols are reaching a higher status in illuminating (i.e., providing additional information to) verbal and nonverbal texts. Teachers and students increasingly are using original art, clip art, icons, pictures, and other graphic elements on web sites and in-class literacy activities.

THE REBUS

You can adapt a traditional strategy that teachers have used for many years by using both static and animated graphic elements you can obtain free off the Internet. The strategy is called rebus reading. Rebuses are graphic elements interspersed with print or electronic text to help students in the early stages of reading. These graphic elements are placed among words, parts of words, or letters so students can read without being impeded by words not already in their sight vocabularies. Thus, beginning readers can read for meaning and enjoyment more quickly because they can name the graphic rather than struggle with words they are not capable of reading or decoding quickly. You may choose to give rebuses "just for fun," and that is fine. Students get more value, however, when they discuss the ideas in the rebus stories.

These are some useful sites for working with rebus activities:

- **The Applet Depot**
  http://www.ericharshbarger.org/java/
  You can download applets to use in developing online literacy materials. Word magnets, jumble, image magnets, and more can be downloaded free of charge.
- **Rebus in Your Scrapbooks**
  http://www.gracefulbee.com/features/feature-2–12.html
  This online scrapbooking e-zine offers examples of words that can be used in making a rebus. Encourage students to make their own scrapbooks using the rebus idea.
- **EnchantedLearning.com: Rebus Rhymes**
  http://www.enchantedlearning.com/Rhymes.html
  This site contains a form of rebus, but the words as well as the pictures are seen. There are forty rhymes, many of which will already be familiar to students, in this set.

EMOTICONS, ACRONYMS, AND OTHER CODES

Rebuses are fun to use to integrate nonverbal symbols into messages. But you can also use emoticons, acronyms, and other codes.

Emoticons. E-mail messages tend to be brief, and in brevity there are sometimes opportunities for miscommunication and/or misunderstanding. Somewhere along the line, people started to create faces and related symbols to convey meaning and/or emotion. You can say something rude, for instance, then temper it with a version of the ubiquitous smiley face. This is one example: !;-) You may need to tilt the page to see the face.

You can show students several examples of emoticons, point out the various symbols on a typical computer keyboard, and suggest that they create some of their own. Help them understand that they are creating a symbolic way to communicate that can add fun to their messages. You might want to use these examples to get started:

C=:-)	A chef	[:-]	A robot
*<):o)	A clown	=);-)	Uncle Sam
(;-!	Foot in mouth	‘-)	A wink
8(:-)	Mickey Mouse	= 8–0	Yikes
:—)	Pinocchio		

TEACHING TIPS
(continued)

At **http://www.pressanykey.com/cgi-bin/cgiwrap/pak/emoticons.pl,** you can type in one of the symbols above the numbers on a keyboard, and you will see emoticons that contain the symbol.

Acronyms. You might be familiar with acronyms such as ASAP (as soon as possible), FYI (for your information), and AKA (also known as). People joke about there being too many TLAs (three-letter acronyms), although WYSIWYG (What you see is what you get) proves that acronyms can be more than three letters. You and students can have fun exploring this form of abbreviated communication. Students can understand how the world around them works as they learn that Colonel Sanders' Kentucky Fried Chicken is now more commonly known as KFC. BTW (by the way), exploring systems that enable quick communication (without having to keyboard a lot) is worth doing. Here are a few examples:

B4	Before	4EVER	Forever
BCNU	Be seeing you	CUL8R	See you later
IDK	I don't know	OIC	Oh, I see
IOH	I'm outta here	WTG	Way to go
LOL	Laughing out loud		

Another Code. There is also a "new Morse code" for the digital age. Students sometimes leave cryptic messages on people's digital pagers using numbers to convey a thought. For instance,

1776 means "You are revolting." (American Revolution)
66 means "Let's hit the road." (Route 66 was once a major American highway)
1040 means "You owe me big time." (This is the number of the U.S. individual income tax form)
13579 means "You are really odd." (Odd numbers)

If you get a strange number on your pager some day, *think about it!*

INSTRUCTIONAL CLOZE FOR WORD MEANING

The cloze strategy is versatile as a way to study context clues and word meanings.

Cloze activities for developing word recognition skills, described earlier, help students attend to phonic elements and context conjointly. From these activities, students can learn to rely on semantic, syntactic, and phonetic cueing systems to help them read. Cloze is also a useful technique to help students learn to attend to vocabulary and words in context. You can create and use several varieties of cloze activities to develop word meanings, for example, by deleting individual words, phrases, clauses, portions of sentences, or entire sentences. Starting with general context cloze passages, teach students to begin thinking about how context clues help them decide which words to choose. Students supply the very last words of sentences using all available context. Examine the general context passage and the other examples in Figure 5.4 for patterns to use in creating vocabulary building cloze activities for comparisons, contrasts, multiple meanings, synonyms, and antonyms. You can make web forms for cloze activities using FrontPage and let students submit their online responses

FIGURE 5.4

Using Cloze Passages to Develop Word Meanings

PART 1: GENERAL CONTEXT

Directions: Write in words that complete the sentences.

My Birthday

When I turned eight, I had a birthday __________. We played lots of __________. My team won the treasure __________. I blew out the candles on my birthday __________. My friend Sam gave me eight pats. Then he gave me one more for good __________. That was a great party! [The words, which would *not* be shown to the students, are *party, games, hunt, cake,* and *luck*.]

PART 2: COMPARISONS

Directions: Write in words that show comparisons.

Old and New Things

I got some new things for my bedroom. My old things were **nice,** but the new things are __________. My old pillow was **soft,** but the new one is __________. My old blanket was **warm,** but the new one is __________. My old rug was **clean,** but the new one is __________. My old curtains were **pretty,** but my new ones are __________. I really like my new things. [The words, which would *not* be shown to the students, are *nicer, softer, warmer, cleaner,* and *prettier*.]

PART 3: CONTRASTS

Directions: Write words that contrast the two places.

City or Town?

Would you like to live in a **large** city or in a __________ town? A big city has **many** people. But a little town has a __________ people. It is often **noisy** in the city. A town, however, is often __________. Most towns have only **one** movie theater. On the other hand, a city has __________ theaters. At night a town is **dark.** But, a city has lots of __________ lights. [The words, which would *not* be shown to the students, are *small, few, quiet, many,* and *bright*.]

PART 4: MULTIPLE MEANINGS

Directions: One word will fit on all of the blanks. Write it on the blanks.

The Drama Club

The Drama Club is going to put on a play. Tryouts were held today after school. Many students showed up to take __________ in the play. The director, Mrs. Palmer, said, "There are too many people here. Only a __________ of this

FIGURE 5.4
(continued)

group can be in the play. The play I have chosen is about two friends who __________ company in the end. Only twelve people will get a __________ in the play. Many of you, however, can be members of the stage crew. We will need painters, ushers, and lots of other helpers. We will have a wonderful play, if we all do our __________."

1. To be in an activity is to take __________.
2. A portion of a whole is a __________.
3. To separate or go away from each other is to __________ company.
4. A role acted in a play is a __________.
5. Doing your share is doing your __________.

[The word, which would *not* be shown to the students, is *part*.]

PART 5: SYNONYMS

Directions: Replace the words with other words with the same meaning.

An Ice Cream Sundae

Kelly works in an ice cream store. One day she decided to make the world's __________ (biggest) sundae. First, she made sure the front door was __________ (shut). Then, she __________ (started) her work. Kelly got a big bowl. She put twenty scoops of ice cream in it. She poured syrup all over the ice cream. Then she put whipped cream and cherries on top. Then, Kelly opened the front door. She invited her __________ (pals) to help her eat the sundae. Everyone had a __________ (wonderful) time. [The words, which would *not* be shown to the students, are *largest, closed, began, friends,* and *great,* but students may think of and will want to discuss equally acceptable words.]

PART 6: ANTONYMS

Directions: Replace the boldfaced words with a word that means just the opposite.

A Spelling Contest

Brad is very **happy** __________ today. Today is the spelling contest at school. Brad is a very **good** __________ speller. The contest started. Brad thought the words were **easy** __________ to spell. The teacher was not surprised when Brad **won** __________ the contest. He came in **first** __________. [The words, which would *not* be shown to the students, are *sad, bad* or *poor, hard, lost,* and *last,* but students may think of equally acceptable words.]

to a database that you can show students and use to discuss their responses. The Auburn University Knowledge Design page "How to Create a Cloze Exercise" at **http://www.auburn.edu/~mitrege/knowledge/cloze.html** offers an excellent explanation of how to make cloze activities using HTML language to create forms. You can learn prerequisite skills through a link to background information. Also, see this book's web site for additional examples of cloze activities.

The complexity of comprehension cloze activities depends on the age and grade level of your students, but you can create cloze comprehension passages focusing on author's purpose, main ideas, details, sequence, cause and effect, making inferences, drawing conclusions, relating information from two or more sources, analogous relations, and classification. In general, arrange the cloze passage in a way that omits whatever you want students to learn. For instance, for a cause-and-effect cloze activity, find or write a passage that has several causes and effects stated. Then, using a word processor, type the passage, deleting some of the "cause" words or phrases and some of the "effect" words or phrases. Present the passage using a computer video projector so students can make their ideas known, and follow the activity with a discussion of any alternative ideas that were offered. As another example, if you want students to think about author's purpose, leave out words from a passage that can be replaced by "nice" words if the author is friendly or "grumpy" words if the author is grouchy. Use your imagination and have fun making cloze activities for your class.

Developing Reference and Study Skills

When print texts in classrooms and school libraries are the major sources of information, pre- and in-service literacy teachers typically spend time helping students learn to use glossaries, tables of contents, footnotes, indexes, and appendixes. In the library, students use dictionaries, encyclopedias, and other reference materials. Students learn to use the card catalog, *Who's Who,* a thesaurus, and indexes such as the *Readers' Guide to Periodical Literature.* You can also use collections of CD-ROMs and the WWW to access these same kinds of resources while at the same time helping students learn to use new electronic study skill strategies.

All the major types of reference materials are now online or on CD-ROMs.

ELECTRONIC REFERENCE SKILLS

Following are a few online resources students can use to locate information. Some of them are appropriate for younger students, while others are more useful to middle school and older students. Most will help you plan instruction and help individual students locate information they need for learning activities and experiences. Some categories overlap because web sites often contain several types of reference materials. You might want to consult several teachers and librarians about how students can profit from using specific resources.

Dictionaries

Sometimes, concern about phonic skills overshadows the fact that there are other aids to dealing with unfamiliar words. Context ("Read to the end of the sentence and see if that helps.") or structural analysis ("Take off endings or break words into smaller parts.") can help. But students can also use electronic glossaries and dictionaries when they encounter words they need help either pronouncing or comprehending. We suggest that you select an online dictionary and either bookmark it or keep its URL prominently displayed in the classroom to use as needed (or both). Also, you can help students use the built-in Thesaurus feature on major word-processing programs such as Word and WordPerfect. If students cannot learn a definition from electronic references, they can try one of these sites: Ask An Expert at **http://njnie.dl.stevens-tech.edu/askanexpert.html,** Ask Jeeves at **http://aj.com/index.asp,** or Ask Jeeves for Kids at **http://www.ajkids.com/index.asp.** After exhausting other strategies, it is all right for students to ask, but they should first try to help themselves.

Examine several online dictionaries to see electronic features you can use to develop literacy skills and the variety of activities you can choose. See Merriam-Webster Online at **http://www.m-w.com/dictionary** or see Houghton Mifflin's American Heritage Dictionary of the English Language at **http://www.bartleby.com/61/.** See other references listed on this book's web site.

WWW

Encyclopedias

Some of the better-known encyclopedias are on the Web. Students can use electronic search features and keywords to quickly locate electronic text about many subjects. Students who need up-to-date information not available in outdated classroom or library encyclopedias may find it online because online encyclopedias are updated frequently. See Encyclopedia Titanica for an unusual reference at **http://www.encyclopedia-titanica.org/**.

Almanacs

Almanacs include calendars, weather forecasts, and tide charts, as well as information about specialty topics and other features. One good example is the AFRO-American Almanac web site at **http://www.toptags.com/aama/index.htm**. This site, a page of which is shown in Figure 5.5, contains a wealth of information from books, documents, and historical events. The purpose is to examine the African-American experience from slavery days to the present.

Maps and Atlases

Students can find foreign countries, their own state, and even their own neighborhoods using online maps. The Virtual Reference Desk of the McFarlin Library at the University of Tulsa includes a page with links to major map sites; it can be found at **http://www.lib.utulsa.edu/eresources/refcenter/maps.htm.**

FIGURE 5.5

AFRO-American Almanac

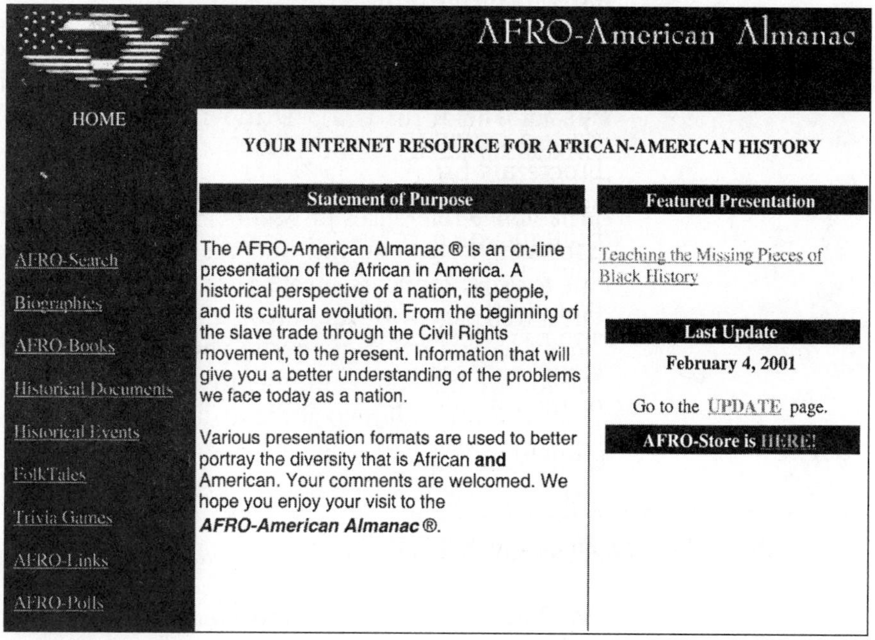

Source: Used by permission of Donald E. Jones.

Newspapers

Some of the major popular newspapers are online, and they feature not only news stories but also typical newspaper features. Students can learn about ongoing major events because online newspapers update frequently while stories are breaking. See Newspapers.com at **http://www.newspapers.com/** for links to USA and international online newspapers.

Magazines

Not all students buy magazines, but you can help them learn about traditional and emerging features of magazines by accessing online magazines. Students can keep current or find archived stories by looking at online magazines such as Time For Kids at **http://www.timeforkids.com/TFK/** or USNEWS.com at **http://www.usnews.com/usnews/home.htm.**

Directories

Some online directories help you locate people, products, and information, and you can find the exact location of schools at the American School Directory (**http://www.asd.com**). Students can maintain information about their own schools.

Special References

Some of the familiar or traditional references are now available online, but new types of electronic references are emerging. The Plumb Design Visual Thesaurus is a 3-D moving web of words. See it at **http://www.visualthesaurus.com/.**

The above references just scratch the surface of the kinds of online electronic materials you and students can use. Bookmark references appropriate for your students, create a database or wall chart of their URLs, or create a web page with your favorite links so the references are easily available to students. Introduce sites to your students via a computer projector or by connecting your computer to a large television set. By exploring a site's features, you will help students learn where to turn for factual information to use in their language arts activities.

ELECTRONIC STUDY SKILLS

We have discussed the importance of helping students become excellent searchers for information using online search engines and menu features

Electronic features in word-processing programs can be used as study skill strategies.

on CD-ROMs to get to materials quickly. These are critical reference skills for the information age. Once they find materials, however, students can use online features to keep track of and organize ideas. Digitally enabled features can help students make electronic comments; use color, copy and paste materials; summarize; and create outlines. We will discuss several of these briefly here.

Commenting

The good, old-fashioned way to take notes was to write ideas and quotes on three-by-five-inch cards. Now you and students can make comments in electronic texts. Major word-processing programs permit you to add comments directly within electronic text. We used Word to prepare this text, and as we worked, we clicked on "Insert," then clicked on "Comment." This opened a comment box into which we placed reminders or thoughts. At the place where the cursor was located, a yellow rectangle with [wjv1] in it indicated that my first comment was located there. The rectangle held my initials and the number 1. We read the comment by holding the cursor over the yellow rectangle until the comment appeared. When we were finished with the comment, we deleted it by using the BACKSPACE key. When they prepare documents using a word-processing program, students can take advantage of this feature to make notes, summarize, or add comments as they work with it. When they write electronically for you, you can add comments and suggestions to their stories or reports so they can see your thoughts in the text. If they cut and paste electronic text from other sources into a word-processing program, they can use the Comment feature to help them study for tests or to prepare the materials for use in reports or other projects.

Highlighting with Color

In books or on photocopies, students can underline to help fix ideas in their mind, to mark information they want to use in further work, or to leave a trail to review for a test. Word lets you underline words, but it also has two special features that make text stand out even better. One feature lets you change the color of text. On the toolbar is a large letter "A" with a black bar under it. To the right of that is a down arrow. Click on the arrow to pull down a color palette. To color words, sentences, paragraphs, or more, select them, pull down the color palette, and choose a color. The selected text will turn that color, and the bar below the "A" symbol will now show the selected color. Want text black again? Select it, pull down the colors, and click on the little black square. A second feature lets you make blocks of text stand out. To use this feature, which is called highlighting, select some text and click on the highlight feature on the toolbar. The default setting is white, so pull down the palette and choose a color. Students can experiment with ways to use one color to mark main ideas, another color to mark ideas they do not agree with, and so forth. The features just described help students locate important information quickly when they are scrolling though electronic text.

Copy and Paste

In addition to commenting and using color, students can copy information from one source and paste it into another. Computers have a feature called a Clipboard, an electronic file into which you can temporarily copy information. Perhaps students are on the WWW and see some text or a graphic they want to either use immediately or place into a temporary document to use later. With both a web browser and a word-processing program open, they can select (highlight) and then copy the web text to the clipboard. They then can paste the information into their own document.

Summarizing

Summarizing is a valuable aid to retaining major thoughts, and it is taught in most schools. Teach students to create summaries by using the Comment feature described above or by organizing notes they have cut and pasted from various sources into a "working" document. While word-processing, we often open two documents at the same time. One holds the materials we want to summarize, and the other is blank. We scan the document for notes and reminders, then toggle to the blank document and write sentences that will eventually become the summary.

To make effective summaries, students should learn to delete redundant details and less important information, collapse lists by using an all-encompassing term that subsumes the exemplars (i.e., categorize information), and find or create topic sentences that get at main ideas (Vacca & Vacca, 1999). Then they can use keywords and main ideas to write and polish the summary statements.

Outlining

Some software programs let you view information in an outline form. In Word, for instance, click on the "View" pull-down menu and then click on "Outline." You will see the document in outline form. You and students can use this view to determine if you are creating an effective, complete outline and to determine if the information is in logical order. You can add numbers or roman numerals in the outline view, also.

Recent versions of PowerPoint have an outline view where you and students can check the effectiveness of the organization of information. You can click on the "Outline View" button at the bottom left-hand area of the screen to activate the outline form and see the number, title, and content of each slide. With this feature, you and students can discuss the flow of a presentation they have created. Help students take advantage of the features they find in electronic materials. Future generations will put these organizational and study skills to good use both at work and at play.

SUMMARY

- Whether you use a synthetic, analytic, or analogy approach, you can find appropriate online ideas and software to help students learn word recognition strategies.
- Effective use of databases and word-processing systems can help you and students engage more easily in language experience, cloze, and other word recognition activities.
- Abundant online reference materials can make vocabulary building and word study both educational and fun for students.
- Electronic features of word-processing programs, web browsers, and other programs enable students to mark, cut and paste, and organize electronic materials for study purposes.

ACTIVITIES

1. Examine online or offline phonics lessons to determine their type (synthetic, etc.).
2. Choose some cloze examples from here or from the book's web site and try them with first- or second-grade students.
3. Use the comment, color features, and other special features in a document. Send it to your instructor.

SOFTWARE

Several important things to consider when buying any type of word recognition or vocabulary software are (1) the scope and sequence of the program, (2) the ages of students for whom the program was designed, and (3) whether the content of the program has a good "fit" with your curriculum objectives. Some programs are designed to *introduce* students to a particular skill or topic, others *provide practice or repetition* with a skill, and still others encourage students to *apply* their knowledge to new circumstances. The software programs listed below deal with developing word recognition skills through phonemic awareness and phonics, using a whole-word emphasis, using cloze procedures, and more. It bears repeating that you should evaluate software to ensure that it suits your overall teaching strategy.

A to Zap!, Sunburst Technology, Pre-K–1
This program provides an introduction to letters, sounds, words, and numbers.

Alphabet Express, School Zone Publishing, Pre-K–3
This program contains activities to learn uppercase and lowercase letters of the alphabet.

Blue's ABC Time, Humongous Entertainment, Pre-K–3
Letter identification, phonics, rhymes, and silly stories are part of this program.

Bubbleland's Word Discovery, Sunburst Technology, Pre-K–2
This program contains a picture dictionary and interactive word recognition, pronunciation, and spelling activities.

Carmen Sandiego Word Detective, The Learning Company/Broderbund, 4–9
This offering from the popular Carmen Sandiego *series teaches grammar.*

Chicka Chicka Boom Boom, Knowledge Adventure, Pre-K–1
This program, based on the popular book, is designed to help students learn the alphabet and phonemic awareness, matching, following instructions, and more.

ClueFinder's Reading Adventure, The Learning Company/Broderbund, 4–7
During CD-ROM travels, students can learn reading comprehension, spelling, grammar, vocabulary, and critical thinking.

Consonant Blends and Digraphs, Tenth Planet/Sunburst Technology, 1–2
Students see and hear consonant blends and digraphs in activities in this program.

CornerStone Reading, SkillsBank/The Learning Company/Broderbund, 3–8
This program presents 1,100 key vocabulary words and 2,000 other vocabulary words in 140 lessons.

Dr. Seuss's ABC, The Learning Company/Broderbund, K–2
This program contains entertaining alphabet activities based on the book.

Earobics, Cognitive Concepts/Don Johnston, Pre-K–5
This is a systematic, individualized phonemic awareness program that adjusts to a student's skill level and progress.

Edmark Reading Program, Edmark/Riverdeep Interactive, All
This sight-reading system takes a multisensory approach that incorporates short instructional steps, repetition, and constant positive reinforcement.

Emergent Reader, Stepping Stones/Sunburst Technology, K–1
This program develops sight vocabulary using twenty picture-book stories with highlighted text. Students record their own voices.

First Phonics, Sunburst Technology, K–2
Initial-letter grapheme-phoneme learning is the goal of this program.

Funny Monsters for Tea, Sunburst Technology, K–4
This program features interactive rhymes. Activities include telling time, spelling, math, writing and hearing poems, and creating music. Students can make their own colorful monsters.

Grammar for the Real World, Knowledge Adventure, 4 and up
Students can learn to proofread, edit, and revise their work at a pretend Hollywood studio.

I Love Spelling!, DK Family Learning, 2–5
Students can learn and are tested on more than 5,000 words in an intergalactic game show format.

Inside Stories, Mimosa Technology, 1–4
Classic stories (e.g., "The Gingerbread Man," "Cinderella," etc.) are the basis for this program's interactive activities, which balance word recognition and comprehension activities.

JumpStart 1st Grade, Knowledge Adventure, 1
First-grade fundamentals are included in eighteen modules. (Versions of JumpStart are available for grades K–6.)

Knock Knock, SunburstTechnology/Houghton Mifflin, Pre-K–2
There are 350 activities designed to develop early literacy capabilities in this program. Students can learn sight words, letter-sound correspondences, rules for phonics, and more.

Leap Into Literacy, LeapFrog SchoolHouse, Pre-K–2
Students can manipulate items in the teaching kit in this comprehensive program to develop phonemic awareness and phonics skills.

Leap Into Phonics, Leap Into Learning, Inc., Pre-K–2
This program introduces phonemic awareness and phonics skills.

Let's Go Read! 1: An Island Adventure, Edmark/Riverdeep Interactive, Pre-K–K
This program presents letter names, shapes, and letter-sound relationships for consonants and short vowels. It also allows students to build three-letter words and develop basic comprehension skills. Some 175 lessons are included in twelve interactive books. Students can record as they read using speech-recognition technology.

Let's Go Read! 2: An Ocean Adventure, Edmark/Riverdeep Interactive, K–1
This program presents long vowels, beginning and ending blends and digraphs. It helps students build three- to five-letter words. It helps students expand vocabulary and deals with longer words, high-frequency words, and long vowels.

Letter Sounds, Tenth Planet/Sunburst Technology, Pre-K–1
This is a basic consonant sound–symbol association program.

Little Monster at School, The Learning Company/Broderbund, Pre-K–3
(Available in "Living Books Library" only) This program deals with the ABCs, numbers, and more. It is available in English and Spanish.

M-SS-NG L-NKS, Sunburst Technology, 3–8
The program contains passages from award-winning novels but with words and letters missing (a type of cloze strategy). As students work, a picture is revealed.

My First Incredible Amazing Dictionary, DK Multimedia/Interactive Learning, Pre-K–3
Students can learn the alphabet as they see and hear letters and letter names. The program builds on pictures and sounds with words.

My Reading Coach, Mindplay, 1 & up
This is a phonics-based beginning reading program.

My Silly CD of Opposites, Harmony Interactive, Pre-K–6
Students can learn about opposites with sound effects and illustrations in this program. (English and Spanish)

Phonics Alive!, Forest Technologies/QuickMind, K–3
This is an interactive, self-paced phonics program dealing with single sounds and sound blends.

Phonics Alive! 2 The Sound Blender, Forest Technologies/QuickMind, 1–6
This program builds from Phonics Alive! as a program of sound blending. Twelve modules deal with rhyming, blending, and keyboard exercises.

Phonics Alive! 3 The Speller, Forest Technologies/QuickMind, 2–12
This is a basic spelling program.

Phonics Alive! 4 Grammar, Forest Technologies/QuickMind, 3 & up
Fourteen modules introduce the basics of grammar on board the "Spacestation Grammatica."

Reader Rabbit's Reading 1, The Learning Company/Broderbund, K–1
This beginning program introduces children to letters and phonics.

Reader Rabbit's Reading 2, The Learning Company/Broderbund, 1–3
This higher-level sequel to Reader Rabbit 1 includes blends, vowels, digraphs, rhymes, and homonyms.

Reading Who? Reading You!, Software for Success/Sunburst Technology, K–2
This program offers basic phonics instruction through games and activities.

Roots, Prefixes, and Suffixes, Tenth Planet/Sunburst Technology, 1–3
Activities in this program can help students develop knowledge of parts within polysyllabic words.

Schoolhouse Rock: Grammar Rock, Creative Wonders/The Learning Company/Broderbund, 1–6
This program is designed to help students build grammar skills.

Simon Sounds It Out, Don Johnston, K–2
Students can learn phonological awareness and phonics in a tutorial program. The program is designed to teach letter sounds and word families.

Simon Spells, Don Johnston, Pre-K–2
This program is designed to help students learn 1,000 Dolch sight words and basic spelling. It has an on-screen tutor, data collection, assessment, and student tracking features.

Sound It Out Land Reading Kit, Forest Technologies/QuickMind, Pre-K–1
This is an introductory word recognition skills program using songs to help students learn.

Sounds Great!, Wright Group/McGraw Hill, K–2
This interactive phonics program deals with phonemic awareness, letter-sound knowledge, print concepts, sight vocabulary, and grammatical awareness.

Spelling Power, Curriculum Associates, 1–8
This program includes activities for spelling, meaning, and writing. It uses a test-study-test approach to spelling.

Spelling Spree, Houghton Mifflin, 3–6
Students interact with things at an amusement park to engage in spelling instruction.

Spelling ToolKit Plus, The Learning Company/Broderbund, 1–6
You and students can design and print puzzles, tests, and spelling study sheets with this product.

Thinking Out Loud, (Little Planet Literacy Series), Sunburst Technology/Houghton Mifflin, 1–2
The program is designed to develop oral language skills. Students engage in six multicultural activities involving folktales and fables. Sequencing, logical thinking, and listening skills are included.

'Tronic Phonics, McGraw-Hill, 1–6
Phonics and other word recognition strategies are included in this program.

Vowel Patterns, Tenth Planet/Sunburst Technology, 1–3
Students can learn letter patterns associated with vowel sounds, including the vocalic r.

Vowels: Short and Long, Tenth Planet/Sunburst Technology, K–2
Students can identify and sort by long and short vowels. They can sort pictures based on like vowel sounds, build and read words, and make rhymes.

Word Parts, Tenth Planet/Sunburst Technology, 1–3
This is designed to help students break words down into smaller components and use phonics to decode them.

Wordsearch Deluxe, Forest Technologies/QuickMind, All
You can create puzzles and update them through the Internet using this program.

Working Phonics, Curriculum Associates, K–6
Phonemic awareness and basic phonics skills are included in this program.

FOR FURTHER READING

Marcovitz, D. M. (1997). I read it on the computer, it must be true: Evaluating information from the web. *Learning and Leading with Technology, 25*(3), 18–21.

CHAPTER 6

Using Technology to Develop Writing Abilities

INTRODUCTION

Writing, speaking, and constructing verbal and nonverbal messages permit us to share our knowledge and ideas with others. Until the advent of the telegraph, information traveled at the speed of the fastest horses. Today, people communicate through e-mail and on the Internet at the speed of light. While much electronic text is informal (e.g., e-mail), there is a growing sense that matters of style, grammar, spelling, accuracy, and intelligent writing and constructing are more important than ever in the information age. This is especially true when students' works appear on the World Wide Web. Educators are conveying this idea, and students are reacting positively. Students recognize that family, friends, and others can see their work, and they want to make well-prepared contributions.

Prior to word-processing and other computer software programs calling for **keyboarding** (i.e., typing and using function keys), many students saw writing as a major chore. Students would handwrite a single draft and hope it was acceptable because rewriting was "boring." Students reasoned that they were mainly writing just for their teachers. Perhaps an occasional assignment or writing contest required the major polishing of a piece of writing, but that was not the norm. When students shared their work, it was often through reading it aloud.

Technology has had a major impact on students' production of messages. Today, students can create work on a computer that they then can print and distribute easily; project onto a television monitor or onto a screen through a computer projector; or place on the Web. All of these are authentic reasons for students to write and construct—and to do so well. Other factors operate today that make writing and constructing more central to classroom events. Not only are students working collaboratively in ways that foster greater communication, they now have access to technologies that help them organize and communicate their ideas through the use of graphics, photos, animations, videos, colors, and sounds as well as text. Instead of helping students become print-based writers only, preservice and in-service teachers are now helping them become multimedia producers, even in the primary grades, and the ways students communicate ideas keep on evolving as computers, hardware, and the capabilities of the Internet and computer technologies continue to evolve.

Writing includes constructing verbal and nonverbal messages.

Researchers and practitioners of literacy are grappling with how technology is changing the nature of reading (see chapter 1). We must also determine how technology is changing the nature of writing. The speed of locating and organizing information to write about, the ease of editing and polishing, and the opportunities to convey ideas using numerous symbol systems in multimedia formats are influencing the writing process and the production of polysymbolic materials. Electronic materials have evolved from simple pages of printed text that were digitized and placed online to being dynamic, multimedia presentations. You can think of the Internet as containing a gigantic collection of files that anyone can read and view, download and print, or use in his or her writings. Computer software has evolved from "drill-and-grill" behaviorist-based software into various complex applications that students can use to create effective presentations. In short, opportunities for writing and constructing are abundant!

In this chapter, we will discuss keyboarding skills and the stages of the writing process. We will suggest a variety of software and online e-materials you can use to help students develop writing and constructing capabilities. Chapter 7, which deals with listening and speaking, as well as chapter 8, which addresses the concept of visual literacy, also contain suggestions for helping students construct verbal and nonverbal messages.

Keyboarding

I learned how to type when I was almost twelve years old. At that time (long ago), such a feat was fairly impressive. Today, third-grade students, many of whom can keyboard quite well, would consider me disadvantaged to have gone that long without learning to type. Keyboarding is a valuable skill because it helps some students write faster and easier without having to form letters by hand. Keyboarding helps other students because their typing can keep up with their thoughts better than their handwriting can (Bitter & Pierson, 1999, p. 49). Some students are more willing to insert, delete, and move around words and ideas while editing than they would be if they had to rewrite their work using a pencil and paper (Burns, Roe, & Ross, 1999).

Keyboarding skills are basic to communicating with others today.

With computers being nearly ubiquitous, the question is not *if* keyboarding needs to be taught, it is *when.* Keyboarding instruction can start anytime a child is interested, but as Simonson and Thompson (1997, p. 169) state, "many elementary schools have instituted programs to teach keyboarding in grades 3 and 4 [and] have reported positive results from these programs." Instruction is necessary for typing letters, numbers, and punctuation as well as using the special function keys on a keyboard. While there is some concern that young students' hands are not big enough to handle a standard keyboard, there is equal concern that delayed instruction may lead to bad habits such as looking at the keys and "hunt-and-peck" behaviors. Breaking bad keyboarding habits that develop over time is quite difficult (Ellsworth, 1997; Simonson & Thompson, 1997), so it is important to begin keyboarding instruction early. Kindergarten instruction often centers on using the left hand on the left side of the keyboard and the right hand on the right. Also, correct wrist position and using the ends of the fingers to type are taught (Baugh, 1999–2000). Such early instruction in these basics readies children for formal instruction later.

Keyboarding software often engages students in adventures to make practice more fun.

Keyboarding requires a great deal of practice and repetition of keystrokes and can be quite boring. Some software programs employ a game or story adventure to help students stay entertained while they learn and practice keyboarding. For instance, Read, Write & Type! teaches students in grades 1–3 keyboarding, phonics, and writing in an adventure setting, and Knowledge Adventure's Typing Tutor, for grades 5 and up, uses a game setting. Some programs teach a traditional approach to typing, but others use such tactics as teaching the letters in alphabetical order and teaching students to divide the keyboard into left-hand and right-hand portions. It is important to ensure that a consistent approach is used throughout the grade levels. More information about keyboarding is available at the following web sites.

WEBLIOGRAPHY

- Keyboarding Olympics
  http://www.crpc.rice.edu/CRPC/GirlTECH/joleland/Lessons/olympics.html
  Teacher Jo Leland describes how she rewards students' keyboarding improvement by calculating their improvements and awarding either gold, silver, or bronze medals.
- NimbleFingers
  http://www.nimblefingers.com/
  This site presents animated dexterity-improving keyboarding exercises accompanied by music. There are tips and suggestions as well as information about carpal tunnel syndrome.

THE INCREASING NEED FOR KEYBOARDING SKILLS

As students' literacy capabilities develop, they need valid reasons to communicate and their keyboarding skills become increasingly important in helping them create verbal messages. Encourage students to write letters to one another, to family members, and to students in other classrooms. Students can keyboard autobiographical sketches or request information from classmates. They can write letters to the editor of a school or local newspaper about an environmental issue or ask an expert questions. Students can send e-mail to their e-pals, but as one teacher notes (Horban, 1998, p. 32), they "should do more than write each other. I want my students to share their reading and writing experiences with their pen pals." She reports that students learn much about both reading and writing through e-mail interchanges. There are countless reasons for students to create formal and informal messages, so keyboarding skills are valuable and become increasingly so as students move through the grades.

The Writing Process: Traditional and Electronic-based Experiences

There are five stages that direct important aspects of the writing process. They are prewriting, drafting (or constructing), revising, editing, and publishing. In the process approach to writing, students choose topics, consider the audiences for whom they plan to write, and then develop their ideas from the prewriting stage through to publishing their work (Burns et al., 1999). The writing process is **recursive**; that is, students may be working in various stages as they deal with several pieces of writing, and students may be working on different stages of development within a single writing project as it nears publication. Writing is a constructive process, and you will want to give students ample opportunities to create meaning (Cooper, 1997). Students must be at the center of the writing process, taking responsibility for generating and sharing knowledge with and for others.

Help students use technology at all stages of the writing process.

You make valuable contributions by helping students learn both the stages of the writing process and how to use technology. Technology assists students in organizing their thoughts before and during the creation of a work, and it can make editing easier. It can help students publish for genuine audiences. Your use of technology throughout the stages to help students plan, produce, and publish their works foreshadows the increasing reliance society is placing on technology to help people communicate in the information age or, as some people are now calling it, the knowledge age. In short, you are helping students develop writing and constructing abilities and technology skills while at the same time preparing students to live and work in an era when strong communication skills are highly valued.

INSTRUCTIONAL PLANNING AND PREPARATION

Students ultimately are responsible for how they create messages, but you often set parameters for productive work in a classroom. When you create overarching themes for units of work (see chapter 1), you give students some leeway to select topics of interest to them that fit under the umbrella theme. Think of strategies you can use to include technology as you prepare a unit. In planning for a unit about an author, for instance, you could take these steps:

- Visit your school and local libraries to determine which of the author's books or stories are available on CD-ROMs.
- Find the author's web site to determine what it contains (e.g., games, autobiography, and so forth).
- Look for other audiovisual materials by or about the author.
- Make a personal contact to try to arrange e-mail or other correspondence with an author.

- Determine where the author was born or now lives so students can study those places.
- Locate biographical information from the Web or some other reference (e.g., a book jacket).
- Identify other authors who write about the same topics or have similar writing styles so students can make comparisons.
- Search the Internet for pertinent web sites about topics in the author's books, organize your findings, and bookmark the sites for students.

Next, think about possible projects students can create, remembering that today creating involves not only writing, but also speaking and constructing messages using nonverbal forms as well as text. For example, students might (1) make a HyperStudio presentation that includes narration, (2) keyboard a biography with scanned-in pictures of the author, or (3) create and illustrate a story in the style of the author for placement on your class web site. Even as you find ways to integrate technology into writing activities, students will likely suggest other ways they would like to construct messages and share them. See the Teaching Tip "Creating an Interactive Electronic Story" to learn how one teacher handles electronic stories.

Consider the hardware and software available to students before making a list of possible projects. You should also think about students' technology skills to determine what types of direct instruction you may need to provide while they create their projects. Once you set overall parameters, students are ready to begin using the stages of the writing process.

PREWRITING STAGE

Prewriting involves much pondering, organizing, and the jotting down of ideas.

"Prewriting is the getting ready to write stage" (Tompkins, 1990, p. 72), and your goal is to help students make important decisions about the topic of their work, its purpose, its audience, and the form the work will take. Be prepared to help students identify topics when they have difficulty deciding what to write about. Students need to determine what purpose their work will serve—to entertain, inform, persuade, and so forth. Their purpose may suggest the form the message will assume (e.g., letter to the editor, fairy tale, newspaper article, hypertext page for the class web site) as will the audience for whom they are creating the work. They might decide to write a speech, a poem, a secret message, or a nonfiction report. They will want to decide if their audience will be fellow students or whether it will be anyone in the world. What the final project will be will determine how it is prepared and organized.

TEACHING TIPS Creating an Interactive Electronic Story

As a computer technology teacher, I am always looking for new and interesting projects that integrate core curriculum with computer technology. Process writing can easily be combined with computer skills. I soon realized that students could learn and apply computer code, use art tools, create animations, play with and incorporate sounds, have fun, and practice process writing all in one project. What an ideal way to consolidate language arts and computer skills! However, thinking through ways to present the activity, I realized that providing only the big picture, the final goal of an electronic story, might overwhelm the middle school students in my classes. Thus, the idea of a checklist began. The checklist breaks down the assignment into small segments of easily achievable goals. The checklist seemed to help students feel more secure in pursuing the overall project. Once implemented, the checklist—along with grouping students into teams—appeared to have a significant influence in helping students stay on task. There were few or no cries of "What do I do now?"

While I created the checklist to help the students, I soon realized it was helping me, too. At first, it helped me set priorities and mentally establish the sequence of events that needed to occur for students to have successful results. The checklist also helped me track the progress of each student team, and it helped students in each team see how much progress they were making as they completed each segment of the assignment. The checklist emphasizes the process of the entire project, as well as the process of writing. Utilizing technology as a means of communication also involves process. Students benefit from understanding the process of computer literacy.

At the beginning of the project, I distributed the checklist and told students to concentrate on just getting one thing done at a time. As each team completed various tasks—such as brainstorming ideas, making storyboards, and delegating teammates' responsibilities—documents were attached to the team's checklist. Student teams picked up their checklist packet each day before beginning their work. The packets were the tiller of the students' electronic stories. As I circulated throughout the classroom, I checked each team's progress and initialed the checklist. Students were soon encouraged about how much progress they made, and they were soon immersed in creating sounds and animations for their electronic stories. I believe my students learned the process of writing as well as the process of technology as literacy.

CHECKLIST FOR MAKING AN ELECTRONIC STORY

Set your priorities and make your story decisions.

1. _____ Choose your team members.
2. _____ Brainstorm story ideas.
3. _____ Decide on story elements: setting, characters, plot.
4. _____ Draw a storyboard—a one-page drawing of each screen.
5. _____ Circle three things on each page you will be animating.
6. _____ Add one or two sentences to each page of your storyboard.
7. _____ Select and assign responsibilities to teammates (art, code, proofing, sound, etc.)
8. _____ Critique your storyboard and storyline with your teammates.
9. _____ Make changes as needed.

Begin your project on the computer.

10. _____ Start a stack.
11. _____ Create a title page—story title, authors, and illustrators. Add a graphic (optional).
12. _____ Create a new background.
13. _____ Create all the pages (foreground cards) needed for the new background.
14. _____ Create the next background.
15. _____ Create all the pages (foreground cards) needed for that background.
16. _____ Create the next background.

TEACHING TIPS
(continued)

17. _____ Create all the pages (foreground cards) needed for that background.
18. _____ Create any additional backgrounds and their foreground pages.
19. _____ Create the foreground art work.
20. _____ Add the story's sentences.
21. _____ Add buttons that move the reader forward and backward through the story.
22. _____ Create a stack for your first animation.
23. _____ Create a stack for each animation.
24. _____ Decide on and/or start creating sounds.
25. _____ Add sounds as desired.
26. _____ Add one final page with credits (which people did the writing, sounds, animation, code).

Source: Barbara Gibson, technology resource teacher, Townsend Middle School, Tucson Unified School District #1, Tucson, Arizona. Used by permission.

As part of prewriting, students read, talk to others, jot down ideas, or create crude diagrams as ways to start organizing their thoughts. Sometimes, when groups work together, you and students may want to brainstorm and organize ideas using a software program such as Inspiration—or, for younger students, Kidspiration. With such programs, you can create diagrams as visual organizers, and students often see relationships they might not otherwise notice. See one teacher's use of Inspiration in the Teaching Tip "Writing Adventures in Grade Three."

Brainstorming and organizing will eventually reveal the scope of a unit and help students become motivated to participate. Brainstorming sessions help them decide what aspects of the overall theme or project they want to study and share with others. The San Diego County Office of Education has a helpful web site that gives definitions and examples of twelve strategies to use in organizing information. Strategies include clustering, fishbone, anticipation and reaction guides, and Venn diagrams, among others. Graphic Organizers (Teacher Directions) at **http://www.sdcoe.k12.ca.us/score/actbank/torganiz.htm** is where you can see this information and examples.

Students will learn to use new technology applications and strategies to convey their messages, using several symbol systems that enable them to include both verbal and visual aspects of communication (see chapter 8). One strategy they can use to prepare for a project is **storyboarding.**

Storyboarding

Storyboarding helps students make decisions about both verbal and nonverbal content.

Storyboarding is a strategy commonly used in video production (Valmont, 1995), and knowledge of this strategy is becoming more and more valuable as students become multimedia authors. It involves creating a series of print or electronic cards on which students place information about what an audience will *see* and *hear* as they work their way through a project. Even younger students making Kid Pix, HyperStudio, or PowerPoint projects can benefit from instruction in making storyboards. Storyboarding not only helps students place ideas in order (e.g., sequencing; logical thinking), it helps them think early on about the visual and auditory aspects of a project or presentation. Storyboard cards, say Bitter and Pierson (1999, p. 218) "can be easily arranged and rearranged in order to arrive at a visual, logical flow of information," noting that storyboarding is "vital to the successful creation of . . . electronic projects." Some students like to start with the verbal aspects of a project and then think of visuals that will add meaning. Others like to "see" (make visual) their project first and then add verbal content. The importance of making a storyboard is that both the verbal and nonverbal aspects are planned *prior* to beginning the actual project, usually heavily influencing the scope of the project (Bailey & Blythe, 1998).

To create a storyboard, students create a set of storyboard cards, each revealing one portion of the project. For instance, to develop a storyboard for three or four web pages, each storyboard card might show, in rough drawings or stick figures, the visual elements the student wants to include

TEACHING TIPS

Writing Adventures in Grade Three

As a third-grade teacher, I engage my students in a variety of learning experiences designed to increase literacy as they study the theme "Adventures Along the Sacramento River." Students publish their own computer-generated and illustrated river stories using ClarisWorks, Microsoft Word, and Kid Pix. For students with motor or reading difficulties, I type dictated stories at least once a week, and I pair third-grade students with first-grade pals for several projects to enable the third graders to teach the first graders how to compose using a computer. They create Kid Pix illustrations with their word-processed story, a "Just Say No" poster, and a "Thankful" poem. Students work with parents to create a family letterhead, and they write letters using a word-processing program. They also create multipage storybooks using Storybook Weaver, and their books become part of the classroom library.

Students write weekly letters to their keypals in another state. They use a word-processing program so they can spell check the letters. Then they cut and paste their letters into the e-mail system. Students print their own letters and their keypals' letters and place them in scrapbooks to read over and over again. With a camcorder, students record other students giving reports and reading aloud their own books. Groups sometimes videotape their puppet plays.

Students conduct Internet and CD-ROM research about birds, and all students create HyperStudio presentations about the birds they study. Internet research provides opportunities for students to learn and practice many practical reading and writing skills. All students search the Internet for information using a search engine, and they skim to find the best sites for information. They glean important information and record it on information sheets. They also use bookmarked sites to find information we use in class. Students love to read what they "publish" to themselves and others.

Source: Linda Gail Johnson, third-grade teacher, Project City Elementary School, Redding, California. Used by permission.

on each page. On each card, the student lists keywords or phrases to indicate what the text, audio, video, and animations will be about. If the project were to be done using Kid Pix, for instance, the full storyboard could show how each screen in the presentation would be arranged, and a few words would tell what the computer users would see and hear. Storyboarding usually helps students see gaps in presentations, and students then can easily move, add, or eliminate individual cards until a complete, well-thought-out project takes shape. Thus, productive, logical thinking is encouraged. The "Guide for Storyboard Editors" at **http://www.matter.org.uk/storyboard/storyboard_guide.htm** is a resource containing advice about making storyboards. Another helpful resource, the Maricopa Center for Learning Instruction's Studio 1151 "Guidebook," located at **http://www.mcli.dist.maricopa.edu/authoring/studio/guidebook/index.html,** describes storyboarding as a preproduction activity.

DRAFTING (CONSTRUCTING) STAGE

Mechanics, spelling, and total correctness are not important at the drafting stage.

The goal of the drafting stage is for students to get their ideas on paper or in electronic format. At this point they are creating *rough* drafts, and neatness is not important, nor is spelling, grammar, and so forth. Students need to deal with *content* as opposed to *mechanics.* They can jot down keywords, ideas, and phrases, or they can develop topic sentences. They can rough out graphics or make other marks to remind them to develop nonverbal ideas. Drafting helps students recognize what they both know and do not know. It also gives them a chance to rethink their prewriting ideas about form, function, and the like. Drafting using technology involves locating not only ideas for inclusion as words in the final project, but also photos, animations, video, sound, and graphic images. When you encourage students to be multimedia producers, the concept of "drafting" includes constructing nonverbal messages.

REVISING STAGE

Input from others helps writers at the revising stage.

The goal of the revising stage is to react to what one has already produced and to determine some of the changes that need to be made. Additionally, revising involves making changes based on feedback from teachers and peers. After letting a little time pass so they can look at their work anew, students can reread their rough drafts and start adding words and features, deleting some items, moving others around, and substituting words, phrases, graphics, and so forth. Word-processing programs are very common in schools, making it easy to cut and paste, or delete and add, ideas.

Revising often means conducting further research to gather additional information as well as engaging in more thinking about how to make a project better, more complete, and clearer. For multimedia productions, revising and editing may involve searching for better graphics, sounds, and so forth to strengthen the project. At some point, however, students need to receive feedback that will help them make additional modifications. You and peers can review the draft and offer constructive suggestions, which the author-producer can ponder and deal with as necessary. Revising is a recursive process, so feedback and modification activities may run through several cycles.

EDITING AND PROOFREADING STAGE

The editing and proofreading stage prepares the work for public consumption, and communication standards are now important.

The goal of this stage is for students to make their work ready to communicate to others by following standard spelling, punctuation, capitalization, and other conventions of the English language. The editing stage is quite possibly the most effective time to teach such skills (Tompkins, 1990), or as some would say, the "teachable moment." Encourage students to locate and correct as many problems as they can. Then, have them turn to their peers or you for additional help. Students need to receive feedback from others about what is unclear or overblown. You, knowing students' capabilities, can plan appropriate minilessons and create appropriate classroom checklists about punctuation, spelling, and so forth. You can teach students to understand and use proofreading symbols by displaying them in the classroom.

Students can use spell checkers to locate typos or alert them to words they need to learn how to spell. Invented spellings may be appropriate for in-class communication with beginning writers, but when projects will be shared outside the classroom, standard spellings should generally be used. Students must learn to be careful of homonyms and typographical errors that result in real words that spell checkers cannot detect as errors because spell checkers cannot tell when a correctly spelled word does not fit in the context of a sentence. Some students like to use a grammar checker to see if their writing mechanics are "up to standard." Others like to use the built-in Thesaurus feature to find more descriptive or precise words. Word-processing programs today have features such as these to help students revise their writings, and they can foster better writing. The Guide to Grammar and Writing site at **http://ccc.commnet.edu/grammar/** is a source of information about grammar and various forms of writing, and you can even download PowerPoint lessons. It also contains a detailed index, making it is a useful reference for preservice and in-service teachers and may be helpful to some middle school students.

Spelling Consciousness and Spelling

Determining the correctness of one's own spelling develops spelling consciousness.

Proofreading involves looking at verbal and nonverbal messages to detect errors. This implies that students not only can recognize errors, they can correct them as well. By helping students develop **spelling consciousness**—an awareness that they have spelled words correctly or incorrectly—you help them improve their editing and spelling capabilities (Cramer, 1998; Fox & Mitchell, 2000; Valmont, 1972). In general, students want to spell words the right way because they recognize that misspelled words can embarrass them. In other words, they have a **spelling conscience** that says, "I want to spell words correctly." Spelling consciousness is the ability to know that a word (1) is spelled right, (2) is spelled wrong, or (3) is spelled either right or wrong, but the speller is unclear as to which. When there is uncertainty, a word could be spelled right, but the student thinks it is spelled wrong. Or, the word could be spelled wrong, but the student thinks it is spelled right. Usually, when students doubt a spelling, the word is spelled incorrectly. See a fuller explanation and examples of ways to teach spelling consciousness on this book's web site.

In addition to teaching students to use online dictionaries to help with spelling (see chapter 1), you can encourage students to engage in online activities that make spelling important all of the time—not just when they are revising their own writing. The following web sites demonstrate a variety of activities you and students can use to learn to spell words; let students have fun with spelling; and offer ideas you as a teacher might use to create similar activities.

WEBLIOGRAPHY

- FunBrain.com
  http://www.funbrain.com/
  Click "Free Games" and go to the "Words" category. Select "Spell Check." In the game, a form of spelling consciousness, you identify words that are misspelled. The "Spellaroo" game also promotes spelling consciousness.

- **National Spelling Bee**
  http://www.spellingbee.com/
  This site is maintained by Scripps Howard, which sponsors the event. See also "Previous Logodaedalyland Topics" at **http://www.spellingbee.com/previous_logoland.htm**, a section that deals with the etymology of words.

PUBLISHING STAGE

A student's work can now be accessed by audiences worldwide.

Word-processing and software programs help students publish professional-looking projects.

Today's students want to publish for valid reasons and real audiences, and the goal of this stage is to put ideas into a form that others can access. Traditionally, publishing meant creating a neat draft on paper and placing it on the classroom or hall wall. For longer works, students used bookbinding techniques such as gluing and sewing to create books that were placed in the classroom or school library. Students can continue to publish in these ways, but they also can use word-processing and other programs to help them generate books electronically. Microsoft Word, for instance, lets you create page layouts suitable for binding. You can add a **gutter,** an extra space in a margin for binding pages without covering text. You can add columns and page numbers, insert graphics, use interesting fonts, and so forth, to re-create features found in printed books. Check the manual for your word-processing program to learn its bookmaking capabilities.

"Even if your classroom has only a single computer, you can still set up a publishing center," according to J. M. Wood (2000, p. 64), who said, "By installing a simple bookmaking program . . . children can transform their stories and illustrations into polished, printed works to be shared throughout the school." For instance, Easy Book Deluxe is useful for students in grades 3–8 who want to make and print books. The Amazing Writing Machine allows K–8 students to write and publish stories, letters, journals, essays, and poetry. Technology has made bookmaking fun and easy. In addition, students can work in electronic formats that enable them to send their works as e-mail attachments, burn (place files on) their own CD-ROMs, or publish on the Web. Chapters 7 and 8 discuss making presentations and constructing electronic materials for publishing or sharing with others. See the Student Project "The Safari" for a story created using HyperStudio. This is just one example that demonstrates how students can write and construct messages electronically.

Class, school, and district web sites are increasing in numbers each year, and publishers and other organizations are making it possible for students to place their works online. Writing and constructing nonverbal images for publication on the Internet gives students genuine reasons to learn about and write about their own communities as well as to study and write about the entire world community. Given opportunities to do so, students are eager to contribute something worthwhile to the world's body of knowledge. Publishing information they create, such as compiling local scientific data, helps students understand that they can add value to the knowledge of the world. What can be more authentic than that?

THE SAFARI

by Erika Spreiser

Erika's comment: I really enjoyed HyperStudio! I liked how I could illustrate all the cards, and I liked making up an adventurous story. I thought it was really cool because I learned that making up stories can be really fun, and I think that I'll make a sequel to my story.

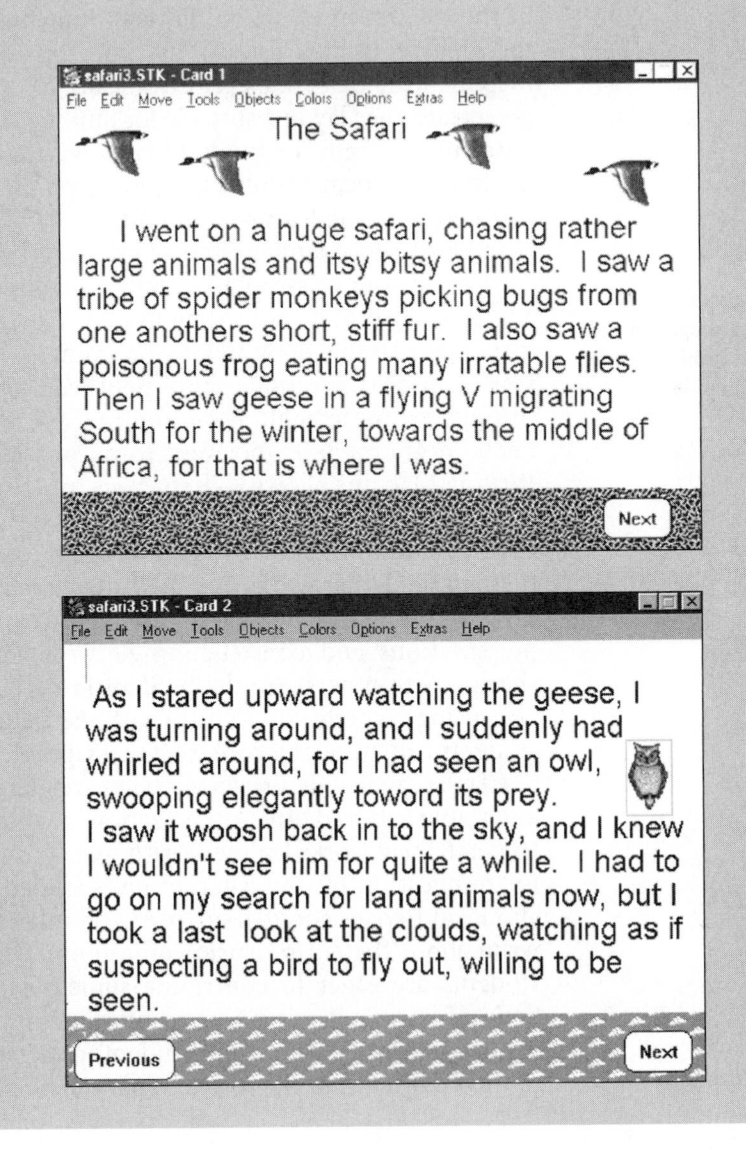

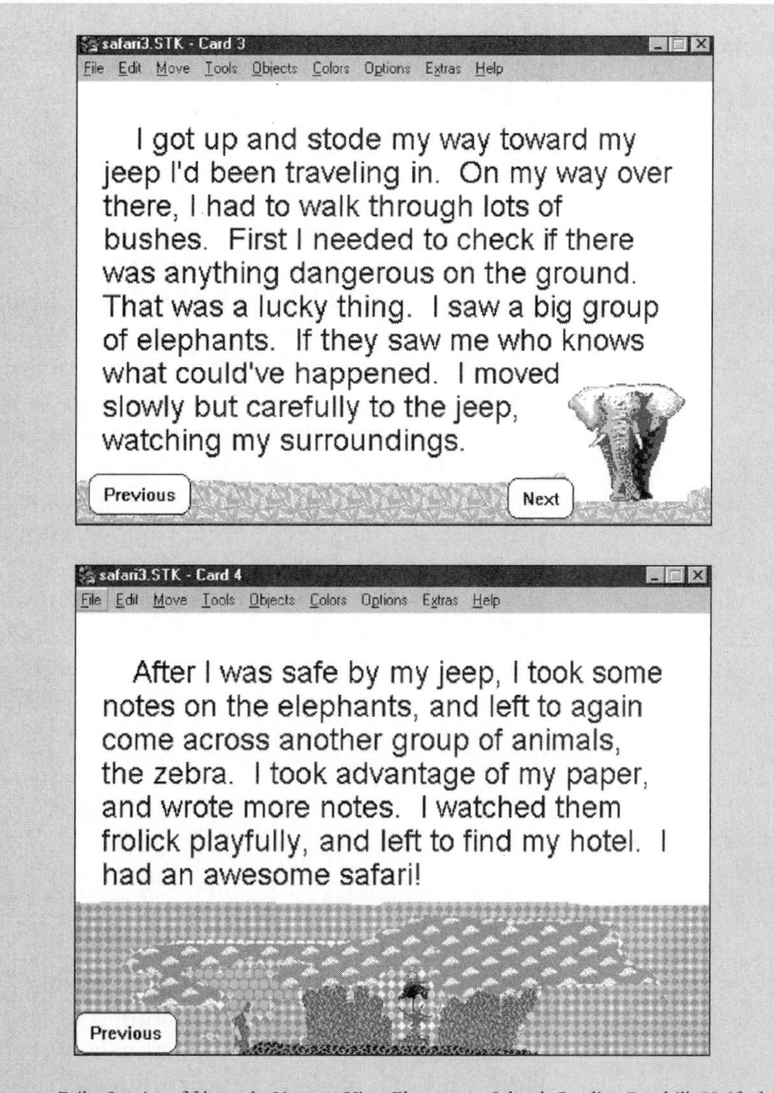

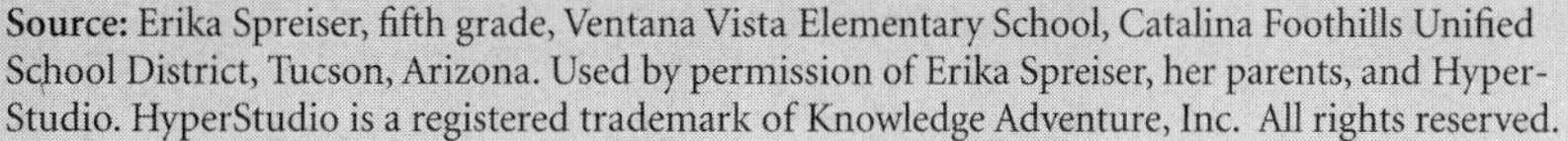
Source: Erika Spreiser, fifth grade, Ventana Vista Elementary School, Catalina Foothills Unified School District, Tucson, Arizona. Used by permission of Erika Spreiser, her parents, and HyperStudio. HyperStudio is a registered trademark of Knowledge Adventure, Inc.

Before ending this section, we would like to mention a valuable web site where you can review the ideas presented here and expand your knowledge of the writing process. See ABC's of the Writing Process at **http://www.angelfire.com/wi/writingprocess/** for many helpful ideas.

Technology-Related Means for Encouraging Students to Write

In addition to having students write as part of unit or thematic explorations, you can use a variety of online strategies and learning experiences to encourage students' writing. You can visit an excellent online source for additional writing ideas at TeachNet.com at **http://www.teachnet.com/lesson/langarts/writing/index.html.** The remainder of this chapter includes ideas about writing and composing, and we suggest ways to use technology to encourage students to write and construct meaning. You can use e-mail to help students learn to deal with informal writing and as a way to contact authors. Students can use online and software applications to write and construct interesting book reports and reviews, providing opportunities for students to share using new media. Show students that there are a variety of electronic ways, including online newspapers, newsletters, and e-zines, to produce messages by demonstrating effective ways to use e-cards, practicing storyboarding while making a commercial, and writing secret messages or filling in words to make Mad Libs. You and students can learn about online forms and ways to complete exercises online to take advantage of online opportunities to communicate. These and many other developing writing opportunities are available and should be explored.

E-MAIL

Teach students how to use online features to communicate with others.

Through sending e-mail and e-mail attachments, students can write to other students (e-pals, also called web-pals, keypals, or net-pals), family members, authors, experts and other adults, as well as you. Their electronic communications will reflect their writing development from struggling with invented spellings in informal communication to eventually crafting polished, well-developed communications. Here are some suggestions about writing e-mail messages:

- Help students realize that when rushed, many of us make typos, forget to check the spelling of words which should be checked, or make other errors. We *all* need to proofread!
- Encourage students to improve the quality of e-mail by having them first compose using a word-processing program where they can write more leisurely and use the spell checker. They can copy and paste messages into the e-mail program later.

- Convey the idea that e-mail tends to be terse writing, meaning that the receiver may easily misconstrue a sentence that does not clearly express the writer's intended thoughts.
- Suggest using emoticons (;]) or words in parentheses (ha ha!) to help readers understand a message. (To see dozens of emoticons, visit Bronwen & Claire's Really Huge Emoticon Collection! at **http://www.angelfire.com/hi/hahakiam/emoticon.html.**)
- Encourage students to reread all messages for completeness and clarity before sending them.
- Suggest that students ask for clarification from people who send them unclear e-mail.

Synchronous chat rooms permit more than two people to communicate and generate numerous messages in a short period of time, so some of the above points apply to these electronic interactions as well. Students need supervision and must learn of dangers that might exist when interacting with others on chat rooms because people are anonymous and may not be who they represent themselves to be. We discussed Internet safety previously, but it bears repeating that you should caution students about divulging personal or school information, and you should encourage them to inform you immediately if anything appears online that makes them uncomfortable. Be certain to check school policies about using chat rooms and whether or not parental permissions are needed for students to engage in online conversations.

Synchronous communications afford countless opportunities for misunderstanding. This is especially true when several people send thoughts about more than one topic at about the same time. Messages to and from the person you are communicating with will likely be intermingled with other people's messages, making it more difficult to follow the thread of your own conversation. Students can communicate with one another at the following and similar sites: KidsCom at **http://www.kidscom.com/**, a site where students can chat with others, play interactive games, and send e-cards, among other activities; and Cyberkids at **http://www.cyberkids.com/**, a site where young students can interact with one another and play games.

As will be noted in chapter 9, some authors and illustrators with web sites and e-mail addresses encourage students to write to them. If students read a book and want to tell the author how much it meant to them, or if they want to ask a question that was not resolved in a book, they have legitimate reasons for sending e-mail to an author. Encourage students who have comments or questions for an author to pool them and send just one e-mail so the author will not be overwhelmed. The following sites will lead you to many authors and illustrators.

WEBLIOGRAPHY

- **Authors and Illustrators on the Web**
  http://www.acs.ucalgary.ca/~dkbrown/authors.html
  This site contains an extensive list of web addresses of authors and illustrators, as well as links to other, similar sites.
- **KidsReads.com**
  http://www.kidsreads.com/
  Click on the "Authors" button for links to dozens of authors' addresses, and biographical sketches.

BOOK REPORTS AND REVIEWS

Experts in children's literature describe specific strategies students can use to share their knowledge of and reactions to stories they read (Norton & Norton, 1999; Short, 1997). Many of these strategies can be modified so they can be shared electronically. Sites such as the following afford opportunities for students to learn about making book reports and sharing stories with others.

WEBLIOGRAPHY

- **Just for Kids Who Love Books**
  http://www3.sympatico.ca/alanbrown/kids.htm
  Students can read numerous book reviews and contribute their own. There are also links to dozens of author sites as well as to literature sites dedicated to specific characters, titles, and series, ranging from the Berenstain Bears, to *Heidi*, to the "Goosebumps" books, many of which offer activities and teaching ideas.
- **TeachNet.com - Lesson Ideas - Reading**
  http://www.teachnet.com/lesson/langarts/reading/bookrepts1.html
  This site offers more than 340 ideas for alternative ways to make book reports, including many that require writing.

ELECTRONIC CARDS (E-CARDS)

Students can send free static or animated electronic cards for birthdays, holidays, special occasions, and so forth from dozens of Internet sites. Use these for opportunities to help students develop writing and social skills. Encourage students to check several sites, examine a variety of cards, and make *thoughtful choices that personalize the cards* for the people who will receive them. For instance, if Dad is a tennis player, the student can look specifically for a special Father's Day card with a tennis theme. Most e-cards let you personalize a message by filling out an online form. Some forms do not provide much space for messages, but others do. Regardless, you can help students learn to use the *entire* form to create thoughtful messages that say more than a simple "Happy Birthday!" Many of the e-cards contain a second space where additional messages can be placed. Again, have students use such spaces to personalize the card, perhaps by telling someone why they are loved, liked, missed, enjoyed, and so forth. Students can write messages using a word-processing program and then cut and paste them into the online form. Be sure to have students preview cards for completeness and spelling before sending them.

You will want to visit electronic card sites prior to suggesting them to students. While some sites offer appropriate subjects for students, perhaps some e-cards may not be appropriate. Students can find free e-cards at these sites.

WEBLIOGRAPHY

- **AwesomeCards.com**
  http://www.marlo.com
  This site includes an "All 4 Kids Cards" section.
- **MoMA E-Cards**
  http://moma.e-cards.org/
  This site, sponsored by the Museum of Modern Art in New York City, has e-cards using well-known artwork and information about the art. The recipient also receives a description of the art.

ONLINE FORMS

There are two types of online forms. The first are forms students can print and fill out with a pencil or a pen, just as they would any printed form. For instance, government agencies are placing forms online for people to read or print using Adobe Acrobat Reader, which is free. You download the forms into your computer. The second are interactive forms that are filled out online and submitted electronically for processing. E-cards, described above, contain this kind of form. Airlines also have interactive online forms you can fill in to determine whether you can travel on the dates you wish to travel. You will want to show students examples of forms that companies are placing on the Web to conduct business. Amazon.com (**http://www.amazon.com**) uses forms to help you order books.

You and students can create forms for your school's web site using HTML or through the use of a web page creation program such as FrontPage or SiteCentral. Consult a technology specialist to determine how to create the correct form for a school or district web server and how to place the contents returned from the form into a database for access and action. These two sites use forms.

WEBLIOGRAPHY

- **Southwest Airlines**
  http://www.iflyswa.com/
  This is the airline's web site.
- **50states.com Directory of State Tax Forms**
  http://www.50states.com/tax/
  Students can use Adobe Acrobat Reader to look at or download tax forms. There are also links to lists of state birds, songs, etc., and various activities.

MAKING COMMERCIALS

Use web sites' unique features to help students have fun communicating with others.

Students can write captions and use storyboarding skills to create a commercial at a site designed to sell food. This is an excellent activity for introducing students to storyboarding. Students create a story line, decide which pictures to use, and choose a logical order for them. They also must create appropriate dialogue so their commercial makes sense. You can have students work independently on commercials, print them out, and

MAKING A COMMERCIAL
by Ray Sosa

Ray Sosa, a sixth-grade student, does not have very many opportunities to work online, and he had never before seen a web site quite like the chefboy.com site, which is highly interactive. He studied the twenty-four pictures, which are presented in random order. He then chose the allowable eight pictures and arranged them, adding words as he went. Ray's idea was that the man was hungry and did not want to let anything keep him from eating. He chuckled at the picture of the can starting to fall, and I think Ray really "became" the hero catching it.

Teacher. *What did you learn when you made your commercial?*
Ray. *I learned that it is very easy to make a commercial, but also hard because you have to pick the right setting and wording. I found that it was very fun and exciting.*
Teacher. *Have you ever made a commercial before?*
Ray. *No. The hardest part was picking the wording. I chose the pictures by the expressions on their faces.*
Teacher. *Why did you place the pictures in the order you did?*
Ray. *It is showing that he's hungry, and he wants to eat fast.*

Source: Ray Sosa, Sierra Middle School, Sunnyside School District, Tucson, Arizona. Used by permission of Ray Sosa, his parents, and Chef Boyardee, a product of ConAgra Grocery Products.

share them with the class, explaining how they arrived at the commercial they made. See the Student Project "Making a Commercial" (which uses the Chef Boyardee Online site at **http://www.chefboy.com**) for an example of this learning experience. Go to the Arcade section and click on "Make Your Own Chef Boyardee Commercial." Students also can use a variety of objects to make a comic book–type story.

CREATING NEWSPAPERS AND NEWSLETTERS

By writing newspapers and newsletters, students learn that the *form* of writing influences the thinking needed to produce it. Specifically, this genre requires writers to summarize, use precise language, and carefully select details (Dexter & Watts-Taffe, 2000). There are CD-ROM and online sources you can use to introduce students to writing various kinds of newspaper articles and features. Among the software programs for designing newspapers and newsletters are Classroom Newspaper Workshop, a program for grades 3–7 that guides students through the stages to create a class newspaper; The Print Shop, which students in all grades can use to create greeting cards, newsletters, signs, web pages, banners, and more; and Ultimate Writing & Creativity Center, a program that includes writing projects, idea starters, editing tools, and multimedia tools. Students in grades 2–5 can make newsletters, journals, storybooks, reports, and signs with this program.

Students can examine the web sites of major newspapers (e.g., *The New York Times, The Washington Post*) to glean ideas for features they might want to include in class newspapers. Here are some other helpful online sources.

WEBLIOGRAPHY

- **Create Your Own Newspaper**
  http://www.crayon.net/
  As the title conveys, you can create a free class newspaper as well as link to other sources of news.
- **E-Newsletters**
  http://training.peoriaud.k12.az.us/Newsletters/default.htm
  Advice about creating electronic newsletters appears at this site.
- **Fujifilm PhotoPals**
  http://www.fujifilmphotopals.com/
  You can fill in a form to become a PhotoPal, or try other activities at this site. The teaching part of the site contains "how-to" ideas for using photography in schools.

CREATING E-ZINES

Middle school students can read, contribute to, and create electronic magazines, also known as e-zines or webzines. Seventh-grade students at Flowing Wells Junior High in Tucson, Arizona, created a webzine under the guidance of Maya Eagleton (1999), who said,

> The webzine project was a positive experience for the seventh graders . . . because it met their affective needs to be active, to learn new things, to have new experiences, to feel motivated and interested, to be social, to have freedom, to feel proud and to have a sense of audience. It also stimulated the cognitive processes of generating ideas, collaborating, problem solving, representing concepts, and monitoring their own learning. (p. 10)

You can see the students' *Electronic MagaZEEN* at **http://earthvision.asu.edu/~maya/e-zeen/.**

E-zines provide valid reasons for students to engage in a variety of original writing activities. Students can write news and features; assemble and describe relevant links to sites that deal with their own topics; and publish the best student work from their own school. Students determine the content before producing the actual web site. Before deciding what to include in their own e-zine, students can look at a variety of styles that are already online. They can then decide how they want their own site to appear and choose the "departments" they want, such as school sports, art projects, poetry, frequently asked questions about their school, and so forth. You must decide how long the e-zine will remain on the Web before it is either changed or removed. While some e-zines are revised on a frequent basis, some have become **cobweb sites** with no revision since they were created.

Brainstorming and storyboarding skills, Internet search strategies, and knowledge of the writing process can all be used to create e-zines. Working with some combination of digital cameras, scanners, HTML, and a web page development program will also be necessary, as will the ability to place electronic files on a server for people to access. See information about digital images on this book's web site.

You and students will expand your technological capabilities tremendously through creating e-zines. In addition, you can use e-zine authoring as a valid reason for studying the media, advertisements, and other journalistic topics. These web sites should be helpful.

WEBLIOGRAPHY

- **Magazines**
  http://www.eduplace.com/kids/links/kids_4.html
  Use this list of online magazines, compiled by Houghton Mifflin Company, to locate sites for your class to examine.
- **MidLink Magazine**
  http://www.cs.ucf.edu/~MidLink/index.html
  This is a web-based magazine by and for students ages 8 to 18. Contributors—both teachers and students—are from all around the world.

SENDING ASSIGNMENTS TO TEACHERS

The same technology that permits the gathering of information from online forms is being used by schools to let students go to a web site, complete homework, and send it to you. Welcome to Web School at **http://webschool.wash.k12.ut.us/** shows how you can create such assignments. It has lessons for reading, language, spelling, and other school subjects.

WRITING SECRET MESSAGES

Students like to keep secrets from teachers, parents, and brothers and sisters. Thunk.com's "Secret Messages for Kids Only" at **http://www.thunk.com/index.cgi** will help them make secret messages, but you will know how to decode them!

FILLING IN MAD LIBS®

Students supply missing words in stories using a strategy that has been around for many years. Often, Mad Lib stories are humorous when they are read, usually aloud. Students can now complete such stories online. Working at their own pace, they can be selective about the words they choose, and if they want to change their mind after reading the story, they can press the "back" button, change the words, and generate the story again. BAB Books: On-line Stories for Kids at **http://www.amtexpo.com/**

babbooks/ is one site you can use. Click on the "Adlib" link for a form that lets you place words, by part of speech, into a story. The web site then generates the finished story. These stories are appropriate for elementary school students.

WRITING POETRY

There is much poetry on the WWW; at some web sites, students can submit their poetry for possible inclusion. Jay Stailey, a principal from Friendswood, Texas, won the International Reading Association's 1999 Presidential Award for Reading and Technology for creating a web site and updating it every few days so his students could follow his trip to Japan. The site includes examples of tanka poetry (poems that have 31 syllables arranged 5–7–5–7–7) and haiku poetry (poems that have 17 syllables arranged 5–7–5). Visit Welcome to Jay Stailey's Amazing Japanese Adventure at **http://www.friendswood.isd.tenet.edu/ba/japan.** Also visit Yahooligans! at **http://www.yahooligans.com** to see a site that has Internet search capabilities. Click on "Language Arts" for a link to haiku poetry.

BALANCING FICTION AND NONFICTION WRITING

Students can engage in a myriad of writing experiences using either fiction or nonfiction topics they find in print books or in electronic materials derived from CD-ROMs or the Web. They can follow the writing process stages to develop fanciful stories or to create research accounts about real people and events. It is important for you to encourage students to write, construct messages, and share fiction and nonfiction works at all grade levels. Take advantage of electronic reference materials and tap into the thousands of sites containing nonfiction topics.

You will see in chapter 9 that fiction is plentiful online, as it is on CD-ROMs. Fiction may inspire students to write their own. Students can use a word processor to craft reports and stories, or you may want to invest in software programs specifically designed to help students create and illustrate stories. If students want to be very creative, they can work with multimedia programs that let them use all of the visual and auditory features of such programs to build their reports and stories from blank pages, a process we will discuss in more detail in the next two chapters.

SUMMARY

- Technology is changing the nature of writing because students can readily include both nonverbal and verbal symbols as they construct meaning for others.
- Keyboarding is a crucial skill students must learn in order to communicate through technology.
- Writing and constructing messages appears to be somewhat easier and more positively received when students use technology.
- Technology enables students to access and organize information in the prewriting stage, and word-processing programs, in particular, aid students in the drafting, revising, editing, and publishing stages.
- Storyboarding helps students learn to attend to both the verbal and nonverbal aspects of writing and constructing.
- Spelling consciousness helps students recognize their correct and incorrect spelling.
- Web sites and software applications can be models of effective writing and constructing.
- You can take advantage of online writing opportunities to help students learn about and use forms and other emerging types of electronic writing.

ACTIVITIES

1. Discuss keyboarding with several K–6 teachers to learn how they teach it.
2. Using the writing process stages, help students write and construct original stories.
3. Create three or four spelling consciousness activities and try them with students.
4. Visit several sites and plan how you can use them to encourage writing and constructing.

SOFTWARE

All the Right Type: School Version, Ingenuity Works, Inc., 4 & up
This is a basic keyboarding program.

Author's Toolkit, Sunburst Technology, 4–8
Students learn to write in an organized fashion. This program has text-to-speech capabilities.

Blue's Birthday Adventure, Humongous Entertainment, Pre-K–3
Make a birthday card and engage in other creative activities with this software.

Draft:Builder, Don Johnston, 2 & up
This program allows students to see and develop an outline, take notes, and use both views to draft their report.

Herzog Keyboarding, Herzog Keyboarding, 3 & up
This program uses special "hub keys" on the letters D and K to help students keep track of finger placement. Letters are learned in alphabetical order.

Hollywood, Grolier Educational, K–8
Students produce, write, and direct animated shows. The characters are animals.

Imagine Express Series, Edmark/Riverdeep Interactive, K–8
Create your own interactive stories, both electronic and printed, based on a destination theme. Destinations include the ocean, a Panamanian rain forest, and a medieval castle.

JumpStart Typing, Knowledge Adventure, 2–5
Students develop keyboarding skills while competing in arcade-style games.

Kid Works, Deluxe Knowledge Adventure, Pre-K–4
This is a multimedia program students can use for creative writing.

Language Skills CD-ROM Series, Curriculum Associates, 3–6
Lessons that deal with grammar and usage, sentences, and mechanics are part of this program.

Mavis Beacon Teaches Typing! for Kids, The Learning Company/Broderbund, K–3
This is a keyboarding program for young students. Mavis Beacon Teaches Typing! (3 & up) is a keyboarding program that adapts to the usage patterns of the user.

Media Weaver, Humanities Software/Sunburst Technology, 3 & up
Integrate pictures, groups, sounds, and movies for multimedia writing and publishing with this software.

MP Express, Bytes of Learning, 3 & up
Multimedia authoring with narration is possible with this program. People of the World: The Americas is a CD-ROM specifically made to use with it.

My First Amazing Diary, DK Interactive Learning, K–3
Students can enter facts about themselves and, sometimes, the information appears in other activities in the diary.

PostCards: A Writer's View of Mexico, Ghana, Japan, and Turkey, Curriculum Associates, 5–8
Students read and write as they take virtual fieldtrips. The program includes scaffolded postcards in four genres: narrative, compare and contrast, persuasive, and descriptive.

Secret Writer's Society, Forest Technologies/QuickMinds, 3 & up
This writing fundamentals program helps students plan, draft, revise, edit, and present their works.

Spelling Blaster Ages 6–9, Knowledge Adventure, 1–4
The program has more than 1,700 words and a word editor you can use to customize spelling lists.

Stagecast Creator, Stagecast, Inc., 4 & up
This is a tool for creating simulations and games. You can save files to the WWW using this program.

Storybook Weaver Deluxe, MECC/The Learning Company/Broderbund, K–6
This is a multimedia creative writing and storytelling program with English and Spanish spell checkers.

Student Writing & Research Center, The Learning Company/Broderbund, 4 & up
This product combines Student Writing Center software program and Compton's 1995 Concise Encyclopedia *for research and writing.*

Student Writing Center, The Learning Company/Broderbund, 5 & up
This is a word-processing and desktop publishing program.

Sunbuddy Writer, Sunburst Technology, K–2
You can use large text and simple icons to make rebus sentences and stories with this product.

Type to Learn, Sunburst Technology, 2 & up,
Students learn keyboarding skills while engaged in "time-travel mission." For younger students, try Type to Learn Jr. (K–2) and Type to Learn Jr. New Keys for Kids (1–3).

UltraKey, Bytes of Learning, 3 & up
This keyboarding tutorial offers 3-D animations, virtual reality, and live videos.

UltraWriter, Bytes of Learning, 3 & up
This writing program uses the writing process approach. A second window opens to reveal templates and writing instruction. The program can speak the directions and words. (Mac version only)

Word Munchers Deluxe, MECC/The Learning Company/Broderbund, 1–5
Students practice reading, grammar, sentence completion, phonics, and other skills using a game format.

Writing for Readers (Odyssey of Discovery Series), Pierian Spring Software, 7 & up
Students use the program to develop plot, setting, characters, and more.

Writer's Solution, Prentice Hall School, 7 & up
This is a writing course that includes software and a textbook.

Writing Trek, The, Sunburst Technology, 4–6, 6–8, 8–10
Students learn different writing genre while engaging in various writing and skill-building (project-based) activities at several levels.

FOR FURTHER READING

Bolter, J. (1998). Hypertext and the question of visual literacy. In D. Reinking, M. McKenna, L. Labbo, & R. Kieffer (Eds.), *Handbook of literacy and technology.* Mahwah, NJ: Lawrence Erlbaum Associates.

De Moll, C. (1998, May/June). Publishing student work online: Investigation, assimilation, and self-expression. *Information Today, Inc. 5*(3), 8–10.

Land, M., & Turner, S. (1997). *Tools for schools: Applications software for the classroom* (2nd ed.). Belmont, CA: Wadsworth Publishing Company.

Reissman, R. (1998). Technology-transformed dictionary compilation. *Learning & Leading with Technology, 26*(3), 35–38.

Reissman, R. (2000). Priceless gifts. *Learning & Leading with Technology, 28*(2), 28–31.

Using Technology to Develop Listening and Speaking Abilities

INTRODUCTION

The language arts develop in a predictable order, with listening being the first to develop. Next, in an amazingly short time frame, students learn to speak ("Mama," "Dada," "milk"), speaking being the second language art to develop. In a few years, children begin reading and writing. Basic listening and speaking abilities emerge well in advance of formal schooling, but you will need to help students extend and refine these critical abilities. Guidance in the language arts should continue through all grade levels, starting with informal experiences in kindergarten, building to formal presentations in middle school, and evolving into advanced debate tactics in high school. Higher-grade speaking skills might include speaking persuasively, conducting sales presentations, and interviewing for a job. The roots of advanced speaking activities, however, are developed throughout elementary school. Some of the ideas you will find in this chapter will help you model effective listening and speaking strategies. Other ideas are meant for students.

Listening is an active process, just as reading is, and a person's mind must be actively engaged in listening. A reader must comprehend ideas being conveyed via paper or electronic print. If a person is merely "calling the words" (pronouncing them) without understanding (comprehending), reading is not occurring. Rather, the person is simply **recoding** from one symbol system to another without understanding. Likewise, a listener must comprehend ideas being conveyed orally. If the person is merely "hearing sounds" without understanding, listening is not occurring.

Critical listening involves active thinking about what you hear.

You can influence students' listening capabilities, starting with improving listening at literal levels of complexity through levels of **critical listening.** Critical listening requires that the listener actively be aware of the speaker's logic, attempts to persuade, and so forth. This chapter suggests strategies and activities you can use to help students become progressively better critical listeners.

You can influence speaking capabilities by using increasingly more structured and formal classroom activities. Thus, for example, beginning at kindergarten, you can help students develop speaking capabilities with self-introductions, show-and-tell sharing, and brief presentations to others (e.g., telling about a picture). Group language experience activities offer some of the earliest opportunities for students to share ideas in a more formal instructional setting.

Students gain confidence through engaging in many speaking experiences.

Speaking is sometimes extemporaneous and sometimes planned, and you should provide opportunities for both types of speaking at all grade levels. Students are often shy or embarrassed about standing before their peers. Help them overcome these feelings by modeling effective speaking behaviors such as using a strong voice, using presentation programs confidently, and rehearsing. Students will gain self-assurance when they learn how to use successful strategies to act in Readers' Theatre or plays. Help students learn the basics of acting, including how to move around on a stage and how to project their voices loudly for an audience. Show them how to "become" a character from a story (or become a tree) and help them understand how nonverbal behaviors such as gestures or movement add to speaking.

Students will gain poise and confidence in their presence before an audience only through careful planning. Model positive group interaction skills and help students feel comfortable expressing ideas in group settings. Demonstrate for students how to give and receive constructive criticism. As you will learn, technology can help you find and use materials, activities, and other resources to enhance listening and speaking abilities.

A Climate for Listening and Speaking

In some classrooms, students are not encouraged to talk. In fact, talking is often discouraged. Establish a climate that encourages speaking and listening by giving students many and varied opportunities to do so. For instance, working together around computers invites communication and cooperative learning, and that evokes speaking and listening.

Promote both formal and informal types of speaking. Students need ample opportunities to speak with one another, to talk in small groups, and to make formal and informal presentations to the entire class. Throughout the school day, students can engage in interpersonal communications as well as give speeches or make presentations. Speaking and listening are social interactions, and you want students to feel free to discuss their interests with one another, pose questions they want to answer, and present information they want to share with others. Students need frequent opportunities to engage in speaking and listening because they get better with your guidance and as they practice and develop effective habits. There will be some personal communications throughout the school day, but that is natural in a friendly atmosphere conducive to conversation. After all, socialization is an important part of schooling. See "What Affects Your Listening Habits" on this book's web site.

WWW

Encourage students' speaking and listening by helping them locate information and talk about topics of interest as part of your thematic or unit work. The Internet and CD-ROMs contain tremendous amounts of information on thousands of topics, so students should not have difficulty talking about or listening to a wide variety of subjects. Once you encourage students to actively pursue those topics that are important to them, they will want many opportunities to share their findings with others either formally or informally. Having an active voice in topic selection during thematic units of study helps students use their voices to share with others.

Students will want to talk about topics that interest and engage them in research.

You set good examples of speaking and listening as you model effective teaching and communication behaviors: speaking loudly and clearly, emphasizing certain words for effect, speaking at a pace that lets the class follow your ideas. You model when you listen attentively to student presentations, plays, Readers' Theatre, and so forth, as well as when you take notes or otherwise act upon things you hear so you can remember them better.

One important thing you can do is help students learn to organize and present information in logical order so that their listeners can follow their arguments or lines of reasoning. Using any of the major organizational or presentation software products, you can guide students to consider the logical progression of presentations they are creating. Gathering unorganized information from web sites or CD-ROM materials, sifting it, and arranging it for sharing with others are intellectual skills you can help students develop.

Encouraging Listening

Infants immediately start to sort out the sounds in their surroundings, and in a short period of time they start to babble in the primary language they hear. Listening is how children learn the sounds of their language, and it is extremely important in the development of auditory discrimination and phonemic awareness. Through listening, children learn new words and the syntax of their language. Therefore, even after students come to school and began to read, it is important for them to be exposed to environments that are rich in language. Your story reading and storytelling provide some of the richness.

Effective listening involves thinking and searching for meaning.

Effective listening is less dependent upon listening to words than it is on uncovering the speaker's intended meaning. Effective listeners listen for key ideas, fix those ideas in their minds, and give the ideas a different weight or importance than that given to the ideas in between the key ideas. Encourage students to ask questions or repeat main ideas or keywords to themselves during the act of listening. Figure 7.1 is a self-rating quiz about listening skills. Have students take this test and then discuss with them the reasons behind each point.

FIGURE 7.1

How Are Your Listening Skills?: A Quick Self-Rating Quiz

Source: Kathie Reed. Used by permission of Taft College and Kathie Reed. The site is located at http://www.taft.cc.ca.us/lrc/quizzes/listtest.htm.

The following quiz is designed to show you what skills are necessary to be a good listener.

Answer these questions by grading your Listening Behaviors. Read the question and think about whether the statements are true of you. If the statement is always true of you, select an "Always" from the menu under the column that says "my grade." If the statement is not always true of you, then choose "Sometimes." "Rarely" would indicate that you would rarely or never listen that way.

Listening Behavior	My Grade
1. I allow speakers to complete sentences before I speak.	Always Sometimes Rarely
2. I make sure I understand the other person's point of view before I respond.	Always Sometimes Rarely
3. I listen for the speaker's important points.	Always Sometimes Rarely
4. I try to understand the speaker's feelings.	Always Sometimes Rarely
5. I attempt to visualize my response before I speak.	Always Sometimes Rarely
6. I visualize the solution before speaking.	Always Sometimes Rarely
7. I am in control, relaxed, and calm when listening.	Always Sometimes Rarely
8. I use listening noises such as yes, gee, I see.	Always Sometimes Rarely
9. I take notes when someone else is speaking.	Always Sometimes Rarely
10. I listen with an open mind.	Always Sometimes Rarely
11. I listen even if the other person is not interesting.	Always Sometimes Rarely
12. I listen even if the other person is a moron.	Always Sometimes Rarely
13. I look directly at the person speaking.	Always Sometimes Rarely
14. I am patient when I listen.	Always Sometimes Rarely
15. I ask questions to be sure I understand the speaker.	Always Sometimes Rarely
16. I do not allow distractions to bother me when I listen.	Always Sometimes Rarely

GRADING INFORMATION

If you have mostly **Always** (14 to 16) you are an excellent listener. If you marked 11 to 13 statements as **Always** you are a good listener but could use some help in a few areas. If you marked **Always** for 7 to 10 statements, you are a fair listener. If you marked **Always** for 4 to 6 statements, you are a poor listener. Less than 4 indicates an extremely poor listener.

USING TECHNOLOGY TO ENHANCE LISTENING OPPORTUNITIES

Use technology to help ensure that students are exposed to a variety of listening experiences. You are probably fairly well versed in employing films and videos in educational settings, and you might have a collection of talking books, audiotapes, or CD-ROMs. You can draw on electronic books, according to Fernandez (1999, p. 34), "to expose children to a greater number of stories and enhance the possibility for improved literacy. Also, the value of electronic books in terms of children's exposure to repeated readings cannot be ignored."

Reading to students is an important professional skill, and there are ample online stories you can draw on. Not only are the classics available to you; stories by new or unpublished authors are also available to read to or be heard by students. (See chapter 9 for examples.) We recommend storytelling as an effective strategy to help students develop listening abilities.

Students of all ages like to hear you or others tell stories, and by hearing a variety of selections, students learn to listen as an audience. Students gain skill in listening to fictional materials by following the plots of stories, feeling emotions, detecting humor, noting voice inflection, and so forth. They gain skill in listening to nonfiction materials by focusing on key ideas and trying to fix important points in their minds. You might like to visit **http://www.audible.com** for information about audio books.

Audio technologies can expose students to models of effective speaking.

There are many opportunities to enlist technology in the development of listening skills. Students can listen to any of the following:

- Stories read aloud on CD-ROMs and audiotapes
- Stories that are accompanied by **streaming audio**, sound that plays through a computer's speakers directly from the Internet while the file is being transmitted
- News and music played over the Internet
- Something you recorded for them to hear
- Words or sentences being pronounced (e.g., keywords in CD-ROM materials)
- Students from higher grades presenting their multimedia works
- Original stories or excerpts that other students recorded
- Reports of students' online research projects
- Online plays

Listening is an active search for understanding and is sometimes hard work, but all students can learn to become better listeners—if they avoid developing bad habits. Over the years, students can develop poor practices such as allowing themselves to be distracted by a speaker's mannerisms or daydreaming. Sometimes students overreact to ideas and become emotional, letting their biases interfere with a message. Conduct a brainstorming session using a graphic organizer to bring these and similar negative behaviors out into the open for discussion. Print and post the graphic you create.

STRATEGIES FOR ACTIVE LISTENING

Just as there are before-, during-, and after-reading strategies (Vacca & Vacca, 1998) to help students read more effectively, you can use similar strategies to encourage more effective listening.

Before Listening

Students can profit from taking certain actions before, during, and after listening.

It is just as important to *identify and clarify purposes for listening* as it is for reading. You can teach before-listening strategies such as (1) pre-thinking a topic, (2) making predictions based on a topic or title, and (3) predicting from **advanced organizers,** which are short summaries designed to overview and provide structure to upcoming materials. The K-W-L strategy (Ogle, 1986) is a tactic used to help students prepare to deal with expository materials, and it can be used to help students get ready to listen as well. *K* stands for "What we know"; it activates a student's current knowledge of a subject. *W* stands for "What we want to find out," which leads to the development of student questions for which answers can be sought. *L* stands for "What we learned and still need to learn"; it signals students to either terminate their work with the topic or continue seeking additional information. Before listening, students can brainstorm what they know about a topic using a graphic organizer program and predict what the presentation might contain. Further, they can discuss what they hope to learn from the presenter. All of these strategies help students tune in.

During Listening

Encourage students to support the person making a presentation by paying close attention. Urge students to take notes about important ideas as they hear them and to make quick notes to remind them of something they want to ask the speaker after the presentation. Model the act of paraphrasing speakers' ideas and let students know that putting ideas into their own words helps them remember better. Also, teach students to ask themselves good questions as they listen. They can ask: "What does the speaker mean?" "What are the main points?" "How can I use what I'm hearing?" "Does this seem logical?" "Did the speaker miss any important parts?" "How do the things I am hearing fit together?" "Does the presentation fit with my criteria of a fine presentation?" Questions such as these help students engage in higher levels of thinking, such as application, analysis, synthesis, and evaluation (Gage & Berliner, 1998).

After Listening

Encourage students to summarize, rethink key ideas, or write additional notes about the main points. Encourage them to relate the points to other things they know. After a presentation, encourage students to assess its completeness and to determine whether it was sufficient or whether there is more they want to learn. Encourage students to frame and ask questions of the speaker when given opportunities to do so after listening.

While there is no reason for them to remember everything they hear, students do need to develop skills that will help them listen to and retain information from lectures and nonfiction presentations. Learning about and using before-, during-, and after-listening strategies will help.

THE LISTENING-THINKING ACTIVITY

LTAs involve thinking and predicting based on hearing fiction or nonfiction.

Directed Reading-Thinking Activities (DRTAs) were discussed in chapter 4, and Seeing-Thinking Activities (STAs) will be discussed in chapter 8. Listening-Thinking Activities (LTAs) foster logical thinking through oral-aural learning experiences. An LTA is virtually the same as a DRTA, *only you or a recorded voice read the story aloud.* Your practiced, expressive delivery of a narrative and your enthusiasm during discussions will positively affect your students and will enhance their enjoyment of the story. Well-narrated online tales such as "June the Prune" (see chapter 4) make electronic tales models of effective reading, also. Your guiding of the prediction process will help students learn to internalize effective listening behaviors.

In an LTA, students listen to an entire selection, stopping from time to time to discuss and revise predictions. Viewing the title, the opening scene of a CD-ROM or web story, or one or more pictures (or graphics), and your telling students how the story starts, are all ways of providing students with initial evidence for making predictions. After students hear the first portion of the story and gain more evidence, you should stop them briefly to verify their ideas or to make new predictions. This listening-and-discussing cycle then continues until the end of the story. See the Teaching Tip "LTA Teaching Strategy." Any story you read to students or have them listen to electronically will have places to stop for predicting (e.g., right before or after a turn of events), and the content of stories will suggest logical questions for students to predict about. You can influence various levels of comprehension (e.g., literal, figurative) through astute questioning.

LTAs may be used not only at the earliest stages of reading instruction, but at all levels of development. Predictive and inferential skills nurtured through the use of LTAs can help students develop better listening habits. Many electronic children's stories can be used as LTAs, whether they are fully illustrated or not.

The key to conducting LTAs resides in your selection of appropriate stopping places and the skillful revealing of evidence so that students predict and discuss their ideas. Determining stopping places is crucial. A useful point at which to stop and obtain predictions is just before or after a plot turn in the story. In stories with chapters, stopping to predict at the

TEACHING TIPS

LTA Teaching Strategy

Here is an example of an LTA teaching strategy created for a longtime popular children's book, *Nobody Listens to Andrew* by Elizabeth Guilfoile. This story is about a boy who is ignored until he loudly declares that there is a bear in his room. Creating such a strategy helps you plan stopping places and reminds you to keep students actively predicting and thinking their way through stories. It also helps you identify important aspects of a story that you might want to highlight. In this story, the character's feelings receive special attention because of the questions being asked. Although a book is used in this example, LTAs also can be planned for CD-ROM stories or stories found on the Web.

You can see a transcription of students discussing the "Andrew" story on this book's web site.

Suggested Teaching Strategy

- Tell students the title of the book and show its cover. Ask, "What do you think this story might be about?" Have a brief discussion.
- Say, "What ideas does this picture give you?" Discuss the ideas briefly.
- Read pages 5–11 and ask, "How do you think Andrew feels when nobody listens to him?" Ask several students to answer why they think what they do.
- After a brief discussion about Andrew's feelings, ask, "What do you think Andrew will do?" Obtain a few predictions, then say, "Let's find out." Read page 12.
- Ask, "How many of you believe Andrew?" Then ask, "Why might Andrew be telling a lie?" Have a brief discussion of these questions. Then ask, "What do you think the people will do?" After a brief discussion, read pages 13–21.
- Ask, "What do you think the people will find?" and "How many of you think the bear is there?" After taking the vote, read pages 22–25.
- Ask, "Do you think Andrew's family will listen to him now?" Get ideas. Then ask, "How do you think Andrew feels now?" Then ask, "Why do you think he feels that way?"
- Read page 26 and discuss the story as the students' interests direct.

end of each chapter is effective, but when a good stopping place occurs within a chapter, be sure to take advantage of it. In some Internet stories (e.g., "June the Prune"), the size of the sound file determines where the sound stops. You can hold brief discussions before starting the next sound segment. After you access the next page and click on the sound button, the story continues. Online and on some CD-ROMs, you can easily pause the sound. In nonfiction materials, study the material to choose effective stops.

LTAs ready students to employ thinking strategies when they can read for themselves.

LTAs are especially helpful preliminaries to DRTAs in which students do their own reading. The problem of word recognition is eliminated so that all students may concentrate largely on thinking. Thus, helping students improve their thinking and comprehending abilities is not delayed until students become more fluent readers. A pupil's thinking performance during LTAs can also reveal a readiness to profit from DRTA instruction. Even after students learn to read independently, LTAs continue to be valuable listening experiences.

The following guidelines should help you refine your skills in conducting LTAs.

- Select materials that are within students' aural understanding.
- Select materials appropriate to students' age and interests.
- Estimate the amount of time needed for listening. Generally, short selections are best for LTAs because ample time should be allotted for discussions.
- LTAs can continue to a second or subsequent day. Refresh everyone's memory by reviewing previous predictions before students hear more of the story.
- Determine beforehand what to offer as initial evidence, where the good stopping places are, and alternative strategies to use if students experience difficulties understanding the story or making logical predictions. The basic question to ask students is "What do you think will happen next?" This question will help students think about logical possibilities.
- Decide where to stop near the end of the story to check students' consensus about the ending.
- If there are pictures or graphics, decide when and how you will show them.

Students may have some difficulty proving their predictions because they are not able to refer to an electronic or printed text. If a question occurs or if there is a disagreement among class members, you may, as necessary, reread statements from the story to resolve the matter or go back to the electronic source so students can listen to some portion again. You can read a transcript of a teacher and students interacting with "Bettina Is a Pest," a Listening-Thinking Activity on this book's web site.

WWW

E-MATERIALS TO ENGAGE STUDENTS IN LISTENING

The Internet has stories, directions, music, audio news, and music. Students can listen to video clips from upcoming movies and do much more. Following are some useful web sites that contain listening activities or provide information about such activities.

WEBLIOGRAPHY

- **The International Listening Association**
  http://www.listen.org/
  The association's purpose is to promote "the study, development, and teaching of listening and the practice of effective listening skills and techniques." The listening exercises found here can be adapted to elementary or middle school classes.
- **Midi Karaoke**
  http://www.geocities.com/Broadway/3386/
  You can listen to music and sing along. The words are there for you to read and point to with the mouse. Use a video projector to show a group or the entire class.
- **Welcome to the Adventures of the Bailey School Kids**
  http://www.baileykids.com/
  There are some scripts for plays in the "Fun Things" section.
- **Welcome to the World of Merpy.com**
  http://www.merpy.com/index.html

FIGURE 7.2

Merpy.com Stories

Listen to music while reading interactive stories. Students can read the stories while listening to a narrator. Click on "Text & Audio Only." (See Figure 7.2.)

Source: Reprinted by permission of Marianne R. Petit.

Encouraging Speaking

Both fiction and nonfiction materials may be used as a basis for speaking before others. When printed books were scarce, decades ago, teachers often read stories aloud to children, usually the great classics. Elementary school libraries contained a great deal of fiction materials, but students had less frequent access to a wealth of current nonfiction materials. Nonfiction increasingly appeared in classroom and school libraries toward the end of the twentieth century. Today's students can access more nonfiction materials than ever, from both CD-ROMs and the Internet. These materials lend themselves to the production of new knowledge, and students want to share their newfound learning and ideas. This chapter suggests activities, strategies, and resources to help them do so.

FICTION PRESENTATIONS

Fictional CD-ROM and web materials can be the source of speaking opportunities.

If students have had few experiences acting or speaking in front of others, you will need to help them remember and deliver their lines, improve their timing, make eye contact with others, and avoid being awkward and self-conscious. Take time to coach students when you want them to speak effectively to others. As possible speaking experiences, students can:

- Draw pictures and tell about them. (Either use a drawing program such as Kid Pix, or scan students' drawings into computer files; then have students tell about their illustrations.) For an example of an illustration one student made and used to tell a story to his classmates, see the Student Project "Michael's Island Adventure."
- Speak during brainstorming sessions using a program such as Inspiration.
- Speak during small-group discussions about Internet-based research topics of interest.
- Speak in plays and Readers' Theatre productions.
- Speak to visitors and other adults about research findings from electronic materials.
- Tell stories encountered on CD-ROMs or read excerpts to entice students to use them.
- Read or tell stories found on the Internet.
- Read school news on the school's radio or video newscast.

There are many benefits to having students produce radio shows. "Having your class produce its own radio story will help students sharpen their auditory and imaging skills, develop their critical thinking, and strengthen their confidence in individual expression" (Heistand, 2000, p. 10). Furthermore, writing or adapting stories as plays involves students in many speaking and listening experiences. Students must interact to write, rehearse, and act recordings of a radio show, and they must deal with sound effects, music, and other auditory aspects of the production.

MICHAEL'S ISLAND ADVENTURE

By Michael

This illustration was created and used as a prop by Michael to tell a story to his classmates.

Source: Michael is in fourth grade at Manzanita Elementary School in Tucson, AZ. Used by permission.

Dramatic Play and Creative Dramatics

Technology can help students engage in either rehearsed or extemporaneous acting.

Students can engage in **dramatic play** in which they simulate real-life experiences. For instance, they could improvise helping to clean their house because company is coming, or play the part of an older brother washing a car or a sister giving a pet a bath. Dramatic play is spontaneous and unrehearsed.

Creative dramatics presents another avenue for students to speak. Creative dramatics is unrehearsed, extemporaneous *acting of stories the students know* (Burns, Roe, & Ross, 1999). Using stories you or students find on the Internet or CD-ROMs, you can have students participate in creative dramatics. Creative dramatics engages students in literacy activities that include the visual aspects (acting) as well as the verbal aspects (speaking) of presenting a story. "Creative drama is an effective tool for enhancing learning by creating learning situations in which students are able to make cognitive, emotional, and physical connections between new ideas and what they already know about the world" (Douville & Finke, 2000, p. 370). For instance, after using a CD-ROM of *Arthur's Teacher Trouble,* students can choose characters and act out the story to the best of their abilities. Traditional dramatic activities such as choral reading, pantomime, charades, and puppetry can give students opportunities to speak and act before their peers and others.

Several web sites will help you use a variety of learning experiences involving fiction as the basis for speaking activities: Creative Drama & Theatre Education Resource Site at **http://www.creativedrama.com/** contains information about creative drama, including classroom ideas and a list of plays for performance. Classroom Lesson Plans at **http://www.geocities.com/Broadway/Alley/3765/lessons.html** offers a variety of web sites. The site's main menu links to learning experiences that are categorized by type, age, and content. The premier site, Storytelling, Drama, Creative Dramatics, Puppetry & Readers Theater for Children & Young Adults at **http://falcon.jmu.edu/~ramseyil/drama.htm,** links to a wealth of resources.

Readers' Theatre

Students across many grade levels enjoy creating and participating in Readers' Theatre productions. Often children's literature provides the material from which productions grow, but poems, songs, or short stories—even nonfiction materials—can be used (Young & Vardell, 1993). Students, under your guidance, take the original story and prepare to act it out—or part of it—for the enjoyment of others. One key is to create dialogue so that students can read the scripts aloud in a dramatic style.

Stories, according to Cooper (2000, p. 325), "must have lots of dialogue, strong story lines, and suspense, humor, or surprise." Students discuss the important plot elements such as setting and major characters and events. They can make a graphic of the story line using Kidspiration to help select elements for their script. They decide if and how a narrator can help them tell the story. They choose what simple props (optional) to use, but they do not use scenery or costumes in their adaptation. Some productions involve the use of masks, but masks tend to muffle students' voices.

After dozens of decisions are made about the preceding matters, students write and polish their Readers' Theatre version, rehearse it, and present it to an audience. Your role throughout is to encourage interest and enthusiasm as well as to conduct rehearsals and teach students a little bit of stage presence. You can buy already-prepared Readers' Theatre scripts, and you can even find some on the Internet. Having a sample script or two with which students can familiarize themselves is helpful for those who have never participated in Readers' Theatre before. Author Online! (the web site of children' author Aaron Shephard) at **http://www.aaronshep.com/index.html** is a source of information about Readers' Theatre; in addition, there are some two dozen actual scripts students can use. Likewise, the Institute for Readers Theatre at **http://www.readers-theatre.com/** is a source for locating and purchasing scripts for classroom use.

Storytelling

Storytelling is an especially important way students can learn to speak before others. Younger students can retell familiar childhood tales such as *The Three Billy Goats Gruff*, while older students can tell longer, more complex tales such as *Soap! Soap! Don't Forget the Soap!* There are dozens of strategies for telling stories. Children can tell stories from all major **genre,** or distinctive types, of children's literature. (See chapter 9.) They can choose stories based on picture books; traditional literature such as folktales, myths, fables, and legends; modern fantasy; contemporary realistic fiction; or historical fiction. They can recite poetry as well. Storytelling techniques from Africa and Japan, and Native American multicultural materials on web sites, can help students learn about these cultures while they learn the art of storytelling (Norton & Norton, 1999). See the Tech Tip "What Is a Ring on the Internet?" to learn about the Storytelling Ring.

Student-made art can enhance storytelling. Students can glue drawings of *The Three Billy Goats Gruff* that they make using a paint program to craft sticks and make a bridge from milk cartons to use as props as they tell the story. Students reading *Soap! Soap!* can use a paint or a multimedia

TECH TIPS

WHAT IS A RING ON THE INTERNET?

A ring (sometimes called web ring) is a set of web sites scattered throughout the Internet by different authors but built around a common interest area. If you have a web site that pertains to the topic, you can join the ring. In this case, the subject of the ring is storytelling. A web site is identified as being a member of a specific ring, and there is usually a logo for the ring. Links to other ring members' web sites are provided, and you can move backward or forward through the ring. Not only can you find a great deal of related information at the sites, you can communicate with others interested in the same topic you are.

The Animation Ring:
http://members.tripod.com/Lal_/
The Children's Literature Ring:
http://www.geocities.com/Athens/3777/ring.html
The Graphics Ring:
http://www.graphicsring.com/
The Storytelling Ring:
http://www.tiac.net/users/papajoe/ring/ring.htm
The Animated Dancing Pages Web Ring:
http://members.aol.com/pinkbreez/index.html

software program such as Digital Chisel, MP Express, or mPOWER to add visuals to their retelling of the story of the young man who sets out to buy soap but is easily distracted. You can't lose when you encourage students to tell stories because both the speakers and the listeners profit.

Inez L. Ramsey created a web page about choosing stories for storytelling for the Internet School Library Media Center at James Madison University. She suggests hints for choosing stories for storytelling. See the Teaching Tip "Choosing Stories for Storytelling."

Many of Ramsey's suggestions apply not only to print materials, but also to electronic materials. In chapter 9 you will find that many classics, fables, and so forth are online or on CD-ROMs, and these can be used for storytelling. Some new online stories bear retelling, also.

Technology can publicize or support speaking experiences.

Technology gives students new ways to accompany storytelling with electronic features. Students can use presentation programs such as PowerPoint to create electronic books of original stories to tell others (Hodges, 1999). For example, instead of adding graphics to a feltboard as in years gone by, students can now use clip art or original drawings of a fly, spider, bird, cat, and so forth to make an electronic presentation to accompany telling of the *Little Old Woman Who Swallowed a Fly* story. Cut-and-paste features and image-sizing techniques for repeating

TEACHING TIPS

Choosing Stories for Storytelling

- Choose only the best stories, stories which by virtue of style, theme, and plot beg to be told. Children deserve the best we can give them. Second rate is not good enough. Choose stories from all genre—legends, fantasy, biography, poetry, and so on.
- Investigate classic editions of works rather than the rewritten, watered-down versions so currently popular in the marketplace.
- Choose a story that speaks to you personally. A story you do not love will not be worth the telling since your own emotional involvement with the story is often a keynote to a successful presentation. Also, you're going to spend a lot of time with this story!
- Know your intended audience—age, interests, attention span, previous experience with stories. Trial and error may be your first guide to matching story with audience to find out what works well for you and the children. Do not be afraid to experiment, however.
- Read widely within all areas of literature. Always be on the lookout for the story which begs to be told.
- Develop a collection of stories that fit your personal storytelling style and meet your needs.
- Locate books, cassettes, records, CDs, and other forms of media devoted to storytelling. Choose good stories from these sources as well.
- Attend storytelling conferences and performances to listen to stories done by master storytellers. With their permission, often you can tape a story to learn later or buy a premade cassette or CD.
- Test your selections with the type of audience for which you intend to use it. Try your story, refine where necessary, or discard it if it does not meet your needs. There are many books, tapes, and CDs in the marketplace on stories and storytelling. Go to your school or public library to see what types of story collections, books on how to tell stories, and other materials are on hand. I'm sure you'll find a treasure trove at the library.

Source: Inez L. Ramsey. No date. Used by permission.

graphics, as well as animations, can enhance the telling of that story. Students can make a book jacket or poster using a program such as Kid Pix to interest other students in hearing a story they want to tell. Similarly, they can make maps to create the town or neighborhood of the characters in their story. They can find Aesop's fables online, cut and paste them into a Word document, and illustrate them to share electronically; then, after they tell the story, they can print it and give it to other students. Students can research storytelling from other cultures online. Japanese *kamishibai*, for instance, is a form of storytelling based on the use of illustrated cards that have the story written on the backs. Students can use a paint program to illustrate such cards as they tell a Japanese story. Sound clips and musical effects can be built into PowerPoint slides made with storytelling in mind. It is fun to create a slideshow for which the storyteller uses one voice in the recording and another, live voice during the actual performance, for an antiphonal arrangement for choral reading. Further, music and sound effects spruce up and augment the telling of stories. Check these helpful sites.

WEBLIOGRAPHY

- **The Art of Story Telling**
  http://www.seanet.com/~eldrbarry/roos/art.htm
  This site has links to resources for storytelling as well as links to storytelling groups and associations.
- **Digital Storytelling Festival**
  http://www.dstory.com/dsf6/home.html
  Not only does this site announce an annual storytelling event, it links to storytelling sites and activities. See the Teaching Tip "Digital Storytelling" for additional information.
- **The Kids' Storytelling Club**
  http://www.storycraft.com/files/welcome.htm
  This site has information about creating stories as well as hints for becoming a better storyteller.

TEACHING TIPS — Digital Storytelling

A new form of storytelling called digital storytelling is emerging. Digital storytellers are combining their text stories with photos, videos, or other graphics that are scanned and turned into electronic files for inclusion in a digital story. You can either start with the photos or illustrations and then write an appropriate story, or you can write the story and then draw illustrations or take digital photos that enhance the story. Digital stories are biographical or autobiographical in nature, perhaps because of the ease of placing original, digitized photos or videos online.

Digital storytelling is very likely to gain popularity quickly. "Digital storytelling begins with the notion that in the not too distant future, sharing one's story through the multiple mediums of digital imagery, text, voice, sound, music, video, and animation will be the principle hobby of the world's people." [Joe Lambert. Memory Box. **http://www.storycenter.org/memorybox.html**]

For more information about digital storytelling, contact The Center for Digital Storytelling at **http://www.storycenter.org/** or Joe Lambert and Nina Mullen, The Center for Digital Storytelling, 1803 Martin Luther King, Jr. Way, Berkeley, CA 94709. Telephone: 510 548-2065. Fax: 510 548-1345.

Plays and Acting

Children engage in more carefully structured speaking activities when they act in plays. Rehearsing and memorizing are part of preparing to appear before others to act, and this requires more cognitive effort. Use camcorders to record student plays, and then help students hone their acting skills by showing them how they look and sound during rehearsals. If students in your class have few experiences with acting, you will need to address such matters as self-consciousness, line memorization and delivery, eye contact with other actors, missed cues, and awkward-looking entrances and exits (Valmont, 1995). All of these, plus other aspects of play production, can be the subject for research and discussion. Children's Creative Theater at **http://tqjunior.advanced.org/5291** and Creative Drama and Theatre Education Resource Site at **http://www.creativedrama.com** are two web sources that will help you and students use plays as opportunities to speak before others.

NONFICTION PRESENTATIONS

Technology can help students make formal or nonfiction presentations.

One exciting development made possible by the WWW is the abundance of nonfiction materials now within the grasp of students everywhere. A wealth of information is available on the Internet, and once students gather information, they are often eager to share it with you and their peers. Often this sharing may represent the culminating stage of the writing process, the publishing stage (discussed in chapter 6). One way for students to "publish" their material is by giving an oral presentation. Several software programs facilitate the organization and sharing of information. Word and WordPerfect (word-processing programs); HyperStudio, AppleWorks, and PowerPoint (presentation programs); and SiteCentral and FrontPage (web page creation programs), among others, are computer applications that enable students to present their ideas before audiences. Students can make presentations while using a video projector to show electronic text documents, electronic slideshows, or online Internet pages—right from the Web.

Writing was discussed in chapter 6, but writing that accompanies oral presentations of information calls for a few additional considerations. Unlike many of the speaking activities using fiction, presenting nonfiction materials often calls for more sophisticated organizational skills and a more formal or structured type of presentation. Students may need help choosing or narrowing a topic that reflects both your curriculum and their interests. Ask students to use the K-W-L technique to tell what they know and what they want to know more about. Demonstrate for students effective ways to conduct research using both print and electronic sources. Guide them in taking and organizing notes, and coach them in successful presentation strategies.

Stress to students that they must be well prepared and that they must organize their presentations to help listeners understand their topic. An audience must believe that presenters know their subjects. Listeners must believe that the topics have some value for them, and they must want the speaker to help them learn. Help students understand that a strong introduction is important to "hook" the audience and pique their attention quickly. Remind students that the audience, throughout the presentation, has to understand the major points they make, that repetition helps fix ideas in listeners' minds, and that a summary aids retention. In other words, speakers help others remember better when they:

1. Prepare a strong introduction to the topic.
2. Use a logical progression to reveal major points.
3. Repeat ideas, facts, and major points.
4. Recap, or summarize, main points at the end.

Nervousness is generally a problem when students present, so teach them ways to relax both themselves and their audience. A joke sometimes helps both speakers and audiences loosen up. Humor throughout a presentation helps people pay attention because they do not want to miss a joke when others are laughing. Some students like to use presentation programs because the audience tends to pay attention to the projected images, helping the speakers feel less in the spotlight or under a microscope. Asking questions or otherwise engaging people in some interaction (e.g., voting) is another way to help audiences feel more comfortable.

Many presentations today are given using a computer connected to a television set or a computer video projector, formerly known as an LCD panel (liquid crystal display) before the technology evolved from showing light through a panel to casting computer images onto screens. Students need to be versed in a few important strategies when they use projection units.

Presentation Pointers

Here are a few general and a few specific pointers for using presentation hardware and software.

- Do not read the screen if the audience is capable of reading it.
- Do not stand between the projection unit and the screen or the audience and the screen.
- Speak clearly (articulate).
- Speak at a good tempo—not too fast or slow.

- ◆ Speak loudly enough for all to hear.
- ◆ Use graphics, sound, and props (when appropriate).
- ◆ Make your voice interesting (expression and tone).
- ◆ Use appropriate gestures (to emphasize points).
- ◆ Learn to use the presentation or other program well so you can use it very effectively.
- ◆ Rehearse and either cut or lengthen a presentation to the desired or required time.
- ◆ Do a trial run. (Have a friend listen and make suggestions.)
- ◆ Anticipate questions and prepare possible answers.

To *articulate* is to speak words clearly and distinctly. *Enunciating* means pronouncing words with precision, saying them without dropping sounds or endings (e.g., saying "going to" instead of "gonna"). Working with technology stimulates speaking, and you can encourage students to speak using effective enunciation skills when they share information. A word of caution is called for here. Home, community, and culture heavily influence students' pronunciations of words and their word usage (grammar). Unless articulation or enunciation problems are *major* barriers to communication, you may wish to deal with these matters only in response to a child's desire to use more formal language.

Presentation Software Programs

Software applications and computer video projectors help students share information.

Students can use computer software applications such as WiggleWorks, PowerPoint, HyperStudio, Digital Chisel, and mPOWER to create presentations. WiggleWorks, for instance, allows students to record into the computer and listen to themselves, rerecording if they want to sound better. Some of these programs can create HTML files that can be placed on a class or school web site. All are being used creatively to help students share stories and information with others.

Many students today are sharing their ideas with their peers and others because they can connect computers and computer video projectors. The ability to project computer images and the development of software applications that permit people to make fast and easy presentations have changed the way many students present their research findings or other projects. Here are a few points to consider:

- ◆ Keep text very brief.
- ◆ Use color to emphasize keywords or thought units.

- Use graphics to support or add to print ideas.
- Sound, video, and animations give additional dimensions to meanings being conveyed.

In helping students compose presentations for projection, you can discuss how to identify strong keywords or phrases to use as "headlines" or "bullets" on a screen. Single words, phrases, or sentences may convey major points, but each must communicate ideas succinctly. Point out to students that although they may use longer quotes, audiences tend to prefer having those read aloud. Aside from text, other symbols used must be clear, relevant, and easily discernible. **Navigation aids,** such as "forward" and "backward" buttons, are best kept small and out of the way of other objects on the screen. (See chapter 8, which deals with graphic and visual literacy, for additional ideas.)

SUMMARY

- Because of increasing opportunities to hear and speak to others, effective listening and speaking skills are growing more essential in the communications age.
- Classrooms must promote many and varied speaking and listening experiences so teachers can nurture the developing confidence and capabilities of young listeners and speakers.
- You can discuss and influence important understandings, skills, and attitudes to help students before, during, and after speaking and listening experiences.
- Multimedia computers deliver sights and sounds as well as permit electronic sharing opportunities, providing opportunities for many oral-aural classroom events.
- Listening-Thinking Activities help students learn to think during the electronic or personal presentation of both fiction and nonfiction materials.
- The Internet and other electronic materials contain rich resources useful for speaking.
- Presentation and web construction programs now make sharing electronically possible for wider audiences.
- You can teach students effective ways to use technology for presenting to others.

ACTIVITIES

1. Make lists of learning experiences you can use to encourage speaking and listening.
2. Choose a story at **http://www.the-office.com/bedtime-story/reference.htm,** then rehearse and read it to a group of students.

3. Find another story at that site to present as a Listening-Thinking Activity. Plan your strategy for stopping for discussions and predictions.
4. Help students use a program such as Kidspiration to design props for telling a fable.

SOFTWARE

AppleWorks, Apple, 6 & up
AppleWorks lets you place text, spreadsheets, digital photos, images, sounds, and movies into a document.

Digital Chisel, Pierian Spring, 6 & up
You and students can create multimedia projects and save them to disks or the Internet.

FrontPage, Microsoft, All
This is web page production software that permits you to create pages and forms, and it permits you to save information from users in databases.

HyperStudio, Knowledge Adventure, All
This multimedia creation program can be used to convert products into HTML files for posting on the WWW.

In My Own Voice, Sunburst Technology, 7 & up
Contemporary poets from all different ethnic backgrounds read their own poetry.

Julliard Music Adventure, Grolier Educational, K–8
Students solve musical puzzles.

Kid Pix Studio Deluxe, The Learning Company/Broderbund, K–8
Painting, animation, multimedia tools, and more are part of this popular program.

MovieWorks, Interactive Solutions, 8–12
You can make multimedia projects with sound using this authoring program.

MP Express, Bytes of Learning, K–12
This program allows students to narrate their presentations.

mPOWER, The Learning Company/Broderbund, K–12
You can make multimedia presentations using audio, video, graphics, and text, and convert them to HTML for publishing on the Web.

Music Loops for Multimedia, FTC Publishing Group, K & up
This has more than 300 royalty-free music bytes for use in multimedia projects.

Naturally Speaking for Teens, Dragon Systems, 6–9
This is speech-recognition software for teenage voices.

PowerPoint, Microsoft, All
This is a widely used presentation program.

Primary Reader's Theatre, Curriculum Associates, 1–4; ESL
Students can develop oral expression while acting out fables and fairy tale plays.

Romeo and Juliet: Center Stage, Sunburst Technology, 7 & up
This is the classic shown in script format annotated notes, and video. It includes interviews with the cast and director. Available only for Macintosh.

SiteCentral, Knowledge Adventure, All
You can turn HyperStudio projects into web pages with this creation application.

Sound Companion, FTC Publishing Group, K & up
This program allows students to edit sound files for use in HyperStudio and other programs.

Sound Effects for Multimedia, vols. 1 & 2, FTC Publishing Group, K & up
These are collections of sound effects.

Web Workshop, Sunburst Technology, 2–8
This is an easy program that young students can use to create web pages that you can publish free on Sunburst's web site.

FOR FURTHER READING

Knee, R., Musgrove, A., & Musgrove, J. (2000). Lights, camera, action! Streaming video on your web site. *Learning & Leading with Technology, 28*(1), 50–53.

Pieronek, F. T. (2001). Inservice project: Upper primary Brunei Darussalam teachers' responses to using four specific reading strategies. *The Reading Teacher, 54*(5), 522–532.

Vardell, S. M. (1998). Using read-aloud to explore the layers of nonfiction. In R. A. Bamford & J. V. Kristo (Eds.), *Making facts come alive: Choosing quality nonfiction literature K–8*. Norwood, MA: Christopher-Gordon.

CHAPTER

8

Using Technology to Develop Graphic and Visual Literacy

INTRODUCTION

Long before there was verbal communication, people relied on visual, nonverbal communication. They communicated through body actions and gestures—for example, perhaps running in place to suggest that the group needed to leave an area. Later, people began to use signs, symbols, and drawings to *represent* things in their surroundings. Perhaps the first images were created to evoke the memory of something that had been seen but was not physically present (Hugo, 1996). As is true today, signs and other symbols that were used long ago required *shared meanings* in order for communication to occur. That is, both the creator and the interpreter of a sign or symbol must share a common understanding of what a symbol means.

Today, students are bombarded with thoughtfully planned visual images that try to persuade them to do—or not do—certain things (e.g., images that accompany slogans such as "Got milk!" with a white milk moustache). It is vital for you to help students learn to be both visually literate and media literate. Writer and illustrator Steve Moline supports the trend toward teaching students to interpret and construct visual texts. He is the author of *I See What You Mean: Children at Work with Visual Information* (1995). Moline's book contains more than one hundred examples of student works that illustrate how some concepts are communicated better with visual texts than with verbal texts alone. Students, according to Rakes (1999), "need to be able to think critically about and manipulate visual information and make a solid interpretation of its meaning" (p. 14). Students who engage in creating visual messages learn to understand them better. Graphical user interfaces (GUIs) such as icons, button bars, and other objects that appear on a page, says Rakes (1999),

> are actually altering print-based literacy skills by making visual thinking as important as basic reading skills. In print-based materials, we have

> frequently been able to ignore visual images and get what we need from the text. In the new multimedia environments, graphic images are frequently an active part of the process of interacting with the text. In a hypermedia text, students must understand the visual cues in order to be able to physically move through the text materials available. (p. 14)

Clearly, we live in a polysymbolic world that was not possible before the digital age, and we must help students deal with the new literacies surrounding them.

Visual Literacy

This chapter presents some of the basics of visual literacy. To be visually literate, students not only need to *interpret* other people's nonverbal messages, they must also learn to *construct* effective visuals to help them convey their ideas to others (Bitter & Pierson, 1999; Heinich, Molenda, Russell, & Smaldino, 1999; Rakes, 1999). You can develop **visual literacy** using two major approaches, according to Heinich et al. (1999):

Visual literacy involves interpreting and constructing nonverbal messages.

> **Input strategies.** Helping learners to *decode,* or "read," visuals proficiently by practicing visual analysis skills (e.g., through picture analysis and discussion of films and video programs).
>
> **Output strategies.** Helping learners to *encode,* or "write" visuals—to express themselves and communicate with others (e.g., through planning and producing photo and video presentations). (p. 65)

At all grade levels, you and students can examine the use of basic visual elements in print and electronic materials as part of your efforts to foster visual literacy. Analyzing computer software images and images from the Internet can help students understand (i.e., decode or interpret) visual elements. **Internet literacy** includes "understanding the form the information comes in (image, text, audio, video) as well as the organization of that information" (Flatley, [Online]). Movies, television, videos, as well as photographs, graphics, and illustrations in books are major sources of visual materials to analyze. Students can learn much about visual literacy through learning to use a scanner and manipulating images with software such as PhotoShop. They can shoot and edit videos and use digital cameras. Creating art and visual presentations with software products as well as designing web pages or web sites are excellent ways for students think about and learn visual skills. Encourage students to hand-draw original art that can be digitized for inclusion in their work. Make opportunities for students to engage in photography and video learning experiences, perhaps by having them learn how to digitize such images. Print and desktop publishing software make useful production tools. You can read a discussion about visual literacy and teaching tips by Michael Milone, contributing editor of *Technology & Learning,* written specifically for this book's web site.

BASIC VISUAL ELEMENTS

Artists work with very basic visual elements in multitudinous ways to create diverse art productions. They have invented a truly amazing diversity of styles in a variety of artistic media. Visual elements are the basic building blocks of art, and they are commonly used by artists to evoke certain responses from viewers. That is, basic elements have a "language" of their own. Students must understand and use these basic elements as they construct electronic materials for presentations or web pages. This brief listing names the basic elements and some of the common thoughts they evoke in viewers:

Basic Visual Elements

- **The dot.** The dot catches our attention. Dots in a series suggest motion and direction.
- **The line.** Straight, curved, or with irregular shape, lines link or intersect other elements and often define a space. The thickness of lines can evoke feelings of strength or weakness. Horizontal lines often evoke a sense of balance, vertical lines tend to stop eye movement, and diagonal lines tend to evoke the feeling of movement and excitement.
- **Shape and dimension.** Shape is two-dimensional and encloses space. Circles, squares, and triangles are commonly used shapes.
- **Direction.** Direction is the impression of movement.
- **Value.** Value is the presence or absence of light. Artists sometimes use thirteen steps, or shadings, in value (black to white) to show the degree of lightness or darkness of an object.
- **Hue and saturation.** These are concerned with the makeup of color. The primary ("pure") colors are red, yellow, and blue. The secondary colors—orange, green, and purple—are created by mixing two primary colors. Often, artists refer to the "temperature" of colors, indicating that red, orange, and yellow are "warm" colors, whereas green, blue, and purple are "cool" colors.
- **Texture.** You can touch actual texture in some works of art, but in others the artist creates an "effect" of how a texture might feel if it could be touched.
- **Scale.** This relates to the relative size and measurement of an image.

Students must realize that verbal *and* nonverbal messages communicate to us.

Fostering the development of visual literacy is important both because we learn much of what we know through visual experiences, and because many of today's communications are developed in a multimedia format, with both verbal and visual information competing for our attention and causing us to think. Visual images can be completely nonverbal (e.g., dark clouds approaching or a sneer on a person's face) or contain verbal elements (e.g., logos or icons that include some letters or words). The Teaching Tip "A Middle School Experience with Icons" illustrates some of the value of encouraging students to construct visual images.

As stated previously, even before people spoke words—or made symbols or words—people communicated. Through the years, oral and written language appeared, and literacy came to be defined (until very recently) primarily as one's ability to read and write. The ability to produce and interpret verbal messages has been the hallmark of the educated person, and teaching reading and writing have had high priorities in

TEACHING TIPS: A Middle School Experience with Icons

Maya Eagleton, now a researcher at the Center for Applied Special Technology (CAST) in Boston, helped students at Flowing Wells Junior High School in Tucson, Arizona, create an e-zine (i.e., an electronic magazine) as part of her doctoral work at the University of Arizona.

Four media elements were particularly valuable to the seventh-grade students in Eagleton's (1999) study of e-zine creation by students. They are *text, graphics, photographs,* and *icons* (p. 163). Students' work with icons, in particular, led them to think about communicating visually and making decisions about meanings evoked by icons. Icons, said Eagleton, "are a convenient method for visually communicating a commonly agreed-upon cultural meaning in a small amount of space and are ubiquitous in the world of computers and the Internet" (p. 166). Students in the project created original icons for six sections of their e-zine. The icon for the "Editors" section is an illustration of a computer and mouse. The "People" section icon shows two hands shaking, one black and one white. The "Sports" section shows a basketball. The "Issues" section is a street with buildings on either side. The "Inner Self" icon is a door with a key above it, and the "Writing" section shows a quill and paper. It is interesting that the students saw editors as computer users and writers as quill users. "I think that this extra effort personalized the site and gave them a sense of ownership and control; I also believe that the process of envisioning and designing icons is a valuable cultural literacy activity and demonstrates the power of semiotic transmediation," said Eagleton (p. 167).

Source: Icons reprinted with permission of Maya Eagleton.

schools. The ability to interpret the world through seeing is extremely important, but visual skills have been taken for granted. It is important to consider that when a baby opens its eyes for the first time, it immediately starts to develop visual capabilities that help it make sense of the world. We sometimes forget that people "read" the sway of trees to help determine the current state of the weather. People "read" the struts and swaggers or the timid movements of teenagers to try to decide how adolescents might be feeling about themselves, and people "read" art to sense its meaning. Helping students become visually literate as well as verbally literate must become education's major thrust in preparing people to live in a multimedia, polysymbolic world. The explosion of images on CD-ROMs and the Internet alone behooves us to take immediate steps toward helping students improve visual literacy skills. According to Labbo (2000, p. 545), "Children who are invited to note how multimedia effects are used by software animators may come to appreciate unique aesthetic qualities of digital storytelling related to tone, texture, and mood." In other words, examining media helps students understand and appreciate how the media work.

Several online references may be useful to you in learning more about visual literacy.

WEBLIOGRAPHY

- **Reading Online**
  http://www.readingonline.org/
  This IRA journal's site includes an excellent section called "New Literacies" that contains numerous online articles about visual literacy, media literacy, and critical literacy.

- **Some History of Visual Literacy**
  http://www.asu.edu/lib/archives/vlhist.htm
  This page, an excerpted chapter from a book on the subject, contains a brief history of the importance of vision and the ability to learn and communicate visually.

- **Visual Literacy**
  http://www.people.memphis.edu/~kjob/wbi/VisualLiteracy.html
  This is an outstanding source of information about visual literacy. The site includes definitions and colorful examples of elements discussed in this chapter.

A MEDIACENTRIC WORLD

Students must understand how people try to manipulate them through images.

Students live in a mediacentric world, and computers capable of delivering audio, video, graphics, photographs, and animations as well as text have enabled the combining of the language and visual arts into a single teaching and learning instrument. It is particularly important for you to help students at all grade levels understand that many of the images they encounter have been crafted specifically to influence their thinking, and they must learn to understand, interpret, and think critically about many different kinds of visual images. Students need to recognize that we interpret visual images through the filters of our own cultures, meaning that different cultural groups may see and interpret visual materials quite differently (Heinich et al., 1999). Through discussions, you can help students learn to understand and assess multimedia events and understand how the nonverbal elements they see affect their thinking.

As pre- or in-service teachers, you have perfectly valid reasons to work with art (graphic design), music (a nonverbal communication medium involving aesthetics and emotion), drama (nonverbal behavior), advertising (visual elements of propaganda), and visual sign systems (e.g., the international symbols for identifying restrooms and traffic directions). In fact, some notable literacy educators (Lapp, Flood, & Ranck-Buhr, 2000, p. 318) suggest that the term "literacy" should "encompass competence in all of the 'communicative arts,' including the visual arts of drama, art, film, video, television, and other technological innovations." Others agree, stating, "Visual art is another means of conveying meaning. Just as readers encounter written text, they must also interpret the visual clues and artistic representation" (Johnson, Giorgis, Bonomo, Colbert, Connor, Kauffman, & King, 2000, p. 604).

You can read or download an online report of seven major studies of the impact of arts on learning titled "Champions of Change" at **http://artsedge.kennedy-center.org/champions/.** The report summarizes the research of James S. Catterall, Shirley Brice Heath, and others, indicating that both learning and achievement are enhanced when the arts are integrated into students' educational experiences. "Arts-rich" students outperform "arts-poor" students on a variety of measures, and the arts impact students in positive ways in cities and in poorer communities. Literacy is very much about *communicating,* and improved comprehension comes with the knowledge of a variety of ways to communicate to others and a better understanding of the communication methods other people use.

MEDIA LITERACY

Each medium uses strategies and conventions to help us interpret messages.

While visual literacy encompasses all things visual, media literacy typically refers to knowing how to interpret and create in the various mass communications media. A book is not the only communication medium that has protocols and strategies for conveying meaning. Each medium has its own conventions that developed over time. Therefore, you can study such media as art, music, radio, television, movies (or videos), video games, and online newspapers or magazines to determine what messages (strategies) people creating in those media intend for you to receive. For instance, in film and video, audiences have learned that very rapid "cuts" (i.e., quickly replacing one image with another) convey excitement, suspense, and action. (For example, in the movie *Psycho,* the famous murder in the shower scene used dozens of cuts.) Another common signal is the defocus-focus transition. When a scene ends with an image going out of focus, followed by a new scene that comes into focus from a blur, such a transition often denotes the passing of time. So does a shot of a tall, burning candle, followed by a dissolve and then the image of the same candle now burned almost completely down. A fade-out can signal the end of a scene or even the end of the entire movie (Valmont, 1995). Over time, people become familiar with such conventions and, with little effort, learn to interpret them. Producers and viewers share an understanding about what the conventions mean. Meaning is clear, and confusion is limited.

Because of the tremendous influence of mass communications, more and more teachers and schools are teaching media literacy, and you as a teacher interested in developing various kinds of literacies are in a position to help students learn to deal with our polysymbolic world. You probably know much about how advertisers on television and in printed materials appeal to your various senses (e.g., "very soft tissue"; "tastes like Mom's homemade cooking") to entice you to purchase their wares. You are probably quite media literate about visual elements of propaganda techniques that are especially plentiful around election time (e.g., a candidate for the other party is made to look foolish in photos). You may not have much experience yet with Internet literacy, the ability to interpret and construct the conventions used in web pages and web sites, but many of the same techniques used in other media are being used on the Internet. In addition, some of the "flash and whiz-bang" web capabilities being developed will undoubtedly create new conventions that you and students must come to understand and use.

Students must understand the evolving conventions of Internet literacy.

It is outside the scope of this book to explore media literacy fully because each medium has its own conventions for creating meaning that you could study in depth. You can learn much more about media literacy using online references as well as texts such as those written by Brunner and Talley (1999) and Taylor and Ward (1999). The following online references may entice you to learn more about media literacy.

WEBLIOGRAPHY

- **Just Think Foundation**
  http://www.justthink.org/
  This site, which has lessons, examples of student projects, and a list of resources, is worth visiting.

- **Media Awareness Network**
  http://www.media-awareness.ca/
  This excellent Canadian source of media literacy information has exceptional educational features.

Seeing-Thinking Activities

STAs elicit student thinking and predicting based on visual evidence.

In chapter 4 you learned about Directed Reading-Thinking Activities (DRTAs), and in chapter 7 you learned about Listening-Thinking Activities (LTAs). We will now discuss Seeing-Thinking Activities (STAs) because STAs can help you enhance students' visual literacy and predicting skills at all grade levels (Valmont, 1976). Students improve visual literacy by examining images for clues to help them identify objects and situations, making predictions and inferences based on graphic evidence, predicting possible story outcomes, and using visual evidence to predict events in wordless picture stories. STAs evoke the same behaviors you want students to engage in when they read verbal texts: using evidence, predicting, and confirming or revising their predictions. With STAs, students examine visual, nonverbal information as the basis for thinking. This appears to be nonthreatening and fun for most students and sharpens their attention to visual information.

STAs are easy to make, and we encourage you to use paint and graphics programs to create your own examples. Just as important, encourage students to create *their* own STAs because doing so gives students practice in constructing visual clues and arranging them in logical order, important aspects of visual literacy development. Four kinds of STAs, originally developed for the program See-Listen-Think (Valmont, 1976) are illustrated herein: Simple STAs, Single-Frame STAs, Alternate-Ending STAs, and Multiple-Frame STAs. You can see examples of all four types in a PowerPoint presentation on this book's web site. The PowerPoint examples model one way you and students can create and show your own STAs.

WWW

SIMPLE STAs

Seeing-Thinking Activities can be composed from line drawings, illustrations, or photos. Although examples in this book are from primary-level materials, you can use age-appropriate materials throughout the grades. You conduct a Simple STA by revealing, *in stages,* parts of common objects such as a button, kite, toothbrush, or fork. After seeing the initial piece of the object only, and at every stage thereafter, students examine the available evidence and predict what the illustration will be when they get to see the final image. Start by asking, "What do you think this object will be when I'm finished drawing (or showing) it?" "What makes you think that?" At first, encourage many ideas. *Divergent* thinking is called for at the beginning of the activity, when there are many possibilities. As you reveal each new piece of evidence, stop and discuss the old and new predictions. Some ideas will be dropped because the evidence now rules them out, and other, new predictions may arise. Eventually, *convergent* thinking will lead students to identify the object just before they see the final, complete, illustration. Many common objects can be revealed in four to six stages. Figure 8.1 shows one way to reveal an object in stages. Of course, students cannot see the images out of order or before making predictions about each stage, so you need to cover illustrations or place them on different slides to keep them hidden.

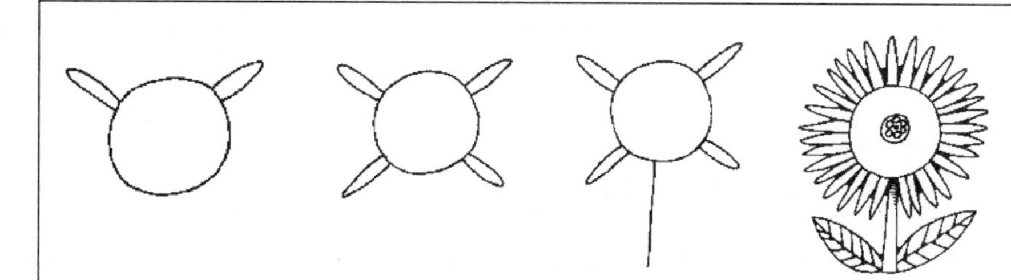

FIGURE 8.1

A Flower Revealed in Stages

Simple STAs are fun to create with HyperStudio, PowerPoint, Digital Chisel, or similar programs. You do not have to be a great artist or have lots of art supplies or computer software to construct your own STAs. Here are some guidelines to help you:

- Select an object that is appropriate for the age and interests of the students.
- Determine the order of revealing evidence, ensuring that the early evidence could lead to the naming of several objects.
- Make the illustration so that the first few lines will positively not reveal the object.
- Experiment with several ways to reveal the evidence until you are satisfied that students will not be able to identify the object too early in the process.
- Present the activity electronically using a computer projector or TV to show the object.
- Tell students that you are going to show them something and that you want them to predict what they think the final drawing will reveal.
- Obtain initial predictions, and then continue to reveal the object in stages, stopping to obtain new predictions and to discuss the various ideas that are expressed.
- Accept predictions that are logically based on available evidence, but challenge ideas that seem frivolous.
- Let evidence speak for itself, and try not to reveal through your verbal or non-verbal behaviors whether students have identified the object before they see the last picture.
- Keep discussions brief enough to sustain interest but long enough to allow all who want to predict to do so.
- After you do several Simple STAs, encourage students to create their own—first on paper while deciding how to break down the object into its parts, then on a computer.
- Tell students how you decided to reveal the evidence the way you did in your STAs so that they better grasp the steps to creating their own.

SINGLE-FRAME STAs

Single-Frame STAs (SF-STAs) give students opportunities to examine illustrations or photos that contain more complex information than a single, simple object. The Teaching Tip "SF-STA—The Jumping Boys" offers

TEACHING TIPS SF-STA—The Jumping Boys

Ms. Kathy Floyd is a fourth-grade teacher at Prince Elementary school in Tucson, Arizona. In the following dialogue, she and five of her students are discussing The Jumping Boys, which I created as an SF-STA.

The teacher shows the SF-STA "The Jumping Boys" to a group of students.

KF. What is happening in this picture?
Jodi. Two kids are jumping on the bed.
KF. If you had a picture to show what happened before this one what would it show?
José. The boys playing.
Tevin. The boys rolling on the floor.
Jodi. The boys were bored.
KF. If you had a picture to show what happens next what would be in it?
Makardo. One boy will get hurt.
José. They will jump off the bed.
Jodi. No, they just fall off.
KF. What do you think, Courtney?
Courtney. I think the two boys were bored and were jumping on the bed.
KF. OK, but what do you think is going to happen next?
Courtney. There's a girl in the background.
KF. How do you know it is a girl?
Courtney. She is wearing a skirt, and it looks like she is wearing high heels.
KF. Where is this girl?
Makardo. I think they are in a store that sells beds. The girl is not their mom, but a saleslady.
Tevin. I think the lady will go get mom or dad, and the kids are going to get a spanking.
Makardo. I think the mom will walk in and tell the kids that they are grounded and can't do any fun stuff that they normally do.
KF. No TV, no phone, no going outside? Those kinds of things?
Makardo. Yes.
KF. One more idea, José?
José. I think those kids are having a sleepover, and those two are jumping on the bed. And the same thing happened as happened in that one song, "Ten Little Monkeys." *(Students sing the song and agree that one, if not both, of the boys will fall off the bed and break his head. Discussion continues.)*

Source: Used with permission of Kathy Floyd.

an example. You and students can draw and digitize your own illustrations or scan photographs or pictures clipped from magazines or newspapers to use as SF-STAs in electronic formats.

To conduct any SF-STA, show students a single illustration or photo and ask, "What is happening here?" Do not identify objects or explain the images. Rather, encourage students to use their ideas and experiences to describe what they think is happening. During the discussion, have students tell you what they might put in a new picture to show what happened right *before* the events in the image they just discussed. After discussion, ask them to tell you what they would put in a picture to show what might happen *next.* Students will use their background experiences and creative ideas to provide content for their hypothetical "before" and "after" illustrations.

Single-Frame STAs provide practice in activating schema (what they already know) as well as having students engage in predicting. Be accepting of all logical ideas, but challenge silly or off-the-wall comments that cannot be traced to evidence in the illustration. Let students' imaginations take flight. Encourage students to look for their own illustrations or pictures and do the same kind of "before" and "after" thinking on their own. Students can also write, word-process, or dictate stories based on these activities.

ALTERNATE-ENDING STAs

As adults, we realize that stories can end in a variety of ways. Alternate-Ending STAs (AE-STAs) demonstrate this idea graphically to students. To conduct an AE-STA, show an illustration or photo that establishes a setting for a story that will be shown in three frames. Next, show a picture that starts some action in the story. Finally, show and discuss, in turn, three possible endings for the story. Show the endings *after* students predict how they think the story will turn out. Often students think of endings you do not have an illustration for. This is a perfect time to assure students that their equally plausible endings show creative thinking and that many stories could conclude in several logical ways. The Teaching Tip "AE-STA—The Paper Bag" contains the establishing illustration, the start of the action, and three possible ways to end the story.

MULTIPLE-FRAME STAs

Wordless picture books can be used as a source of Multiple-Frame STAs (MF-STAs), or you can create your own. We have found that by cutting the same comic strip out of the newspaper over a period of time, we can eventually select six to eight frames that we can use as a story. Of course, we delete or cover words because they would not make sense in a new sequencing of the frames. The major purpose of MF-STAs is to give students opportunities to make predictions and inferences over a series of continuing observations. Start by having students tell what they think is happening in the first frame. Then have them predict what might happen next. After eliciting several predictions, show the second picture. As you go along, make certain students continue to see all of the frames previously

TEACHING TIPS

AE-STA—The Paper Bag

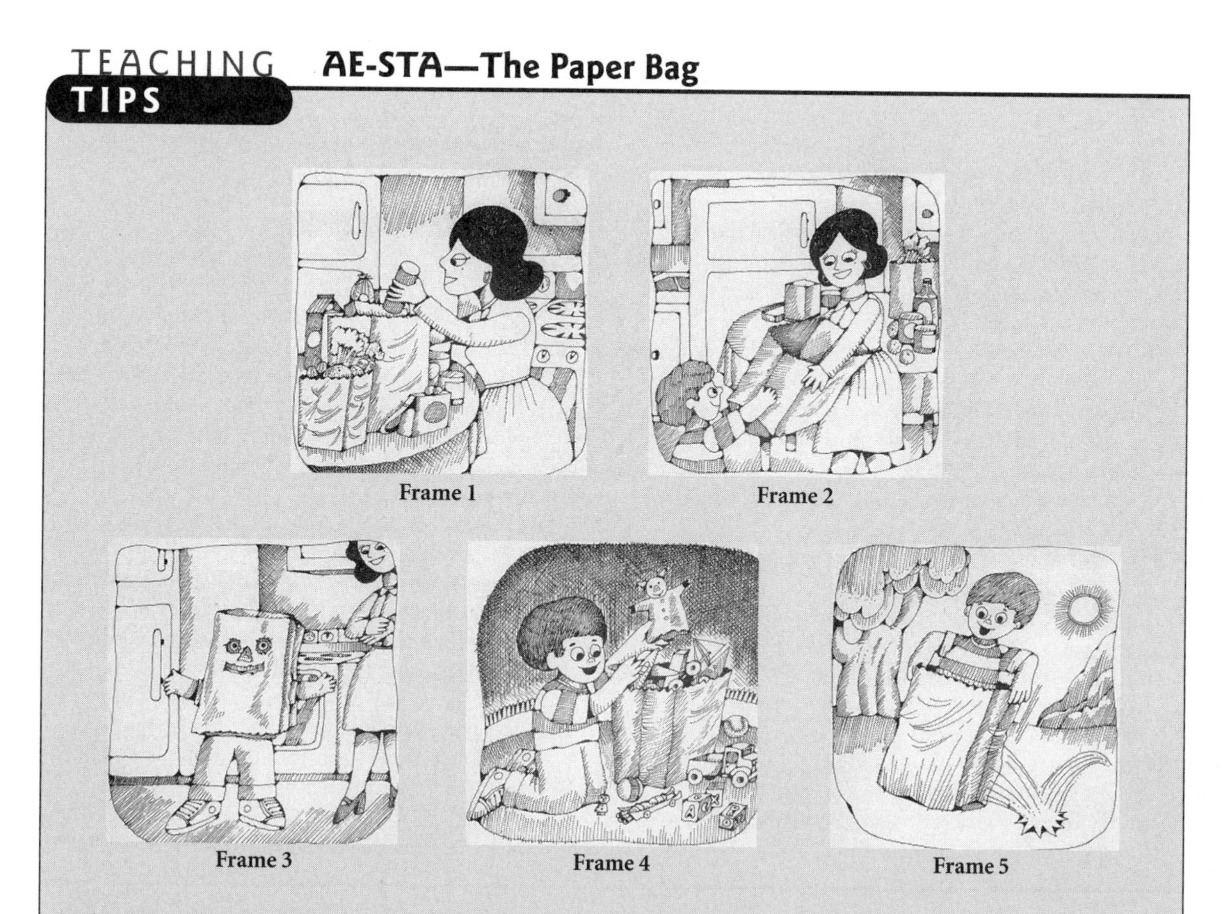

Frame 1 Frame 2 Frame 3 Frame 4 Frame 5

In this dialogue, Ms. Floyd, some of the same students, and some new students discuss The Paper Bag, an AE-STA.

KF. I'm going to give you a look at the first card, and I want you to buddy-buzz with your partner about what is happening. Also discuss what you think could happen next. *(Students talk together.)*

KF. OK, time's up. What do you think is happening in this picture? *(She places the picture on a holder.)*

Makardo. She's taking out groceries and putting them on the table.

Jodi. I think by the way she's holding it, the bag might break.

Makardo. It might slip out of her hand.

Sara. She just got back from the grocery store, and she's taking the groceries out.

KF. OK, what do you think might happen next?

Sara. She will put the things away in the cupboards.

José. I think it is the kid's mom who found him standing on a stool to reach the cookie jar on the fridge. [Note: This refers to an SF-STA that students predicted from earlier. This picture also shows part of a refrigerator, but this is a different story.]

KF. It's the mom from the kid and the cookies. Oh, so you think this picture should have come before the one of the boy trying to get the cookie jar off the refrigerator. Good connection to that other picture.

Tevin. Maybe she robbed all that stuff, and they recognized her dress, and the cops will come to her door and arrest her, and the kid will eat all of the food.

KF. What a great imagination. Here's the next card. It shows you the next part of the story. Tell your partner what you think is happening in the card and then predict what you think might happen next. *(She places the card on the holder to the right of the first one. Students talk together.)*

TEACHING TIPS
(continued)

KF. Tell me what's happening in this card.

Jodi. Mom is giving the bag to the kid, and he's going to put it on the refrigerator.

Tevin. I think she put the groceries on the table and said, "Honey, will you take these out to the garbage?" and he said, "Sure Mom, I'll take this to the garbage."

Andrew. The cookies are in the bag.

KF. You are saying that he is going to put the bag in the trash, or he will find cookies in the bag. Or just do something with the bag. Are there any other possible endings? If we had one more picture over here *(pointing to the right of the two cards on the holder)*, could there be something completely different from what you said might happen?

Sara. He's going to put the grocery bag away.

KF. Let's look at a couple endings that the author thought of. What happened in this ending? *(She places the card to the right of the two cards.)*

Andrew. He made a mask out of the bag.

KF. How many of you have done that? *(Several students say they have made masks.)*

Tevin. I did. I did. My mom told me to put a bag away, but I made a mask instead.

Sara. I brought a grocery bag to school and made a turkey. It ended up being in a play.

KF. How neat. Here's another ending that could possibly happen. What's he doing in this picture? *(She places the card on top of the previous card to reveal a second ending.)*

Nattely. He's putting stuff in the bag.

Tevin. He has an Afro puff now.

KF. Good observation, you're noticing details. In this picture he is putting toys in his bag, so maybe he's organizing or cleaning up. Here's the last idea of what he could do with the bag. *(She places the final card on top of the other two.)* What is this one?

Nattely. It's like what you could play at a party.

Jodi. A potato sack?

KF. Sack races. Good!

Nattely. When all of our family gathered up on New Year's Eve, at nighttime we kids would go outside and play sack races.

KF. Did you like the ideas the author had for ending the story? *(Students agree.)* You had different ideas. Were those good ideas? *(Students say "yes.")* Sure. The ways you said the story could end were good—even if they were different from the author's ideas. Good job! Very nice predicting.

Source: Used with permission of Kathy Floyd.

discussed in case they want to reexamine previous evidence. Encourage students to substantiate their predictions with their observations of the illustrations. Continue this routine through all but the final illustration. Before showing that one, see if there is group consensus about how the story will end. Then reveal the last picture and discuss it as necessary. Students who do not arrive at the ending depicted will feel all right if they have suggested equally plausible endings. This is why working with AE-STAs prior to using MF-STAs is a good idea. See the Teaching Tip "MF-STA—Making a Tent."

Throughout MF-STAs, it is important to encourage as many ideas as possible, to be positive in telling students they are good thinkers with good ideas, and to continue having students think by asking questions such as "What will happen next?" "Let's see if any of these ideas show up in the next picture?" and "How can we find out?"

TEACHING TIPS MF-STA—Making a Tent

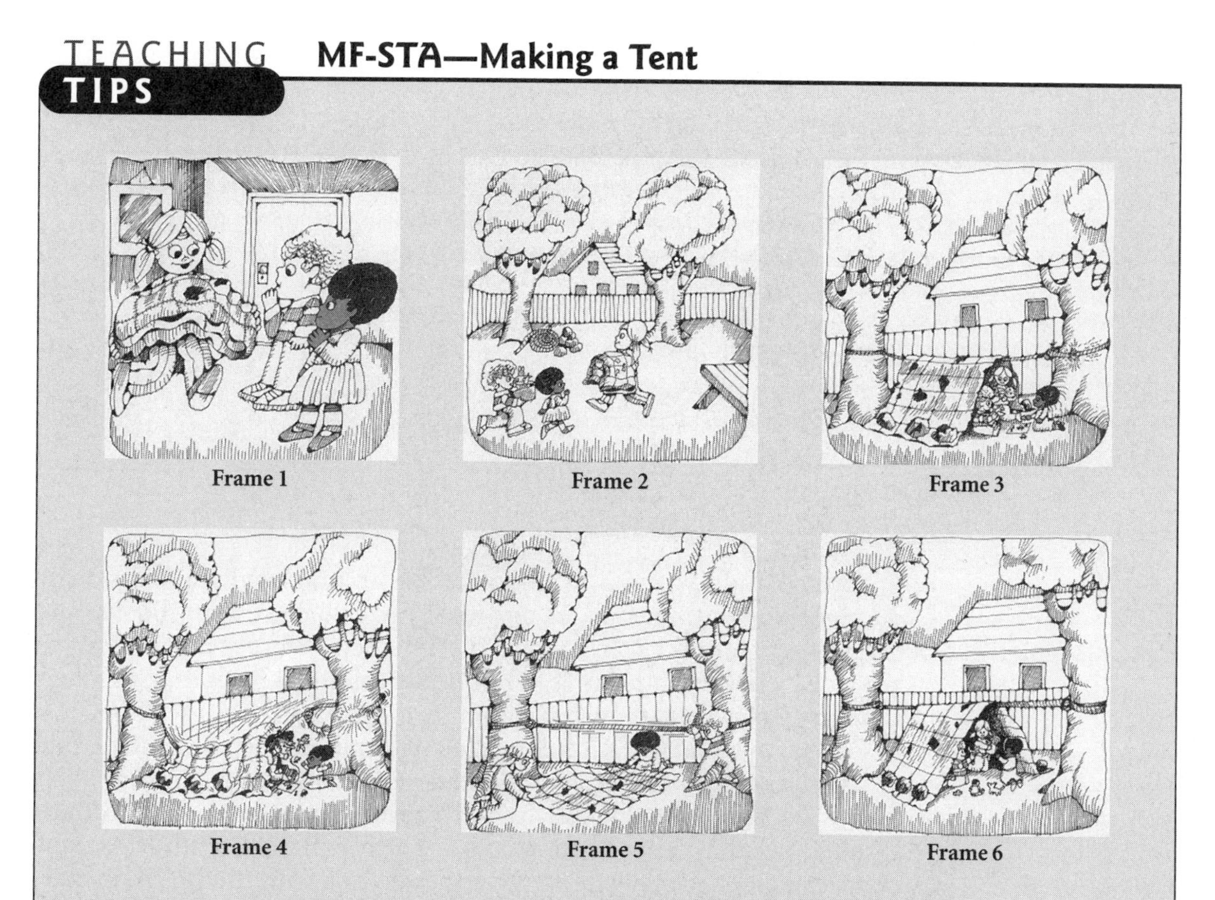
Frame 1 Frame 2 Frame 3 Frame 4 Frame 5 Frame 6

In the dialogue that follows, Ms. Floyd and several of her students discuss Making a Tent, an MF-STA.

KF. Today, we have a whole picture story. I'm going to ask you to predict what you think will happen next each time I show you a new picture. The cards will take up the whole length of this cardholder. Here's the start of the story. *(She places the first picture on a holder.)* Discuss it with your partner and predict what might happen next. *(Students talk together.)*
KF. What do you think might be happening?
Jonathan. Maybe they're going to have a play.
KF. What in this picture makes you think that?
Jonathan. She's got a costume.
KF. She's got a different-looking dress or outfit on. She may use it to act in a play.
Makardo. I think she's going to a sleepover. *(Several students agree.)*
Jackie. Me too! And do their hair.
Roy. They'll have a costume party.
KF. Good ideas! Next one. *(She places the second card to the right of the first.)*
Tevin. Yep, she was right.
KF. Who was right? Which prediction was right?
Tevin. Maybe a sleepover.
KF. So where are they, according to this card?
Several students. At camp. Outside. In the back yard.
Sara. They might have a picnic under the stars.
KF. Makardo said, "I was right. Whoo hoo!" What do you notice in this picture? *(She places the third card on the holder.) (Several students say they are camping.)*
KF. What do you think might be in the next picture?
Jackie. I don't know.
Andrew. S'mores.
Tevin. We make a fire and make s'mores with chocolate on them. We do. *(The students discuss food briefly.)*

TEACHING TIPS
(continued)

KF. Lets look. *(She puts the fourth card on the holder.)* What is happening?

Students. It crashed. The string fell down.

KF. Yes, their tent fell down. It crashed. What do you think will happen next? *(Several students discuss possibilities, but do not agree about what will happen next.)*

KF. Well, their tent just fell. Do you think they are going to fix it? They could say, "Ah, forget it!" *(Several students say, "Fix it!")*

KF. Here's the next picture. *(She puts the fifth card on the holder.)* What's happening?

Nattely. They're trying to fix it.

KF. Do you think they're going to do it? *(Almost all students say, "Yes.")*

KF. There's the final card. *(She puts the final card on the holder.)*

Roy. They fixed it. They made it tighter.

KF. You were all right. Good job of predicting.

Source: Used with permission of Kathy Floyd.

Today's students come to school having accumulated years of experience with visual materials in movies; from billboard signs, books, and magazines; and on television and the Internet. Before students learn to read, or if they can already read but need additional practice in reading-thinking behaviors, they can profit from engaging in the STAs just described. In addition, STAs offer students ample opportunities to discuss visual clues when objects and illustrations are inspected. Creating their own STAs can help students learn to reveal visual evidence to others through deciding what to show and what to withhold. With STAs, students can practice many of the strategies described in the DRTA, including specifically examining evidence, making predictions, and engaging in critical and creative thinking.

STAs are valuable because you conduct them in a nonthreatening, fun way where thoughts are expressed freely. Scanning artwork and adding navigation buttons lets you and students make electronic STAs. Several software programs can be helpful to students in making STAs. Multimedia Projects for Kid Pix (grades Pre-K–6) contains clip art and sounds for multimedia production. Multimedia Workshop (K & up) has multimedia authoring tools, photos, clip art, music, movie clips, and sound effects. Stanley's Sticker Stories (Pre-K–2) has characters students can use to make new animated electronic storybooks. It includes recording, playback, and printing options.

E-materials and Related Activities to Enhance Visual Literacy

An abundance of software and free online sites exist to develop visual literacy.

Many web sites contain arts and crafts activities you can use to help students study elements of visual literacy. At art sites, students can discuss a variety of styles of visually pleasing art from both famous and unknown painters and illustrators. Students can locate specific examples of visual design elements such as color, shape, texture, etc. They can learn that some art is mere decoration, while other art can interact with story plots and can be integral to telling a story both verbally and visually. Students can engage in arts and crafts activities such as printing graphics on transfer paper and ironing them onto T-shirts.

The beauty of sites containing artistic activities is that students can try out the techniques they see. While commercial paint programs have let artistically challenged students use art for making stories or presentation graphics, the downside is that some students may fail to develop their own artistic talents (Meltzer, 1999–2000). Clip art is quick and easy for amateur artists, but you should encourage and help students use all of their potential artistic skills because visual literacy skills develop through practice, and students need to learn to communicate visually using their own constructions. Figure 8.2 shows one student's artistic renditions and the clip art that inspired them.

FIGURE 8.2

Figure Art vs. Hand-drawn Art

Source: Reprinted with permission of Michael Tringali and his parents.

ART ACTIVITIES AND LESSONS

You can find useful software programs to help students learn about art. For example, The Art Lesson (grades K–4) deals with art basics, and Mexico's Day of the Dead (grades 4–9) shows art projects from Mexico and has information about Mexico's annual Day of the Dead traditions. **Applets** add interesting art to web pages; see "Adding Movement to Graphics" on this book's web site to learn ways to obtain some applets from online sources.

WWW

Not all art sites fit into neat categories, but several sites are worth including in your efforts to introduce students to visually interesting web sites.

WEBLIOGRAPHY

- **A. Pintura: Art Detective**
  http://www.eduweb.com/pintura
  This site offers "The Case of Grandpa's Painting," an interactive, branching story. Students make decisions from each story page about what they want to see next. Interactive activities in almost any subject can be a springboard for language arts and visual literacy activities.
- **The Art Teacher Connection**
  http://www.artteacherconnection.com/
  This site, created by Bettie Lake, an elementary arts teacher, has art web lessons, lesson plans, handouts, and links to other sites dealing with the visual arts.
- **AskERIC Lesson Plans**
  http://askeric.org/cgi-bin/lessons.cgi/Arts
  The "Arts" page contains links to art lessons that include step-by-step directions.
- **Crayola**
  http://www.crayola.com
  This site has facts about crayons and fun activities as well as the names of colors used by the company throughout time. Students can mix their own crayon color, color and print pages, and learn facts about colors.
- **A Lifetime of Color**
  http://www.sanford-artedventures.com
  This site, maintained by the Sanford Corporation, includes a timeline of art from 15,000 B.C.E. through the twentieth century. You can learn about the principles and elements of art, color, and various media, styles, and artists at this site.

CARTOONS AND COMIC STRIPS

Cartoons and comic strips can be used to enhance comprehension, and you can study them for their use of basic graphic elements. Understanding of both verbal and graphic symbols often depends on shared knowledge about a character or event from children's literature, a current event, a classic children's movie, or the Internet itself. You and students can search for and discuss meanings that cartoonists and their readers must share to understand and appreciate a cartoon or comic strip. You can view more than sixty different comic strips at **http://www.ucomics.com/comics/.**

One of our favorite cartoonists is Pat Brady, the creator of "Rose Is Rose." The web site, at **http://www.unitedmedia.com/comics/roseisrose,** contains archived cartoons you can study. Brady illustrates his stories using many storyboarding techniques, such as low-angle point of view (POV) (in his case, a cat's-eye view), and he is an expert at using techniques that give the illusion of fluid motion. The cartoons, an example of which appears in Figure 8.3, are full of excellent visual effects to discuss with students.

FIGURE 8.3

"Rose Is Rose" by Pat Brady

ROSE IS ROSE is reprinted by permission of United Feature Syndicate, Inc.

Use cartoons and comic strips to examine illustrations for subtle visual clues, as not all such clues are immediately obvious. Discuss artists' techniques for telling stories in one or more frames, as well as cartoonists' use of color, line, shape, and texture. Students can reach an understanding about why a cartoon is funny, sad, or whatever, and they can discuss what information they needed to know to understand a cartoon (e.g., a movie). Perhaps students can visit the Heathcliff site at **http://www.unitedmedia.com/creators/heathcliff/index.html** and explain why Heathcliff's actions are funny. Students can discuss why they think the cartoonist created a particular cartoon, and they can discuss how they might make a cartoon better for younger students. We recommend having students create original cartoons as well as draw their own cartoons in the style of their favorite cartoonist. Political cartoons and historical cartoons are particularly well suited for analyzing and discussing both their verbal and visual languages.

WEBLIOGRAPHY

- **Political Cartoons.com**
  http://www.politicalcartoons.com
  This site offers archived political cartoons and an index of American, Canadian, and international cartoonists. Lesson plan ideas for teaching with cartoons are also available.

ONLINE MUSEUMS

Use online museums containing art and photographs to analyze cultural influences on art. You can also discuss elements of design, introduce students to famous works and artists, and examine various genre of art.

WEBLIOGRAPHY

- **African Odyssey Interactive**
  http://artsedge.kennedy-center.org/aoi/home.html
  This site is devoted to African and African American art. There are links to art collections in several galleries throughout the United States and elsewhere.

- **The Children's Museum of Indianapolis**
  http://www.childrensmuseum.org
  Use the "Fun on-line" page to engage students in an "Arts Workshop" and have them create an online multimedia puppet show.
- **The Metropolitan Museum of Art**
  http://www.metmuseum.org/
  This site has more than 3,500 images from this New York museum's collections and exhibitions for you to examine.
- **The Virtual Library Museum Pages**
  http://www.icom.org/vlmp
  You can find online museum resources from all over the United States and throughout the world.

PHOTOGRAPHS

Students who want to learn about digital photography and related techniques—sizing or **cropping,** editing out part of an image, incorporating digital images in presentations, and so forth—should examine commercial photography sites. They often contain pertinent visual literacy ideas.

- **Kodak**
  http://www.kodak.com
  The company's web site offers picture-taking tips and information about digital cameras and ways to digitize photographs during film processing. "How to Get Started in Digital Photography" is part of the site. See it at **http://www.kodak.com/global/en/consumer/digitization/.**

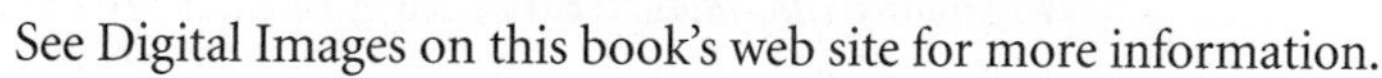

See Digital Images on this book's web site for more information.

THEATER ARTS

Students can use online Readers' Theatre scripts to engage in acting (see chapter 7), and you can use theater arts–related web sites to discuss nonverbal behaviors, pantomime, and other visual movements. Children's Creative Theater at **http://tqjunior.thinkquest.org/5291/** has a history of the theater, terminology, games, and a play's script.

Student Design of Web Pages, Web Sites, and Reports

Students learn much about constructing visuals through creating web pages, web sites, and reports.

Increasingly, teachers are encouraging students to design web pages containing their original works. Students are even helping schools design multipage web sites that present information about the school, the community and its people, student projects, and much more. Students are enthusiastic about being "web publishers" who can share their interests and information with the world, and the educational values evoked by web site creation are high. Students learn a great deal about visual literacy when they plan and produce pages or entire sites because you and they must make hundreds of decisions about both form and content. This means that opportunities to study and use verbal and visual elements abound. There is no one right or wrong way to make web pages or sites, as you can tell from looking at the variety of pages on the WWW. However, some traditional conventions are useful, and new protocols are emerging that can lead to greater success for you and students. You can read "There's No Place Like Home," in which fifth-grade students discuss their working on school web sites, at this book's site.

Among the decisions students will need to make regarding the visual and verbal elements of their web page site are the following:

- The name of the page or web site
- The colors of text, background, or other elements on the page
- The type sizes and font styles they will use
- The graphics such as photographs and logos
- The graphic elements such as dots or lines
- The animation, sound, and video elements they want to include
- The *internal* links to other pages of their site or *external* links to other sites
- The contact information (e.g., including a name, post office address, telephone number, fax number, and an e-mail link to the webmaster)
- Any other elements (e.g., "hit counters" and guest books to collect e-mail addresses of people who visit the site) used

There is much good advice about web design online.

WEBLIOGRAPHY

- **Designing School Web Sites to Deliver**
  http://www.fno.org/webdesign.html
  This site discusses reasons for having a school web site, offers suggestions for creating one, and provides examples and copyright information.
- **Fundamentals of Web Design**
  http://www.eserver.org/design
  The "Favorite URLs" link leads to other pages that demonstrate or explain basics of web site design.
- **Selection Criteria: How to Tell If You Are Looking at a Great Web Site**
  http://www.ala.org/parentspage/greatsites/criteria.html
  This page, which explains why sites were chosen for inclusion in the ALA's 700+ Great Sites listings, contains hints about effective web site construction.
- **Top Ten Mistakes in Web Design**
  http://www.useit.com/alertbox/9605.html
  While several years old, this page has advice that is still pertinent. You and students can decide if you agree with the author's assessment of what constitutes a mistake.

WHAT YOU NEED TO GET STARTED

To create a web site for a class or school, you will need a computer with full sound and video capabilities, ample storage capacity, and either a modem for dialing a local Internet service provider through a telephone line or an Ethernet card to connect the computer to a high speed (T1) Internet line or a wireless system. You will also need a recent web browser such as Netscape Communicator or Microsoft's Internet Explorer (both are free, and Netscape Composer lets you create web pages).

One major immediate consideration is where you will store your web files. Check to see if the school or district has a server you can use. You will need to know how much file space you can use and how to handle graphics, which may need to be limited. You should also find out the features of the web server software and its capabilities to carry out such tasks as placing data from web forms into a database. Technical support of your web efforts is another major consideration. Several sites on the Web house school or class web sites free, but some schools do not permit teachers to

use such sites. GeoCities at **http://geocities.yahoo.com/home/** is one such site. See this book's web site for additional information about placing web pages or web sites online free of charge.

Creating web pages and web sites has become easier with the arrival of friendly educational products.

Some basic knowledge of HTML (hypertext markup language) is worth having, even if you use a software application such as Microsoft's FrontPage that allows you to create and edit web pages. Knowledge of HTML permits you solve problems when you are using a web design program and find something does not work the way you want. Online help is available from "The Bare Bones Guide to HTML" at **http://werbach.com/barebones,** which contains the basic HTML symbols used to turn text documents into WWW documents. The "Interactive HTML Tutorial" at **http://www.coedu.usf.edu/inst_tech/publications/html** is another fine page for a beginner: you get to try out the HTML features.

BASIC WEB DESIGN GUIDELINES

You will want to help students create the best web sites they can produce. One major goal is to make a site that is *legible and easy for visitors to interpret.* Another goal is to ensure that the site will *actively engage those who visit it.* In addition, you should help students create a site at which visitors will focus on the most important parts of each page's message.

Following basic design guidelines leads to better results in designing web sites.

You can combine the basic elements of visual design in countless ways, permitting you and students to create unique web pages and sites. While the following will help you develop attractive, eye-catching, and informative web pages, achieving aesthetically pleasing results involves both art and skill in combining many factors. Unless expert guidance is available, you and students might wish to do a great deal of experimenting before reaching a consensus that you have designed the best web site possible. These are some design basics to consider:

- **Balance.** Balance gives a sense of equilibrium to a web page, making the reader feel comfortable while viewing it. Either symmetrical or asymmetrical balance is pleasing to the eye. With the first, both halves are identical. With the latter, the sides are not identical but have a similar visual weight or attractiveness. You may balance elements horizontally or vertically, or you can radiate objects that are identical (or similar) out from a point that is central in the page.
- **Emphasis.** Emphasizing a portion of a visual image makes it stand out and, therefore, gives it more importance. Artists use contrast as well as isolation to provide emphasis, or they place information in an important location on a visual. Research indicates that people start to read at the top left corner of a computer screen, then they read down the screen, check out the graphics on the right side of the screen, and move to the navigation elements (Korolenko, 1997, p. 152). Using

elements that cause the viewer to converge on a certain spot or using something novel, unique, or out of place helps lend emphasize to a part of a display.

- **Harmony.** When the various parts relate to one another and complement one another, harmony results. You achieve harmony by organizing objects in a display, using color (or not), and repeating graphic elements.
- **Movement.** You can create the illusion of movement in a graphic by repeating an image, changing a shape, using diagonal lines or curves, changing the color of one part of an image, or implying direction (e.g., showing a marching band with members facing the same direction).
- **Perspective.** Artists use overlapping objects to create a feeling of depth. They also use relative sizes to indicate that some things are "closer" than others. Another technique is to make the background "out of focus" while keeping objects in the foreground sharp. Perspective conveys a feeling of reality to an image. In the real world, we know that some things are closer than other things, and we like to see depth in graphic images, also.
- **Unity.** Unity helps all of the graphic elements in a display "work together." Unity results from creating well-organized images, choosing similar shapes or patterns, using space, or selecting common backgrounds on which you place other objects.
- **Variety.** Variety adds interest or novelty to an image. Contrasts in elements, size changes, point of view, and changing angles are ways to add variety to visual images.

LAYOUT CONSIDERATIONS

Using the basic design features just mentioned can help you and students achieve a nice appearance on a web page or web site. The following are some additional suggestions that will be helpful to people visiting your site:

- Use frames and tables to control the layout of web pages. Objects you place inside a frame or table maintain their relationship to other objects in other frames or areas of tables without getting out of alignment. (Note: Some web browsers do not handle frames, so you might want to also create an alternative page without frames for people who cannot access them.)
- Place an easy-to-find-and-read title on each web page. Make the title clear and descriptive of its content.
- Describe the purpose of a web page in the first few inches of the top of the main page. Viewers need to know quickly whether they want to stay at your site or leave to visit other sites.
- Put things in logical order. Make it easy for viewers to understand relationships in the information on your site.

- Avoid visual clutter. Have some areas with no text or graphics ("white space"). Viewers generally tend to avoid extra-full sites.
- Use left-hand justification because it tends to give order to a page.
- Use spacing, lines, borders, and background colors to unify objects.
- Keep graphics small. Use **thumbnail illustrations** (very small renderings) of photographs or graphics. Provide links to larger versions for people who want to see more detail.
- Keep the screen's width useable for most computers. Long lines of print are hard to read.

It is important for you to create web pages or sites that people needing assistive technologies can use. Learn about the Universal Design for Learning and Bobby, a free web service that will analyze your pages, at the Center for Applied Special Technology (CAST) web site at **http://www.cast.org/.**

TYPOGRAPHY CONSIDERATIONS

Typography is the appearance and arrangement (composition) of print or electronic text. The choice of font style (typefaces) and text size, as well as consistent use, are important considerations in web page design. It is best to stay with common, simple fonts because they are usually present on most computers. Unusual fonts cannot be seen if a computer does not have them installed. Consider these important ideas about fonts:

- **Use readable fonts.** Many designers recommend using a sans serif font such as Helvetica or Arial. Times New Roman and Courier New are fonts with serifs that are widely used, also.
- **Use no more than four variations of a font** (Heinich et al., 1999). (Italics, boldface, underlines, outlines, and size changes are all font variations.)
- **Give each style a purpose.** You might use a regular style for running text and italics for emphasis. Regardless, be consistent throughout a web site about the use of font size and style.
- **Avoid using underlining.** People associate underlined words in electronic text with hyperlinks that take viewers elsewhere, and when this does not happen, they wonder why—or they think a link is not working properly.
- **Use 12- or 14-point type.** For most text, these sizes will suffice, but you may have occasion to use a larger or smaller font for special purposes.

The online Web Style Guide at **http://info.med.yale.edu/caim/manual/contents.html** is full of advice on constructing web pages and sites.

You can download from the Internet many free backgrounds, navigation buttons, images, sounds, and so forth, for noncommercial purposes. Of course, you must adhere to copyright laws and ensure that any image you download does not come from a page that contains text prohibiting the copying of that image. Several sites specifically grant you permission to download from their collections. You can find additional sources of free materials at this book's web site.

WWW

WEBLIOGRAPHY

- **Bellsnwhistles.com**
  http://www.bellsnwhistles.com
  This is a premier site where you can find animations, clip art, and much more.

ANALYZING WEB PAGES AND WEB SITES AS AN AID TO WEB DESIGN

Studying visual elements at sites and from presentations aids student production.

You can find excellent sites (e.g., ones that are visually pleasing) and unattractive sites (e.g., ones that have irritating scrolling marquees) through exploring the Web, and you will quickly decide what you think is pleasing and helpful and what is not. Encouraging students to evaluate web sites enables you to emphasize higher-order thinking skills. People have created criteria for assessing web sites, so you and students might want to study such ideas and create a set of criteria of your own. Criteria are meant to be helpful—not to dampen enthusiasm or to stifle creativity.

WEBLIOGRAPHY

- **Evaluating the Quality of World Wide Web Resources**
  http://www.valpo.edu/library/evaluation.html#top
  This site presents evaluation criteria and includes exercises and worksheets for web evaluation.
- **Evaluation of Web Resources**
  http://www.library.csustan.edu/lboyer/webeval
  This very thorough site contains links to other sites that deal with WWW evaluation. It has guidelines for evaluating several kinds of web sites (e.g., business, news, personal sites).

CREATING VISUALLY RICH MULTIMEDIA REPORTS

You can make web pages using several software programs. PowerPoint, Word, WordPerfect, and AppleWorks all can save files as HTML documents. SiteCentral allows you to use HyperStudio cards as web pages. Adobe PageMill has a tutorial that makes the software easy to learn. In addition to web page production products, visit web sites for product information.

WEBLIOGRAPHY

- **HyperStudio**
  http://www.hyperstudio.com
  This site has information about HyperStudio and shows examples of projects created with this software. It also contains a description of electronic portfolios.

- **PowerPoint in the Classroom**
  http://www.actden.com/pp
  This is an online tutorial about PowerPoint's features.

- **Shockwave.com**
  http://www.shockwave.com/sw/home/
  At this site you can learn about and view the Web's capabilities to deliver sound and video. Click on some of the free animations to see their quality and listen to the sound, also.

Visual literacy is now very much a part of planning and preparing electronic presentations for others. Students are learning to share their ideas with their peers and others because of the ability to connect computers to computer video projectors. The ability to project computer-generated texts and images and the increase in software applications that permit people to make thoughtful presentations have changed the way students can present their research findings and other projects. All hints and strategies used to create materials for web sites are equally pertinent when creating presentations. Here are a few other points to consider.

- Because of space constraints, text is generally very brief.
- Appropriately sized fonts are needed for ease of viewing from a distance.

- ◆ Backgrounds must be pleasant but unobtrusive.
- ◆ Color can be used to emphasize keywords or thought units.
- ◆ Colors must contrast well in order to project well.
- ◆ Graphics must support or add to print ideas, not be distracting.
- ◆ Sound, video, and animations convey additional dimensions of meaning.

In helping students construct presentations for video projection, you will want to discuss how to identify strong keywords or phrases to use as "headlines" or "bullets" on a screen. Major points can be expressed as single words, phrases, or sentences, but each must convey ideas succinctly. While students may use longer quotes, audiences tend to prefer having them read aloud.

Software such as Kid Pix, HyperStudio, mPOWER, and PowerPoint are programs used widely in schools to help students create polysymbolic presentations.

SUMMARY

- Computer technology enables instantaneous reception of verbal and nonverbal messages.
- Students must develop both visual and verbal literacy competencies to fully comprehend.
- Interpreting and constructing nonverbal messages aids understanding of how they work.
- Students must understand how media's specific conventions create and evoke meaning.
- Seeing-Thinking Activities help students examine graphics in order to make inferences.
- STAs enable students to examine evidence, predict, and think even before they can read words.
- Ample software and free online web sites exist that can be used in dealing with visual literacy.
- You and students can discuss and develop visual design skills through making web sites.

ACTIVITIES

1. Help students design icons or buttons that quickly convey an idea about a page's content.
2. Use examples of STAs from this book's web site, or create new STAs, and try them with students.
3. Examine software or web sites and plan a lesson about some of the graphics you find.
4. Ask students to find "good" and "not-so-good" web sites and explain why they evaluate each site as such.

SOFTWARE

Digital Chisel, Pierian Spring Software, 7 & up
This is a multimedia authoring tool that lets you publish on disk or as HTML on the Web.

Diorama Designer, Tom Snyder Productions, 2–6
This software contains elements to use in creating dioramas illustrating various historical periods.

FrontPage, Microsoft, 7 & up
This is a web page and web site development tool. No HTML knowledge is needed. You can save data from online forms into Access databases.

The Graph Club, Tom Snyder Productions, K–4
Students can create and interpret graphs, as well as sort and classify information.

Graph Master, Tom Snyder Productions, 4–8
You can make graphs to help analyze data with this software.

Kai's, Corel, 7 & up
This is a graphic image editor.

MediaWeaver, Humanities Software/Sunburst Technology, 3 & up
This is a multimedia word processor for students.

MovieWorks, Interactive Solutions, K & up
You can edit graphics, sound, and QuickTime videos with this software.

QuickTime, Apple Computer, All
This software lets you view online videos.

SiteCentral, Knowledge Adventure, All
Web site creation software that integrates with HyperStudio.

Survival Signs Set, Attainment Company, 1–3
This software helps students learn eighty signs. It is helpful for special needs students, and you can discuss features of the symbols.

Web Workshop, Sunburst Technology, 2–8
You can make web pages without knowing HTML with this software.

Web Workshop Pro, Sunburst Technology, 6 & up
This web design software is for middle and high school students. (You can publish pages free on the Sunburst web site.)

WebPainter, Totally Hip Software, 1 & up
You can make animated clips for web pages with this software.

WiggleWorks, Scholastic, K–3
This software integrates language arts using leveled trade books. Students can listen to stories and record their own voices and stories.

WiggleWorks Plus, Scholastic, K–3
This software contains activities that integrate the scholastic reading program Literacy Place. There are two interactive books supporting every unit.

World Wide Web Weaver, Miracle Software, 7 & up
You can create web pages with this software.

FOR FURTHER READING

Bailey, G. D., & Blythe, M. (1998). Outlining, diagramming & storyboarding or how to create great educational web sites. *Learning and Leading with Technology, 25*(8), 6–11.

Bull, G., Bull, G., Thomas, J., & Jordan, J. (2000). Incorporating imagery into instruction. *Learning and Leading with Technology, 27*(6), 46–49, 63.

Giorgis, C., Johnson, N. J., Bonomo, A., Colbert, C., Conner, A., Kauffman, G., & Kulesza, D. (1999). Visual literacy. *The Reading Teacher, 53*(2), 146–153.

Grabe, M., & Grabe, C. (2000). Designing web pages: Principles for students and teachers. In *Integrating the Internet for meaningful learning* (pp. 192–222). Boston: Houghton Mifflin.

Holzberg, C. S. (2001). Yes! You can build a web site. *Scholastic Instructor, 110*(8), 62–64.

McInwenwy, P. (2000). Worth 1,000 words. *Learning and Leading with Technology, 28*(8), 10–125.

Short, K. G., Kauffman, G., & Kahn, L. H. (2000). "I just need to draw": Responding to literature across multiple sign systems. *The Reading Teacher, 54*(2), 160–171.

Using Technology with Children's Literature

INTRODUCTION

I am often asked, "Why would anyone want to read a book online when they can read the 'real' book?" My first answer is, "Not everyone has equal access to all of the printed versions of books." While there is a tremendous amount of children's literature in print, schools in less-wealthy school districts may not have an abundance of printed books in their libraries. Electronic books and other online materials are valuable to teachers and students who do not have ways to obtain printed stories or nonfiction materials they want to read. Having access to electronic literature online is extremely important in rural areas (e.g., Ajo, Arizona, or on a Native American reservation) or in other areas with no libraries close by. An online version of a story may be the only way that children in such locations can read some of the most praised classic literature. Even when a school owns a print copy of a book, someone else may have it checked out when one of your students really needs it for a project. An online version can be accessed on one or more computers at the same time instead of putting a project on hold until a print version is available.

Another answer to the "why read online" question is that electronic materials are evolving and improving in quality and in their capacity to integrate new features, resulting in better e-materials. E-materials include text, graphics, photographs, video, sound, and animations. These features have an impact upon the user's *comprehension* of the e-materials as well as upon the ways that creative, technically proficient students and teachers can *present* stories and information to others.

Tools for creating multimedia CD-ROMs and web sites have improved dramatically in user friendliness. Until recently, only a relatively few authors and illustrators had the technical skills needed to create major multimedia products, and many authors and illustrators are still learning to use advanced multimedia authoring applications. Online e-materials will become better as today's students and more adults gain proficiency as multimedia authors. For example, some online art is now of very high quality. Just as dot matrix stick figures in early computer software and CD-ROMs have been replaced by colorful illustrations that can be rolled out of laser printers or viewed on color computer screens, online art is becoming as appealing as the most beautiful print illustrations. As an example, see the artwork for *Alice in Wonderland* at **http://the-office.com/bedtime-story/alice-background.htm.** For more about Alice, see the Tech Tip "*Alice* and Her Author Online."

TECH TIPS — *ALICE* AND HER AUTHOR ONLINE

Children's stories have many fans, some of whom go to great lengths to create web sites about their favorite stories and authors. Plain-text versions of classic stories first appeared when early systems of text transmission on the Internet made online publishing feasible. Today, with the advent of HTML and subsequent improvements that enable multimedia productions online, stories now rival printed books. The sites here contain various versions of *Alice in Wonderland*, a fan-created web site with activities based on the stories, an organization that is devoted to the author, and a fourth-grade class project.

Webliography

- **Alice in Wonderland: An Interactive Adventure**
  http://www.ruthannzaroff.com/wonderland/
  There is much for *Alice* lovers to do at this clever site. Interactive activities based on the *Alice* characters and events are certain to interest students.
- **Alice's Adventures in Wonderland**
  http://www.cs.indiana.edu/metastuff/wonder/wonderdir.html
  This Project Gutenberg file is a text-only version of the story.
- **The Pazooter Works: *Alice's Adventures in Wonderland***
  http://megabrands.com/alice/indexx.html
  Clicking the "Alice in Wonderland" button or the picture takes you to *The Dynamic Text Edition* of *Alice's Adventures in Wonderland* by Lewis Carroll. After entering the site, you can hear background music and read an attractive HTML version of *Alice* at this web site. Some illustrations are slightly animated.
- **Lewis Carroll Society of North America**
  http://www.lewiscarroll.org/
  This site, created by a nonprofit organization devoted to learning about Lewis Carroll (real name Charles Lutwidge Dodgson) and his works, has a biography of the author, as well as other interesting *Alice* links.
- **The Many Faces of Alice**
  http://www.dalton.org/ms/alice/
  Fourth-grade classes at the Dalton School in New York present their own illustrated *Alice* text.

You can find similar web sites for other books you and students like. Run an Internet search with Profusion (or another metasearch engine) using the title or a few keywords of the title. Then examine the sites until you are satisfied they will be useful for your students. You can cut and paste the URLs into an electronic document, add anything else you want to (e.g., questions about the different sites or things you want students to ponder), and save the document as an HTML file. You can then place the file on a classroom computer so students can easily access the sites you found. This gives students a good resource and models how to share topics of interest.

Multimedia features illuminate stories in ways that print versions cannot because they can engage readers in interactive, multimodality presentations of the stories. You can introduce students to online children's literature today knowing that more and better quality e-materials are being created all of the time. Some of the web sites you learn about in this chapter contain high-quality children's stories and illustrations that make use of current improvements in web features which help tell stories (e.g., animations and audio). One additional advantage gained by working with electronic stories is that you and students can use the special features built into web browsers and many CD-ROMs. For instance, electronic text is searchable. See "Finding Specific Words Within Text" on this book's web site.

Web sites appear to hold much more nonfiction than fiction, primarily because of the commercial and educational uses people are making of it. Many fine fictional works reside on the Web now, and in the future, with new ways to create and manipulate text and images, authors will develop even more creative online fictional works. To see a story told using **Flash,** a file format that permits authors to place animations and interactivity on web pages, see Buzz Beamer's Animated Adventures at **http://www.sikids.com/buzz/animated/index.html.**

Using Technology-based Instruction with the Genre of Children's Literature

Examples of all major genre of children's literature appear in electronic formats.

Traditional literature (folktales, fables, etc.), modern fantasy, poetry, contemporary realistic fiction, historical fiction, and nonfiction (biographies and informational materials) are the major genre, or classifications, you deal with in teaching children's literature, according to Donna and Saundra Norton in their book *Through the Eyes of a Child: An Introduction to Children's Literature* (1998). You can find examples of major genre of children's literature in movies and videos, as well as on CD-ROMs, and each genre contains multicultural aspects that you can explore with students.

There is a great deal of traditional literature online. In fact, task forces such as Project Gutenberg at **http://www.gutenberg.org/** have a mission of placing materials that are in the public domain online for all to access. The U.S. Library of Congress, **http://lcweb.loc.gov/**, houses a great many nonfiction materials. In addition, many universities make their collections available online, although in some cases only students enrolled at the universities can access the collections. The University of Virginia also makes available a Young Reader's area on its web site. See **http://etext.lib.virginia.edu/subjects/Young-Readers.html** (Bull, Bull, Blazi, & Cochran, 1999–2000).

TECHNOLOGY-RELATED ACTIVITIES FOR EACH GENRE

Nonfiction materials online can be updated and kept current.

Nonfiction as a genre is of growing importance in the information age. Fortunately, national governments, states, and provinces are placing much public information online. Some of it is not specifically intended for K–8 students, but you can guide students in its use. You can help students use real data as the basis of their learning about and using nonfiction materials, and much of the information is as current as today. This is a distinct advantage over print materials that may have taken months or years to become available.

For genre that are fiction, you can deal with all of the usual literary elements, such as plot, characterization, setting, theme, style, point of view, and stereotypes as you discuss web and/or CD-ROM stories. These are traditional areas of exploration by teachers and students studying children's literature. One major difference between print and electronic materials may be that you and students will need to take a more active role in examining literary elements because teachers' guides and suggestions for teachers do not accompany most web e-materials.

You can discuss literary elements in e-materials as well as print materials.

You and students are free to devise ways to discuss literary elements. For instance, students can evaluate e-materials written by other students and authors whose works are not edited by publishing houses. Students can offer their opinions about how well the stories deal with such elements as plot development, growth of the characters, and realistic settings. Students can also express their satisfaction or dissatisfaction with both the content and presentation of original online stories. You and students can discuss illustrators' techniques, and you can examine and discuss illustrations in terms of the visual elements and design that are discussed in chapter 8. Links to an author's or illustrator's own web site can bring added value to author study sessions. See the Teaching Tip "Multimedia Book Reports" for some useful ideas.

TEACHING TIPS Multimedia Book Reports

Children's literature can be the springboard for encouraging students to create multimedia book reports. Students can make story webs using Inspiration, Kidspiration, or similar programs to help them get organized. You can see examples of character webs and other literacy activities at **http://www.inspiration.com/home.cfm.** Students can use presentation or productivity programs such as HyperStudio, scanners, Zip drives, camcorders, web development programs, paint programs, and printers to create their reports. For whole-group presentations, MultiPro Plus or similar products can connect a computer to a television set, or students can use a computer video projector to share their works with others.

Susan Houston, a teacher, has her students make and present nine reports during a school year. A written report, a completed project, and an oral presentation are major avenues for sharing. Activities and the literary genre included in the projects are:

- **Book-in-a-Bag (short story)** Students read books then use paper bags or large envelopes as props for their report. They decorate the outside of the bags and place objects or drawings in them that represent characters, settings, and problems and solutions in the stories they read.
- **Character poster (chapter fiction book)** Students create a poster of aspects of the story.
- **Book cube (nonfiction book)** Using a supplied pattern, students assemble a cube and decorate each side. One side has the title, author, and a drawing. One side is publication information. The remaining sides show facts from the nonfiction book.
- **Greeting card (holiday or season book)** Students illustrate a scene from a story. (For example, students can write poetry or short "greetings" from a character in the book.)
- **Movie poster (chapter book)** Posters are good for illustrating the story's climax.
- **Mind map (chapter book of choice)** Students create a diagram with specific areas such as book information, main idea, setting, characters, plot, and story outcome. (See **http://artfolio.com/pete/MIndMaps/HowTo.html** for hints on making such maps.)
- **Book jacket** (from a book selected by the librarian)
- **Final project** (student's choice)
- "Students gain the experience of exploring a variety of genre as they learn to present themselves orally to an audience of their peers. Listening skill refinement is an added benefit, as well as learning to critique others in a positive, constructive fashion," said Houston, who videotapes the monthly reports, permitting students and parents to view the presentations and creating the development of electronic portfolios that show student growth throughout the school year.

Students also complete three other multimedia projects each year: a presentation about a state of their choice, including geography, population, places to visit, and economics; an autobiography; and a report on women in history.

Source: Susan Houston, fourth-grade teacher, Eddy School, Carlsbad, New Mexico. Used by permission.

Traditional Literature

The genre of traditional literature can help students learn about the views of the world that people held in ancient times and identify universal themes that are expressed over and over again in such stories. As international use of the Web increases, and **translation engines,** software programs that translate from one language to another, improve, people will be able to enjoy classic and contemporary folktales, myths, fables, and legends from around the world. This is the easiest fictional genre to work with online because many classic stories are in the public domain. Specific new versions of the old works in this genre can be copyrighted, but the stories themselves are free for all to read.

WEBLIOGRAPHY

- **Mything Links**
  http://www.mythinglinks.org/reference~teachers.html
  This has an annotated collection of links to myths, and fairy tales, as well as to folklore and traditions.
- **Myths and Legends**
  http://members.bellatlantic.net/~vze33gpz/myth.html
  This is a major source of links to worldwide myths and legends.

Students can access stories, learn storytelling techniques, and tell the stories to others. They can use presentation programs to present high-tech versions of common storytelling techniques such as using felt boards and other props while they tell their stories (e.g., a student can use HyperStudio cards on a computer presentation to add each character as it appears. *The Three Billy Goats Gruff*, for instance, could show the troll meeting each goat in turn). They can analyze, compare, and contrast various international versions of the same story (e.g., *Cinderella*) by placing categories of information from the various versions in databases for ease of sorting while they analyze the various stories (Land & Turner, 1997). See Cinderella Stories at **http://www.acs.ucalgary.ca/~dkbrown/cinderella.html,** a reference site giving Internet and print sources of information about various retellings of the Cinderella story. Learn more ideas about comparing versions of stories on this book's web site.

WWW

Students can videotape pantomimes and other performances of stories. In essence, any of the techniques you typically use with students can be used with the traditional stories you find online. Enhancing your and students' sharing of such stories (e.g., making electronic presentations) is a bonus that current technologies make possible. In one excellent project, a teacher reads a fairy tale to students, who then create a cyberdictionary by writing or dictating sentences and illustrating words from their retelling of the story. They end up with a word for each letter in the alphabet. You can see examples at **http://www.op97.k12.il.us/instruct/ftcyber/next.html.**

Picture Books

Picture books are books with few or no words. Most online e-stories are text or audio stories at this point, but enterprising authors will likely place more picture stories online when they recognize the value of this genre to beginning readers. You can find or make picture stories that illustrate a rhyme or story. Students can create their own alphabet books—some with moving letters you can get from Artie.com at **http://www.artie.com/alpha-index.htm**—and they can see animated words and hear words using RealPlayer.

Concept books fall under the category of picture books. Concept books help young students learn easier concepts (e.g., the color *red*, the *square* shape) or more advanced concepts (e.g., *through* a tunnel, *between* two trees). You can find online collections of concept-building exercises in the "activities" sections of various web sites.

You can use picture books as the basis for dozens of class, group, and individual activities. Just as they can do with printed picture books, students can write or dictate captions for illustrations, stories about characters or objects they see online, or stories to go with wordless stories and illustrations. These days, however, students will likely use a word processor to engage in some of these activities. Of course, students can read aloud any words or sentences they find in those online picture stories, or they can record their ideas into computers or on videotapes and audiotapes.

Modern Fantasy

Modern fantasy stories give you opportunities to help students learn to suspend disbelief about the characters and plots. This genre includes stories with talking animals and toys, strange worlds, ghosts, time warps, and, of course, science fiction. Science fiction fans can learn about authors and their works at SF Authors at **http://www.magicdragon.com/UltimateSF/authors.html.**

You can help students recognize that even though some stories are fantasy, they often deal with universal themes. The popular television series *Star Trek* is noted for its conflicts and attempts at resolutions of universal problems, such as racism, that took place on distant planets. Help students think about how authors create plausible settings or worlds that are quite different from our own world and its laws of physics. Modern fantasy lends itself well to art and drama activities, and the genre is well suited for engaging students in comparisons of "real" science and science fiction as well as social studies topics. This genre lends itself nicely to discussing the ISTE NETS standards dealing with social, ethical, and human issues.

Poetry

Poetry is a genre that students first meet as preschoolers. Mother Goose rhymes and rhyming elements in popular music (rap music) are just two ways students are exposed to rhymes prior to school. Children generally like poetry not just because of the rhyming element, but because much poetry has rhythm, repetition, alliteration, and the playful use of words. Haiku poetry is particularly popular with teachers and students alike, and there are many examples of this kind of poetry online. Students can read online poetry aloud, chant poetry while skipping rope, or act it out. Groups of students can read poetry by speaking in unison or in various patterns of delivery, such as each student reading a single line of the poem, groups of students alternating with each group reading a part (antiphonal reading), or groups joining in one by one until the entire class is speaking. KidLit at **http://mgfx.com/kidlit/** contains stories, poetry, and artwork created by students. You can encourage students to place their works on the Web. Anne Wall, IRA Presidential Award for Reading and Technology Southeast Regional Winner 2000, created Poetry Page at **http://members.aol.com/volsfive2/poetry.html.** This site contains definitions and examples of cinquains, haiku, and limericks written by fifth-grade students. Gloria Antifaiff, two-time Canadian winner of the IRA Presidential Award for Reading and Technology, recommends integrating technology and poetry through using Kid Pix's stamping feature to create shape poems and its slide show feature to create drawn representations of responses to poetry. She also recommends using Kid Pix to make rebus stories and picture poems (G. Antifaiff, personal communication, May 31, 2001).

You can learn about children's literature awards and associations at this book's web site.

Contemporary Realistic Fiction

Contemporary realistic fiction takes place in the current time frame, and authors take great pains to convince readers that a story is true. The story or its events *might* have happened and real-life events may even be incorporated into the plot, but the story is fiction nonetheless. Often controversial issues such as growing up, violence, and death are dealt with in stories of this genre. Beverly Cleary's *Dear Mr. Henshaw,* a story about the divorce of a boy's parents, is an example of one topic you will find in contemporary realistic fiction. Help students recognize stereotypes and evaluate the actions of characters in these stories so that they come to understand better their own feelings and attitudes. Because people and events in contemporary realistic fiction are so lifelike, take opportunities to help students develop critical reading skills through analyzing characters' motives, questioning the inferences they are making about characters and their actions, and reflecting on what the story means to them personally. Since this genre lends itself nicely to discussions, you can arrange telecollaborative sessions about books or themes with students from other schools or between students and college students in literacy courses.

Historical Fiction

Historical fiction helps us imagine people and events from the past. A key concept in working with historical fiction is that historical events, settings, and actions should be authentic to the time period of the story. Authors are telling us a story, but they painstakingly research such things as events, furniture, clothing, and transportation so the story and history are smoothly intertwined. As you might know from first-hand experience, an **anachronism** (e.g., a computer sitting on a desk before computers were even invented) can ruin the authenticity of a story that is supposed to be historically accurate. Elizabeth George Speare's *The Witch of Blackbird Pond* is historical fiction about suspected witchcraft in New England.

The genre of historical fiction is well suited for helping students develop research skills. Much historical information is now found on CD-ROMs and on the Web. You and students can use genealogy sites to trace family histories (e.g., Genealogy.com at **http://www.genealogy.com/index.html** or Ancestry.com at **http://www.ancestry.com/**), and you can examine government sites that contain historical papers (e.g., The Library of Congress at **http://lcweb.loc.gov/**). An excellent factual web site is From Revolution to Reconstruction at **http://odur.let.rug.nl/%7Escholing/usa/.** Students can use the information they find online to write historical fiction of their own, as the following anecdote demonstrates:

Irene Huschak, a technology instructor at Altoona Area High School in Pennsylvania, is the grand prize-winner of the 2000 IRA Presidential Award for Reading and Technology. Ms. Huschak is responsible for the development of a creative, historically accurate web site. The site, Interactive Stories (**http://www.aasdcat/9a/**) was created with the help of local historians, high school English and technology students, and fifth-grade story reviewers. Students participated in the development of nine interactive, historically accurate stories, emphasizing people, places, or events from Altoona's past. Old and new digital photos as well as a few clever animations make the stories visually interesting. Elementary school students are encouraged to log on and then to place their own names and a few other names into an online form. They can then read their *personalized* stories. This model project demonstrates how students can learn about their own localities and then disseminate the information to the entire world as historical fiction.

Writing historical fiction and other works based on their own research, as Ms. Huschak's students did, can help students appreciate this genre *and* make a contribution to knowledge in the areas they study. In another example, students in a second-grade class at Pocantico Hills School in Sleepy Hollow, New York, studied Harriet Tubman. Then they created an extensive web site about her. The site uses a quilt for a border, said Taverna and Hongell (2000, p. 44), "because the station masters used quilts to let the slaves know that the station was safe. We chose bare feet . . . as navigational tools because many slaves escaped on bare feet." The site contains poems, a timeline, character sketches and profiles, crossword puzzles, and much more. The site, which you can visit at **http://www2.lhric.org/pocantico/tubman/tubman.html,** is a good example of how students are using factual information as the basis for creating historically accurate materials.

Nonfiction

Nonfiction information is abundant on the Web. However, topics are often presented more in small "chunks" of data connected through the use of hyperlinks rather than in well-organized and presented chapters or full-length books. Many of today's *adult* readers are not fond of reading electronic text for long periods of time, generally because they grew up reading printed books. Tomorrow's readers, who are growing up reading more and more e-materials, may think nothing of reading novels and other e-materials online. The use of hand-held devices for reading e-books is a rapidly growing area of the technology market, and many of the electronic texts at the University of Virginia's Electronic Text Center at **http://etext.lib.virginia.edu/** are downloadable. Microsoft Reader and Palm Pilot versions are available to read on your own computer or device.

E-books are becoming more popular as the technology evolves.

Because many short web pages contain nonfiction materials, students must learn to collate (assemble) their own "books" or "book chapters" on topics that interest them, using information found in various web sources. The difference between reading a work that was produced by an established author or publisher and creating one yourself may be one of the biggest developments in dealing with nonfiction information in the present and future. Authorship on the Web is possible for *everyone* who can deal effectively with thinking about, using, and creating reliable information.

People interested in history are working to make bona fide information available online. For instance, Lynne Anderson-Inman, Director of the Center for Advanced Technology in Education in the College of Education at The University of Oregon, oversees Web de Anza (**http://anza.uoregon.edu/**). This web site is an interactive study environment on Spanish exploration and colonization of "Alta California" during the period of 1774–1776. The site, which promotes historical inquiry about

Juan Bautista de Anza, contains authentic documents and accounts of his two eighteenth-century expeditions from northern Mexico into northern California. This and similar sites are making historical information readily available to today's and tomorrow's students, who can use the information in their work with nonfiction materials.

Students profit from reading materials in the nonfiction genre because they learn to generate important research questions and understand the kinds of resources that are available for inquiry. Understanding nonfiction materials can lead students to an increased ability to conduct their own research and to write about topics that interest them. Giving students exposure to many nonfiction books serves several purposes, according to Tower (2000):

> Readers use nonfiction for a variety of purposes that include finding information to answer a particular question and browsing through information to satisfy general curiosity about a subject. Students need to be taught the different purposes for using nonfiction, and how these purposes differ from the use of fiction. They need to be taught the various access features of nonfiction, including [the] table of contents, chapter titles, glossaries, sidebars, inserted information, bibliographies, and authors' notes. (p. 553)

Students may not find typical nonfiction print conventions in most online materials (e.g., tables of contents or glossaries), but they should learn of their importance for establishing organization and clarity when they turn the findings of their own research into presentation materials for online delivery or for class presentations.

Reading nonfiction aloud to students, according to Vardell (cited in Tower, 2000, p. 154), can be useful. He listed these strategies for reading nonfiction aloud: "cover-to-cover read-alouds, participatory read-alouds, chapter read-alouds, caption reading, browsing, believe-it-or-not sharing, and introducing structural elements through reading aloud." While reading aloud, you can note and discuss tables, glossaries, and other nonfiction features. You can also model effective strategies such as previewing chapter headings, looking at graphics before reading a chapter, and other study strategies.

MULTICULTURAL EMPHASIS FOR ALL GENRE

Stories are written by and about almost all cultural groups in the world, and these stories and books are often referred to as multicultural literature. Multicultural stories can be created in all the major genre of literature,

Various cultural groups are increasingly represented in online literature.

and as people from more countries place materials on the Web, you will be able to find materials written by and about almost everybody in the world. It is important for you to identify these stories and help students learn about cultures other than their own. Through such reading, students learn about how they are like other people and how they differ in customs, traditions, and beliefs. Discussions of multicultural literature can lead to a better understanding of historical and current events and how all people live today. A good source of information is the "Multicultural and International Children's Literature Links" page at **http://www.home.earthlink.net/~elbond/multicultural.htm.** See the Tech Tip "Pacific Children's Literature Project" to learn about a Micronesian web site.

TECH TIPS — PACIFIC CHILDREN'S LITERATURE PROJECT

The Internet, says Dalton (2000), "has a great potential to address issues of equity and to support efforts that give a voice to those previously unheard, even in their own communities" (p. 684). The Pacific Children's Literature Web Site, developed by Dalton and University of Guam media services director Brian Millhoff, went online in July 1999. See it at **http://www.uog.edu/coe/paclit/index.htm.** The project "is designed to use the Internet as a vehicle for building and sharing the stories and cultures of Guam, Micronesia, and the Pacific. Students and other members of the Micronesian community are the authors of the various web pages constituting the site" (p. 684). This web project, which involved students at the University of Guam, is an example of why the Internet is changing how teachers are preparing students of all cultures for the future. Dalton says:

> First, the Internet is a self-publication tool that makes it possible for all voices to be heard and all peoples to be represented, even when they are few in number, disconnected from traditional print literacies, or marginalized in society. . . . The Internet is a teaching agent; a socializing tool. It can be used to make progress in appreciating another culture's perspective, and perhaps, in making one's own perspective clearer to others. (p. 690)

Students were proud of the project not only for their own accomplishment, but because the web site gave them a way to share their culture with others.

Source: Ideas and screenshot used with permission of Bridget Dalton and Brian Millhoff.

ACROSS-GENRE TECHNOLOGY-RELATED ACTIVITIES

Some technological applications are useful when studying any genre.

As we have seen, each of the genre previously discussed suggests certain technology tie-ins. However, there are also many interest-provoking technology-related activities that are more generic in nature and that can be used with all kinds of children's literature. These are just a few activities various educators suggest:

- Have students create e-mail and snail mail addresses for characters in materials they read (e.g., rabbit@madhatter.com), then write letters or e-mail messages using a word processor, print them, and share them with the class (Heese, 2000). This creative activity will help students think about characters and events more carefully as they prepare their messages. Encourage students to refer back to texts during their drafting of the messages. See the Student Project "A Pretend E-mail to MagicTricks@HarryPotter.com."
- Make a **character web** using Inspiration or other graphics-creation programs. A character web "is a visual representation of the [story's] character with lines coming from the drawing. The lines are used to write words that describe what is known about the character from the text" (Lapp, Flood, & Fisher, 1999, p. 776).
- Encourage students to hold online literature discussions via e-mail or a chat room with other students, college students, or teachers. Sullivan (1998) teamed elementary school students and college students who held literature discussions and found an increase in elementary school students' incentive to read as well as more specificity in their responses.
- Use a dozen or more ways to mine CD-ROMs for opportunities to help student's literacy development. Having students listen to stories, read along, echo read, or read first and then listen are Linda Labbo's suggestions for building fluency and comprehension. Labbo said, "Asking children to explain how events from one screen relate to previous screens may help them learn to make digital intratextual connections that support a metacognitive, strategic approach to making meaning" (Labbo, 2000, p. 545). She proposes having students comment about how special effects in CD-ROM stories relate to the story. This is a valuable suggestion because students can come to realize that they are using knowledge obtained from several information systems (e.g., animations, audio) to comprehend more fully. Using CD-ROMs also provides opportunities to engage students in other literacy activities, such as identifying letters or words, matching sounds within words, and finding rhyming words (Labbo, 2000).
- Create a **CyberHunt** for students. Select ten or more of the children's literature web sites mentioned in this chapter and create questions that students can answer when they access those sites. Use author web sites to ask students questions about the author's life or books, have students read a story and answer a specific question about it, or have them locate a key idea in the story and

A PRETEND E-MAIL TO MagicTricks@HarryPotter.com

by Eric Valmont

Dear Harry,

I loved your magic tricks, like the one trick where you made blank pages of a book turn into colorful pictures. I also like the one where you made the dime pass through the plastic. I thought that one was cool!
I do some cool magic tricks, too. I have this one trick where you make three balls appear out of three cups. That is my best trick. I also have a trick where you make a hat float in the air like magic.
I would like to order the tricks I mentioned in the beginning, the *Book of Color* and the *Magic Dime* tricks. I can't wait to get them. I will be getting more tricks in the future if these go well.
Sincerely, Eric Valmont

You can encourage students to write creative e-mail to characters in stories. Have them create a pretend e-mail address for the character and send some comments. Students can develop their ideas on either an e-mail system (even if it is not connected to the Internet) or by working on a word processor.

Source: Used by permission of Eric Valmont, Pistor Middle School, Tucson, AZ, and his parents.

describe it (Kloza, 2000). You will not have difficulty creating relevant questions as you explore the sites. Make a handout or place your questions on a web page for students to access and answer. (See Kloza's article for a helpful example that you may actually use.)

- Build activities around themes such as differences (*Stellaluna*), slavery, and survival (Wepner & Ray, 2000), or "use the current reading or literature theme and assign students to search the Internet and print sources to find poems related to the theme" (Scolari, Bedient, & Randolph, 2000, p. 30).
- Encourage students to visit web sites with stories and determine into which genre the stories fall.
- Visit authors' web sites during author studies (Wepner & Ray, 2000).

Suggestions such as the above reinforce the idea that you can use many of the traditional strategies teachers have been using for a long time to help develop literacy abilities—only you can now use electronic resources as well as ink on paper. As teachers, you will want to become familiar with the dozens of references and resources to help you integrate technology and children's literature. See "Online Journals and Related Sites Dealing with Children's Literature" at this book's web site.

As they learn about the characteristics of various literary genre, you can encourage students to emulate all types of genre in their writing, speaking, and constructing of messages. Encourage students to submit their fables, science fiction, historical fiction, and so forth for publication online. You can publish their stories on a class or school web site (be sure to follow school regulations), or you can "publish" them on a computer. See the Teaching Tip "Using Technology with Literature" for further suggestions.

TEACHING TIPS Using Technology with Literature

Marsha Strader, now retired, taught seventh-grade reading for many years at the Charleston Middle School in Charleston, Illinois. In an e-mail to me, she explained how she integrated technology and literature. After studying the elements of literature, students worked in groups of four to create illustrated stories that explained an American custom to students in Brazil, Jamaica, or Russia. Students identified and used elements of literature in their text. They scanned photos, used a digital camera, or downloaded images from the Internet. They cropped and otherwise enhanced their graphics using Adobe Photoshop. "Stories were typed, revised, and edited by the group, and then they were evaluated by a peer group," Ms. Strader says. "A comparison of the students' and peer-group evaluations was made, and students had a final opportunity to revise their story before it was put into a spiral bound booklet and mailed," she adds. Students also tape-recorded their stories so students in Russia could hear the stories spoken in English. Students used The Rosetta Stone CD-ROM to learn a few words in another language. (See **http://www.101language.com/rosetta.html.**)

During the poetry study unit, "students wrote poetry utilizing their knowledge of rhythm, mood, repetition, allusion, rhyme, or any other poetic devices they chose," Ms. Strader says. Students illustrated their poems with photos or clip art. "Students were encouraged to experiment with fonts, style, size, and layout to best portray the mood of their poems," she adds. Selected poems were included in a book that was placed in the school's library as well as in local libraries. Another book that included every student's work was created for the classroom. Some students read their poetry to students in lower grades and gave them a signed copy of the poem during a school open house. "To give students a feeling of 'audience,' my home page featured a different piece of student writing each month," says Ms. Strader.

Source: Used by permission of Marsha Strader.

Electronic-based Reading Materials

WEB SITE MATERIALS

Online materials vary greatly in quality and production values.

You can find new stories created specifically for the Web, and you can also find adapted and enhanced older stories. Some of these stories are good models for students to emulate when creating multimedia projects, and others contain features such as loud music that distract from the stories. Students will learn from both good and not-so-good examples. There is a range of "production values" in online stories. Some:

- are simple creations, perhaps text only.
- are text with audio that can be played or not as the reader chooses.
- have music that either distracts from the story or captures its mood.
- have graphic elements that "decorate" but do not add to the story.
- have graphic elements that illustrate the story.
- have graphics that bring characters and/or actions to life (applets, animations).
- have complex animations that enhance and are integrated into the story.
- are audio-only stories (narrated texts).

Regardless of their quality, you and students can read online stories, evaluate them, and create your own that are better and that make use of the latest web applications. As a pre- or in-service teacher, you will always want to examine ahead of time any of the stories listed here and elsewhere throughout this book. Not only can pages and links change, but **hackers,** people who tamper with sites, can alter online materials. Your judgment about sending students to web sites to view electronic reading materials is similar to your role in recommending print materials, and it is even more important for you to screen e-materials. Online web materials, generally, do not undergo professional review, but self-censorship by authors is basically what keeps most materials suitable for elementary and middle school students.

AUTHORS' AND ILLUSTRATORS' WEB SITES

Make lists of authors and illustrators that your students enjoy or of the favorite books that are in your classroom or school library. Then have students search the Web for sites about those authors and illustrators and their works (Scolari et al., 2000).

Many children's literature authors have a presence on the Web (e.g., Jan Brett at **http://www.janbrett.com** and Mem Fox at **http://www.memfox.net**), and you can use these sites when you engage in author-study activities. You can find URLs for several popular authors and illustrators on this book's web site.

You can find extensive lists of authors' web sites and information about authors at several sites. Two such sites are Authors and Illustrators on the Web at **http://www.acs.ucalgary.ca/~dkbrown/authors.html** and a Yahoo! directory of Children's Authors at **http://dir.yahoo.com/Arts/Humanities/Literature/Authors/Children_s/**. On this book's web site are several sites devoted to Laura Ingalls Wilder and to Mark Twain as a reminder to search for multiple web sites for any author you are studying. Also visit this book's web site to learn about the similarities of a Mark Twain story and a recent CD-ROM.

CHILDREN'S LITERATURE WEB SITES

Many new and classic stories appear online for you and students to use.

The old saying about everyone having a story to tell seems truer today than ever. Budding authors are finding ways to place stories online—some with sophisticated multimedia features. Some publishers sample their wares online by placing short selections or chapters online to whet readers' appetites enough to buy a book, and some have developed sites where you and students can learn about books, authors and illustrators, and their related wares. Winslow Press at **http://www.winslowpress.com/** shows its books and permits visitors to engage in book-related interactive activities made with Macromedia Shockwave. You can download teacher's guides for some books as **PDF** (portable document format) images. Figure 9.1 shows the menu for one book, *The Runaway Tortilla.*

Teachers are working alone or with school technology personnel to develop web sites where their students' commentary about children's literature appear. Private and nonprofit organizations place stories online as a service to schools and children. Universities, too, are placing course

FIGURE 9.1

The Runaway Tortilla Web Site Menu

Source: Use of this screenshot from *The Runaway Tortilla* by Eric A. Kimmel, illustrated by Randy Cecil, is courtesy of Winslow Press.

materials online pertaining to children's literature. All of this is good for you as a teacher and for students, too, because they can read classic literature and new works from anywhere and everywhere in the world.

The following are some of the main sites where you can find children's literature and reviews of children's literature.

WEBLIOGRAPHY

- **Absolutely Whootie: Stories to Grow by**
  http://www.storiestogrowby.com/
  This award-winning site (see Figure 9.2) features free, upbeat, nonsectarian, and kid-tested interactive fairy tales and stories illustrated by children from around the world.

FIGURE 9.2

Whootie Stories Web Site

Source: Screenshot of Absolutely Whootie is used by permission of Whootie Owl International, LLC. All rights reserved.

Aesop's Fables Online Collection
http://www.pacificnet.net/~johnr/aesop/
There are more than 600 fables in this collection, some of which you can hear using RealPlayer. The site is relocating to one of these URLs: **AesopsFables.com** or **.net** or **.org**, so try the new URLs if the one above does not work.

- **The Amazing Adventure Series**
  http://www.amazingadventure.com/
  You can read and listen to "June the Prune" and "Blossom's Tale" and see story-related activities at the site.

- **BAB Books On-Line Stories for Kids**
  http://www.amtexpo.com/babbooks/
  Read "Shall We Make a Mad Dash" and "When I Grow Up" at this site. The site also includes a fun "Adlib" link feature that lets you add words to a story. When you finish, the web site generates the story, usually with amusing results.

- **Bartleby.com**
  http://www.bartleby.com/
  Online classics in HTML format—not just text files—appear here. The Harvard Classics and the Harvard Classics Shelf of Fiction are contained in this collection.

- **Bedtime-Story**
  http://www.bedtime-story.com/bedtime-story/indexmain.htm
  This site is one of the best sources of online stories on the Web. These are typically well-illustrated stories that are accompanied by music. See "The Snakeman," in which animations help advance the story, something unique to the electronic story format.

- **Bibliomania**
  http://www.bibliomania.com/
  Here you can read reference materials, fiction (e.g., *Tom Sawyer, The Phantom of the Opera*), nonfiction (e.g., *The Concise Pepys, The Interpretation of Dreams*), and poems (e.g., Walt Whitman's *Leaves of Grass*).

- **Billy Gnome's Bedtime Stories**
  http://www.bgammon.freeserve.co.uk/contents.htm
  This site presents twelve chapters in the life of "Billy Gnome." This original children's story was written by Cindy White, the web site owner's grandmother. You can hear a "bug chorus" and try to solve a puzzle.

- **Childrenstory.com**
  http://www.childrenstory.com/
  This site contains fairytales, interactive stories, and rhymes.

- **Children's Storybooks Online**
  http://www.magickeys.com/books/index.html
  Books, riddles, a maze, and coloring books for young children are included, a number of which are animated. Books for older children and young adults also appear at this site.

- **Electronic Text Center**
  http://etext.lib.virginia.edu/
  This site contains thousands of texts, including many classic books for young adults. For instance, Zitkala-Sa's *Old Indian Legends* and Louisa May Alcott's *Little Women* are online here.

- **The EServer Poetry Collection**
  http://english-www.hss.cmu.edu/poetry/default.html
  This site has a searchable collection of classic poetry, such as *Jabberwocky* and *The Rime of the Ancient Mariner.*

WEBLIOGRAPHY (continued)

- **Find Poetry.com**
  http://www.findpoetry.com/searchnow/Childrens_Poems/
  This site has a wealth of information about poetry and links to poems for elementary school students.

- **Grandpa Tucker's Rhymes and Tales**
  http://www.night.net/tucker/
  This site contains humorous stories and poems. Be certain to read them before the students.

- **Hans Christian Andersen Fairy Tales and Stories**
  http://hca.gilead.org.il/#intro
  This very complete site includes both the tales and information about Andersen's life.

- **Hypertexts (The University of Virginia)**
  http://xroads.virginia.edu/%7EHYPER/hypertex.html
  The Red Badge of Courage, The Narrative of Sojourner Truth, Sister Carrie, and many more stories and books are included. Some contain photographs of illustrations from various old editions (e.g., *Uncle Remus*).

- **The Internet Classics Archive**
  http://classics.mit.edu/
  You can read Aesop's fables, the writings of Homer, Plato, and many more important authors of the ancient classics at this site useful for older, advanced students.

- **The Mother Goose Pages**
  http://www-personal.umich.edu/~pfa/dreamhouse/nursery/rhymes.html
  You can read the words to famous Mother Goose rhymes at this site.

- **The On-Line Books Page**
  http://digital.library.upenn.edu/books/
  More than 15,000 titles are available. Some are PDF images, others are created using HTML, and still others are plain text. The site also uses SGML/TEI (standard generalized markup language–text encoded initiative) and XML (extensible markup language), advanced ways of preparing images and text for web viewing.

- **Rapunzel**
  http://www.newchapter.com/kidz/fairy/rapunzel/
  Middle school students will think this humorous version of Rapunzel is "cool." You will want to read it completely to determine if the humor is appropriate for your students before letting them visit the site. It is a model for encouraging students to update classic stories.

- **Room 108**
  http://www.netrover.com/~kingskid/108.html
  This site contains dozens of stories, plus singing, spelling, and other activities.
- **SurLaLune Fairy Tale Pages**
  http://members.aol.com/surlalune/frytales/index.htm
  This is an excellent site with annotated versions of stories and illustrations from books. A history of each story appears as well as information about stories from different cultures that tell similar tales. *Beauty and the Beast* and *Hansel and Gretel* are just two of the several dozen stories.
- **Welcome to the *Scoop* Adventure Page**
  http://www.friend.ly.net/scoop/adventure/index.html
  This site contains an interactive pirate adventure story. Students make decisions about the progress of the story by clicking on one of two choices at each stopping place. This is one way you can create interactive stories.
- **World of Reading!**
  http://www.worldreading.org/
  You can read reviews of stories such as *Treasure Island* and *Peter Pan* that were written by students.
- **Yahooligans! Directory**
  http://www.yahooligans.com/School_Bell/Language_Arts/Online_Stories
  This site has information about authors, book reviews and awards, books, drama, folk and fairy tales, magazines, poetry, word games, and writing. The "Online Stories" link takes users to stories such as *The Adventures of Shakey Snake* (**http://www.webtownis.bc.ca/shakey/**) and more.

STORY CHARACTERS ONLINE

Popular story character sites are bountiful online.

If a character in a book is popular with students, you are likely to find that a publisher, a fan, or a class has created a web site. Sometimes such sites are primarily intended to encourage teachers and students to buy things, but some also contain games and activities of interest to youngsters. Pages that young students can print and color are popular giveaways at character sites. Students can write about and illustrate the characters' stories.

WEBLIOGRAPHY

- **Arthur**
  http://www.pbskids.org/arthur
  There are many activities at this site featuring Marc Brown's popular character.
- **Charlotte's Web**
  http://www2.lhric.org/pocantico/charlotte/index.htm
  This site was developed by Patricia Taverna and Terry Hongell, 2001 IRA Presidential Award for Reading and Technology Award grand prize winners, to encourage second-grade students to write chapter summaries, a mystery quiz, and puzzles based on the story.
- **Harry Potter**
  http://www.scholastic.com/harrypotter/home.asp
  At this site the uninitiated can learn about Harry Potter stories and J. K. Rowling, author of these books. There are Harry puzzles and games, and you can read a sample chapter from one of the books.
- **Welcome to Berenstain Bear Country**
  http://www.berenstainbears.com/
  Students can read a story and participate in other activities at this site.

CD-ROM MATERIALS

CD-ROM materials may take a back seat to Internet materials.

The development of CD-ROMs brought us electronic, interactive stories and accompanying learning experiences. Technologically savvy fans of children's literature were pleased to encounter such CD-ROMs as the Talking Classic Tales (New Media School House), Annabel's Dream of Ancient Egypt (Texas Caviar), and Cinderella (Discus Books) with its diaphanous pages that "turned." We enjoyed clicking on hotspots in Arthur's Teacher Troubles and Just Grandma and Me. We were happy that companies such as Computer Curriculum Corporation, MECC, and Broderbund were creating story disks and CD-ROMs in the early 1990s. Many of the products are still being used in schools today. Some major educational development companies have moved to creating Internet projects and, unfortunately, some of the pioneer developers are no longer in business. So the future of children's literature in CD-ROM format is unclear as more e-materials move to the Web. We selected and listed at the end of this chapter a number of software products based on children's literature or characters in children's literature that were available as of this writing. You can look at publishers' catalogs or web sites for more information about these and other CD-ROM products.

SUMMARY

- E-materials bring literature to students who cannot access local print library resources.
- Emerging features of e-materials will challenge readers to use new literacy skills.
- The various genre of children's literature are available in electronic formats.
- Children's literature in the public domain is readily available online.
- Individuals, teachers, universities, and others are placing free e-materials online.
- It is easily possible to integrate technology with author and genre studies.
- Authors from around the world are making multicultural e-materials readily accessible.
- Evolving technologies may well make web-based materials the preferred medium for delivering e-materials.

ACTIVITIES

1. Search for one of your favorite fairy tales online and read it aloud to students.
2. Do an online search for your favorite author, illustrator, or poet.
3. Create a list like Susan Houston's tying genre to specific technology applications.
4. Locate a children's literature movie, video, or CD-ROM and evaluate its best features.

SOFTWARE

Aesop in ASL, Texas School for the Deaf, 4–9
Four of the famous fables are told in American Sign Language.

Amanda Stories, Grolier Educational, Pre-K–6
These are ten stories by Amanda Goodenough.

Arthur's Birthday Deluxe, The Learning Company/Broderbund, K–3
Arthur and his friend are having birthday parties at the same time. Other titles in this series of CD-ROMs are Arthur's Computer Adventure, Arthur's Reading Race, and Arthur's Teacher Trouble.

Cat in the Hat, The, The Learning Company/Broderbund, Pre-K–2
This is an interactive version of the story in English and Spanish.

Edward Lear's Book of Nonsense, Maxima New Media, 7 and up
Lear's limericks and illustrations are presented on CD-ROM and with a book.

Green Eggs and Ham, The Learning Company/Broderbund, K–4
This adaptation of the book contains new scenes as well as activities.

Just Grandma and Me Deluxe, The Learning Company/Broderbund, Pre-K–2
The classic CD-ROM is available in "Library" only.

Polar Express, The, Houghton Mifflin Interactive, Pre-K–4
Chris Van Allsburg's story is narrated by Garrison Keillor.

Sheila Rae, the Brave, The Learning Company/Broderbund, K–3
This is the CD-ROM version of Kevin Henkes' story about working together to solve problems.

Stellaluna, The Learning Company/Broderbund, 1–6
(Available in "Library" only) Here is an interactive version of the little bat's adventures.

Stories and More Series, Edmark/Riverdeep Interactive, K–3
This program promotes comprehension, interpretation, evaluation, and appreciation of text using award-winning stories.

Tortoise and the Hare, The, The Learning Company/Broderbund, 1–6
This interactive version of the fable is available in Library only.

Why Mosquitoes Buzz in People's Ears, Scholastic, Pre-K–2
Here's a retelling of the tale of mishaps through the jungle grapevine.

FOR FURTHER READING

Berry, D. (1998). Literature on the web: Guided searching. *MultiMedia Schools, 5*(3), 38–41.

Cockrum, W. (2000). Web site connections. *Arizona Reading Journal, 27*(1), 47–48.

Johnson, D. (1999). Electronic collaboration: Children's literature in the classroom. *The Reading Teacher, 53*(1), 54–59.

Karchmer, R. A. (2000). Exploring literacy on the Internet. Using the Internet and children's literature to support interdisciplinary instruction. *The Reading Teacher, 54*(1), 100–103.

Reissman, R., & Gil, E. (2000). Technology takes on fairy tales and folktales. *Learning & Leading with Technology, 27*(5), 18–21.

Sullivan, J. (1998). The electronic journal: Combining literacy and technology. *The Reading Teacher, 52*(1), 90–92.

CHAPTER 10

Assessment of Student Learning and Achievement

INTRODUCTION

Assessment of literacy today has changed because you and your students can use technology to determine what students know. In the past, literacy teachers often had students read books and make written or oral book reports. Today, to show their understanding of something they read, students can make a multimedia report using a presentation program on a computer, make a video, construct electronic images with a paint program (or freehand using a cursor), create a collage of digitized images, synthesize sounds, and use real-time electronic data from the Web. Assessing students' literacy capabilities just got to be more challenging because of new assessment options.

Today, you need to assess not only traditional print literacy abilities, but emerging electronic literacy abilities and students' use of technological tools as well. You are familiar with traditional print assessment instruments, but you may not have encountered some technology-assisted tests and other assessment instruments. In this chapter, we will briefly define common assessment terms and then present several major ways that technology can help you in your assessment of students.

Computers and the Web will become increasingly helpful as delivery systems for assessment as test manufacturers, publishing companies, and others create online assessment instruments. You, yourself, can create electronic assessments and use databases and spreadsheets to file observations for the ongoing authentic assessments you conduct. Students can create electronic materials or digitize them and place them in electronic portfolios, making it possible for you and others to assess students throughout their schooling.

Basic Assessment Terms and Relationships

ASSESSMENT

Assessment is the process of collecting information about a person's understandings, skills, and abilities, as well as making judgments about that person's performance (see "Evaluation" below). We typically use the information we gather from assessments to help us plan either remedial or developmental learning experiences designed to help students make further progress. Assessments can be either formal or informal.

Formal

Formal assessments mainly involve norm-referenced instruments.

Formal assessment generally involves using standardized, norm-referenced tests. These are created through the statistical analysis of items given to large numbers of students, resulting in an instrument that distributes students along the infamous bell-shaped curve. Some assessments are created by test-making companies or by publishers to accompany their programs. For instance, the Scholastic Reading Inventory works in conjunction with Scholastic's *Reading Counts.* Some states and school districts create standardized tests as well.

Many educators are dissatisfied with standardized tests' being used as the primary way politicians and some members of the public judge schools and student progress. You and most educators recognize that not all of students' knowledge and abilities can be measured with statistically determined, standardized test questions. You also recognize that many of your goals for instruction are not measured by standardized tests at all. For instance, we have never seen a standardized test that measures the love of reading. Standardized tests give a picture of where students stand in relationship to one another on a specific set of items, but informal assessments provide a better way to appraise individual students' abilities and instructional needs because such evaluations grow out of classroom work.

Informal

Informal assessments usually emerge from ongoing classroom learning experiences.

You conduct informal assessments as you use a variety of ways to make judgments about a student's performance. Common formats include checklists, conferences, informal reading inventories, observations, miscue analysis, and portfolios. There are a number of educators who strongly advocate electronic portfolio assessment because students' work over time can be preserved and reevaluated. Later in this chapter, we will discuss this and other ways technology can help you conduct informal assessments. You constantly measure and evaluate students, and informal assessments allow you to view students as they engage in day-to-day literacy activities. Some call this **authentic assessment** (performance-based). (For detailed descriptions of these and other informal assessment techniques such as retellings, process interviews, interest inventories, and running records, see Cooper, 2000.)

EVALUATION

Evaluation involves your judgment of the information you collect regarding how well a student has learned or performs the thing(s) you are assessing. When using formal assessment instruments, the resulting scores, percentages, percentiles, and so forth are intended to help you make judgments about how a student is performing against the normative group's performance. When using informal assessments, you must establish benchmarks or criteria to help you define the degrees of adequacy of student performance. You can use techniques such as **holistic scoring** and **rubrics** to determine how well a student is performing a given task. Holistic scoring involves judging something as a whole and assigning a score from 0 to 4 based on preestablished criteria. The American Library Association defines a rubric as "a scaled set of criteria that clearly defines for the student and the teacher what a range of acceptable and unacceptable performances looks like. Its purpose is to provide a description of successful performance" (ALA, 1998, p. 51). It is very important to establish clear criteria so students know right from the start what they need to know and do to perform successfully. This also clarifies your expectations for both them and you. See the Teaching Tip "Rubrics" for additional ideas, and see a rubric for webfolios on this book's web site.

Formative

Formative evaluations influence instruction; summative evaluations sum up your judgment of the student's performance.

When you use evaluations throughout an ongoing activity, such evaluations are called **formative evaluations** because you and the student use what you discover at that point to help the student be more successful at the finish of the activity.

Summative

If you collect information at the end of an activity, you are using what people call **summative evaluations.** This gives you an opportunity to sum up

TEACHING TIPS Rubrics

A well-known language arts rubric is the Northwest Regional Educational Laboratory's *6+1 TRAITS of Analytical Writing Assessment Scoring Guide.* The rubric areas for assessing and teaching writing, according to this model are "*Ideas,* the heart of the message; *Organization,* the internal structure of the piece; *Voice,* the personal tone and flavor of the author's message; *Word Choice,* the vocabulary a writer chooses to convey meaning; *Sentence Fluency,* the rhythm and flow of the language; *Conventions,* the mechanical correctness; and *Presentation,* how the writing actually looks on the page" (2001, [online]).

A complete set of the rubrics and samples of writing are located at the site, as are a beginning writers' continuum that helps you keep track of writing traits as they develop. See them at **http://www.nwrel.org/assessment/.** In addition, NWREL has a set of rubrics for what they call the six traits of an effective reader. The areas they define, based on extensive research, are decoding conventions, establishing comprehension, realizing context, developing interpretations, integrating for synthesis, and critiquing for evaluation. You can print the rubrics from this location: **http://www.nwrel.org/assessment/scoring.asp?odelay=3&d=2.** The rubrics are designed for various reading areas, including reading informational texts, literary texts, and oral reading.

WebQuests are very popular online activities that became possible only because of the World Wide Web. WebQuests send students to various locations to find information, and you can assess how well students complete their quests. You can also assess how well you and students create WebQuests using "A Rubric for Evaluating WebQuests" at **http://edweb.sdsu.edu/webquest/webquestrubric.html.** A portion of the rubric is shown in accompanying figure.

A Rubric for Evaluating WebQuests

The WebQuest format can be applied to a variety of teaching situations. If you take advantage of all the possibilities inherent in the format, your students will have a rich and powerful experience. This rubric will help you pinpoint the ways in which your WebQuest isn't doing everything it could do. If a page seems to fall between categories, feel free to score it with in-between points.

	Beginning	Developing	Accomplished	Score
Overall Aesthetics (This refers to the WebQuest page itself, not the external resources linked to it.)				
Overall Visual Appeal	0 points There are few or no graphic elements. No variation in layout or typography. OR Color is garish and/or typographic variations are overused and legibility suffers. Background interferes with the readability.	2 points Graphic elements sometimes, but not always, contribute to the understanding of concepts, ideas and relationships. There is some variation in type size, color, and layout.	4 points Appropriate and thematic graphic elements are used to make visual connections that contribute to the understanding of concepts, ideas and relationships. Differences in type size and/or color are used well and consistently. See Fine Points Checklist.	
Navigation & Flow	0 points Getting through the lesson is confusing and unconventional. Pages can't be found easily and/or the way back isn't clear.	2 points There are a few places where the learner can get lost and not know where to go next.	4 points Navigation is seamless. It is always clear to the learner what all the pieces are and how to get to them.	

Source: Used with permission of Bernie Dodge. See the entire page at http://edweb.sdsu.edu/webquest/webquestrubric.html.

how well a student has met the objectives/criteria you established. Report cards and grades are one common vehicle for conveying summative evaluations. As well, standardized tests given at the end of the school year can be considered summative because the bulk of instruction is finished.

ASSESSMENT AND INSTRUCTION

All teachers must become competent at interpreting and applying assessment outcomes to instruction and instructional decisions. Assessment is a natural part of instruction: you constantly assess students as part of the instructional cycle, modifying activities and learning experiences based on what your assessments indicate might help students learn better. This is true not only for individual students, but for the entire class as well. Assessments also let students monitor their own learning, and there is some evidence that frequent assessments help students consolidate learning when knowledge of how well they are doing influences their study habits (Snowman & Biehler, 2000, p. 439).

STANDARDS AND ASSESSMENT

As we explored in chapter 3, national standards by major professional organizations are influencing education in all major curricular areas. Curriculum standards are now common at the state, district, and even school levels. Some states and districts have adopted or modified national standards. Publishers now routinely describe in their catalogs how their products relate to specific national and state standards. Standards are likely to stay with us for a long time, and they are influencing literacy assessment. The so-called standardized high-stakes tests are evidence that politicians want assessment to demonstrate that students are learning the standards they mandate.

With the expectation that your students must pass tests that grow out of standards, you are expected to make connections between classroom learning experiences, teaching-learning strategies, the school's basic curriculum, and the standards with which you are expected to work. Therefore, it is vital for you to know the exact standards you are expected to help students meet. Where standards are specific (e.g., students will be able to recite the alphabet by the end of kindergarten), your classroom activities must also be specific. Where standards are more broadly stated (e.g., students will understand how technology affects society), you can have students engage in many different learning experiences that will prepare them to meet those standards. Looking at just a small sample of the Arizona language arts standards, you can readily see that some standards are broadly stated, and you can have students engage in a wide variety of learning experiences that will help them meet each standard. For instance, Arizona wants students to know and be able to do the following:

Reading Describe the literary elements of fiction and nonfiction; follow a set of written directions.

Writing Apply letter/sound relationships as emergent writers. Write an introductory statement.

Listening/Speaking Follow simple directions. Deliver oral interpretations of literary or original works.

Viewing/Presenting Identify story events or information from visual media. Plan and present a report, using two or more visual media. [Arizona Department of Education (No date). Academic Standards & Accountability: Language Arts Standards. [Online]. Available **http://www.ade.state.az.us/standards/language-arts/** 2001, November 16)].

Arizona's Technology Education Standards, based on the ISTE NETS standards, at **http://www.ade.state.az.us/standards/technology/** are also broad enough to permit you to devise ways for students to meet technology standards. The ISTE technology standards appear in chapter 3 of this book, and you can see how it is possible to integrate technology naturally in thematic units in the *You Were There!* sample unit included in chapter 1. Later in this chapter, we will revisit ISTE standards, thematic units based on them, and their use in assessment.

Assessment is increasingly being tied to local, state, and national standards.

Your assessment practices are increasingly influenced by standards, and you must demonstrate students' progress toward meeting standards such as the above. Some schools and districts have assembled task forces to plan standards-based instruction at each grade level. You can read their reports or clarify expectations in faculty meetings. To ensure coverage of required standards, you, working with other school personnel, can create new activities or modify many of the strategies and activities you already use to develop literacy and technology capabilities. Start with the standards and plan instruction accordingly.

Literacy Assessment and Technology

Some evidence exists that students are motivated by technology and that it aids in the development of some literacy capabilities such as writing (Coley, 1997). Adequate assessment of technology's effect on many literacy abilities, especially higher-level thinking abilities, has been more elusive. One thing is very clear. You cannot wait to use and teach about computer applications and the Internet until researchers resolve all of the issues about how technology influences learning. That may take a long time. Elsewhere I have noted, "It may be years before convincing proof is found, mainly because it will take a thorough study of people growing up immersed in computer technology to examine how they differ in the ways they learn and what they have learned" (Valmont, 2000, p. 167).

Precise knowledge of technology's effect on literacy is elusive.

The rapid changes in computer hardware, software, and innovative uses of multimedia on CD-ROMs and the Internet make it impossible to conduct long-term studies of computer effectiveness. By the time a study progresses over a few years, the hardware and software have changed dramatically, and students are using the next generation of hardware and software. This "moving target" situation of evolving technology makes it difficult to conduct meaningful research (Kamil & Lane, 1998). Others agree. When conducting research about literacy, according to Leu, Karchmer, and Leu (1999, p. 641), "it has become difficult, if not impossible, to develop a consistent body of published research within traditional forums before the technology on which a study is based is replaced by an even newer technology."

In this section, we will take a look at two different aspects of the relationship between technology and assessment. First, we will examine some ways in which the use of technology can facilitate your assessment of your students' literacy development. Next, we will discuss one effective way in which you can assess your students' own learning of technology skills, as well as of literacy skills.

ASSESSING LITERACY WITH THE AID OF TECHNOLOGY

Technology's role, according to *Learning & Leading with Technology* (2000, April, p. 6), "varies from a new delivery system for testing to a vehicle for authentic assessment to a storage-and-viewing system for student portfolios." At this time, there are only a few assessment products for the K–8 market. Several useful products can help you create authentic assessment instruments, and electronic portfolios are quickly becoming valuable for assessing student progress.

Delivery System for Testing

Technology is used as an assessment delivery system for older students and adults.

CD-ROMs and the Internet have great potential as delivery systems of test materials. In fact, colleges and universities are working with several distance learning products (Web CT and Blackboard among others) that include ways students can submit results of quizzes, tests, and essay responses to their instructors via the Web. At this time, however, products for K–12 education are few and far between. This may be true because a sufficient number of good-quality computers, as well as Internet accessibility, are still not available in all classrooms; furthermore, many elementary and middle school teachers have little training in using electronic test-making products. At this point, you can use computers to administer tests. You will, however, most likely have to create them yourself. See the Tech Tip "Creating Online Assessment Instruments" for some suggestions on how to do so.

Software programs such as STAR Reading and Accelerated Reader (both by Advantage Learning Systems) can help you make decisions about placing students in materials at a comfortable reading level and then provide a measure of their success in reading the materials. STAR Reading assesses students' reading by checking their knowledge of vocabulary and paragraph comprehension. It provides an instant analysis for the teacher to

TECH TIPS — CREATING ONLINE ASSESSMENT INSTRUMENTS

Commercial software for assessment of literacy is not widely available for K–8 students, and free assessment materials on the Web are sparse. Colleges and universities are experimenting with online testing, and several publishers are dealing with the higher-education market. Distance learning has piqued interest in long-distance testing, also. For the present time, you might want to experiment for yourself. With some planning of your test items and a little knowledge of a web-authoring tool such as FrontPage, you can create online tests and have students enter their responses directly into a database. Here are web sites that will be helpful to you as you plan and make online assessments.

Webliography

- **Activities for ESL Students**
  http://a4esl.org/
  This extremely useful site has more than a thousand exercises you can use as patterns to create several basic kinds of online quizzes. These were created to help ESL students, but the basic structures are useful for many topics. Most use a cloze format, and some require a Flash Player plug-in you can download free.
- **KnowledgeDesign Instructional Resources**
  http://www.auburn.edu/~mitrege/knowledge/
  George Mitrevski's page at Auburn University contains several tutorials to help you create tests and exercises. This page has links to "How-to Tutorials" for creating cloze exercises, making basic HTML forms, embedding audio in web pages, and more.
- **Sheppard Software**
  http://www.sheppardsoftware.com/contests_trivia.htm
  This site hosts a variety of quizzes (i.e., trivia, word, math) for high school students or possibly advanced middle school students. For a word quiz, you click on a day of the week, and the first word appears. Click the button of what you believe is the correct definition. If you are correct, a box pops up telling you so, but if you are incorrect the definition of the word pops up. There is a running total for your score. These pages suggest ways you can create similar quizzes.
- **Webclass**
  http://www.webclass.asn.au/
  This Australian site has both math and English quizzes. The fun feature of this site is that when correct words are entered into the quiz answer slots, letters also appear in spaces that finish another sentence. First, you select a "puzzle" option; then, before you start, it asks a question. The letters reveal, à la "Wheel of Fortune," the answer to the question. Clever animations make the pages fun.

use as a placement instrument. Accelerated Reader has students read one of more than 32,000 books and then take a test and receive instant feedback about how they did on the test. Teacher reports are also generated. Turtle-back Books sells paperback books with heavily bound covers for many of the books tested by this software. While these programs are a starting place, you will want to conduct additional assessments of both student placement in books and of their successful comprehension of them.

Vehicle for Authentic Assessment

You most likely use authentic assessments to evaluate students' knowledge or skills in actual situations or under realistic conditions. In addition, as mentioned earlier, you use a variety of informal assessment strategies to note student progress. However, in order for such data to be meaningful and useful to you, you must collate, analyze, add comments to, and use your observations to help students. Scraps of paper stuffed in folders may be helpful, but we recommend the use of spreadsheets and databases instead. Once you learn to manage a spreadsheet, you can store and manipulate numbers and other variables from informal assessments such as these:

You can use technology today to help you create and organize informal assessments.

- **Observations.** You observe students daily. You can store your ideas or facts about how well a student reads aloud from a CD-ROM or a web page. You can record information about a student's use of gestures during a Kid Pix presentation. You can make a note about whether a student knows how to save a file to a floppy disk or use the features of a paint program. By building your criteria into a spreadsheet and entering data into it, you can track your observations in a systematic way.
- **Checklists.** Checklists may contain a set of items that you mark when students complete the action called for in the items. You might make simple checklists for the letters of the alphabet, high-frequency sight words, weekly spelling words, or the various types of comprehension abilities (e.g., cause and effect; sequence) you want to monitor. Such checklists are useful when assessing students' writing and speaking or their composing of visual messages. Regardless of the type of content, making checklist templates on a computer and placing your findings into them will permit you to keep good track of both facts and your pertinent comments.
- **Conferences.** Conferences are either structured or informal meetings designed to discuss specific areas of progress. They may be just long enough to review a student's progress in writing a story or working on a web page, or they may be longer to assess a student's success in conducting online research. Regardless, placing information into a word-processing document or a spreadsheet during or immediately after a conference will be most helpful. During conferences, you can track students' progress toward meeting both literacy and technology standards.

- **Journals.** Journals are running records of actions taken, ideas learned, anecdotes, and other observations. Students can create journals with a word-processing program. Then, as you review the journal's entries, you and a student can flag (perhaps in color) items that need to be discussed in greater detail or actions the student needs to take to complete a project. We recommend that students keep a special journal record of sites they visit on the Web while they are preparing reports or any time they encounter online ideas they want to revisit. You may want to keep an electronic teaching journal that you can also add comments to easily.

Observations, checklists, conferences, and journals are appropriate for assessing many of the things you are expecting students to learn. But these informal assessments are not valuable unless you can easily revisit them and use them to guide instruction. Technology can help you get and stay organized. You can find resources to use to create assessments at these web sites.

WEBLIOGRAPHY

- **Exercises, Quizzes, Tests**
  http://eleaston.com/quizzes.html
  This site links you to dozens of online test instruments that you might be interested in using with students or as models to create your own.
- **Hot Potatoes**
  http://web.uvic.ca/hrd/halfbaked/
  You can download and use this product free for nonprofit, educational purposes. It includes six applications. You can make interactive multiple-choice, short-answer, jumbled-sentence, crossword, matching/ordering, and gap-fill exercises to place on a web page.
- **Kelly's Multiple-Choice HTML Quiz Generator**
  http://www.aitech.ac.jp/~iteslj/quizzes/help/write-mc.html
  You can make tests at this site for students to take online.
- **Self-Grading Quiz**
  http://www.webwinder.com/wwhtmbin/jbibquiz.html
  You can see an example of one way to place a quiz online. To modify the example, you will need to know something about HTML and JavaScript web-authoring systems.

Storage and Viewing System of Student Portfolios

Electronic portfolios are effective for storing students' work for future reassessment.

For decades, teachers have collected examples of student writings throughout the year in order to compare students' progress in spelling, penmanship, content, and so forth. Students often kept such materials in folders in their desks or lockers. Teachers routinely encouraged students to take their best work home to share with parents and then to bring it back and put it in their folders or lockers. Students' folders often contained collections of papers, pictures, and so forth. They were difficult to store, and pieces of student work were often discarded or misplaced on the way to and from home. These nonelectronic portfolios were used for assessment and are still being created in schools.

Students, today, can create electronic documents, presentations, web sites, and other electronic products that you, parents, and others can use to evaluate students' improvement over time. More and more, schools are making use of the **CD-RW** (compact disc, rewritable), a readable and writable compact disc onto which you and students can place information. Electronic storage of student materials is gaining in popularity. Compact discs are both durable and portable, making it possible to share a student's work with many people and for students to periodically review their work. With the proper software, students can even add new pieces of work throughout the school year on a single disc. Portfolio assessment, according to the American Library Association (ALA, 1998),

> is a cumulative process in which samples of student work are collected over a period of time to demonstrate the learning that has taken place. The student's portfolio must contain deliberate compilations, not casual collections, of items. The portfolio is a documentation of student growth based on the student's learning goals established at the beginning of the portfolio compilation. The student's own reflection on his or her work is also an important aspect of portfolio assessment. (p. 54)

Electronic storage of assessment materials in portfolios is not only valuable but increasingly necessary as more students present their ideas electronically to others. And because they often follow students through the school years, portfolios allow you and other teachers to assess students development over very long periods of time.

Materials for Creating Portfolios Electronic portfolios, states Barrett (2000, p. 15), "allow the portfolio developer to collect and organize artifacts in many formats (audio, video, graphics, and text)." You and students probably have—or soon will have—ample technology available to create electronic materials to place in electronic portfolios. You need access to a scanner, digital camera, and equipment for digitizing video. The school or district probably has the ability to place digitized files onto a CD-RW. In the classroom, you most likely have a word-processing program (e.g., Word or WordPerfect) that can save materials in HTML format, or software such as PowerPoint or, perhaps, Presentations. Programs such as FrontPage and SiteCentral let students prepare web materials. You may have created templates for students to use as a model for creating portfolios. If you already have these items, then engaging students in portfolio development will be quite feasible for you. If you do not have these materials, determine their availability elsewhere in the school or at the district level. At the very least, students can create their work electronically and store it on floppy disks, zip disks, videotapes, or other storage media.

Content of a Portfolio One definition of a portfolio (as cited in Paulson, Paulson, & Meyer, 1991) reflects the thinking of the Northwest Evaluation Association:

> A portfolio is a purposeful collection of student work that exhibits the students' efforts, progress, and achievements in one or more areas. The collection must include student participation in selecting contents, the criteria for selection, the criteria for judging merit, and evidence of student self-reflection. (p. 60)

Baseline measures of students' literacy efforts can be collected at the beginning of the school year when they create their first electronic materials. Portfolios can include, say Swearingen and Allen (2000, p. 43), "informal reading assessments, teacher observations, writing samples, student self-assessments, audio recordings of student reading, lists of books read by the student, and results of standardized testing." All electronic materials or performances by students are eligible for inclusion in portfolios.

Students assemble examples of their work, which are usually accompanied by their self-reflections and self-analysis of their growth in literacy. Either alone or together with a student, you then review the materials, perhaps suggesting additional items to include in the portfolio. Some educators advocate that very specific things be included. For example, Barrett (1998, p. 7) says electronic portfolios should contain the following:

- learner goals
- guidelines for selecting materials (to keep the collection from growing haphazardly)
- work samples chosen by both student and teacher
- teacher feedback
- student self-reflection pieces
- clear and appropriate criteria for evaluating work (rubrics based on standards)
- standards and examples of good work

Also, some educators like to include parent feedback.

In addition to preserving their work, students gain from preparing electronic portfolios in several ways: students learn to present information in multiple formats; actively select materials for inclusion in portfolios, gaining skills in self-evaluation and assessment; and plan future projects at least as sophisticated as their current projects. They may gain insight into subject matter as they find ways to create projects to share with others (Agnew, Kellerman, & Meyer, 1996).

Portfolio assessment is an effective way for you and students to jointly create and refine the criteria of what constitutes acceptable evidence that students are making progress in developing literacy abilities. You can find a great deal of information about portfolios at Dr. Helen Barrett's web site, How to Create Your Own Electronic Portfolio, found at **http://transition.alaska.edu/www/portfolios/howto/index.html.**

ASSESSING BOTH LITERACY AND TECHNOLOGY SKILLS

Both literacy and technology capabilities must be assessed.

Technology and literacy are intricately intertwined because literacy includes understanding and producing both verbal and nonverbal symbol systems. Students read and hear verbal messages as well as interpret nonverbal messages. They speak and write verbal messages as well as construct visual messages. They receive messages from print as well as electronic sources, and they produce messages for others in both print and electronic formats. Since students are growing up in a computer-dependent world, they *must* use technology skills to learn and to communicate, and you must assess their knowledge of technologies and their ability to use them. Your task, then, is to assess both literacy and technology competencies.

You may find it helpful to administer inventory-like quizzes like the one in Figure 10.1, to get an early sense of your students' computer familiarity

FIGURE 10.1

Self Quiz: Internet Terminology

Self Quiz: Internet Terminology

Please click on the correct answer

---

1 IRC is what?

- A Individual Relay Column
- B Internet Reaction Core
- C Internet Relay Chat
- D Internet Relay Corporation

---

2 What is an electronic bulletin board?

- A A board that uses computer components as pushpins.
- B A place on the Internet where you can post and read messages.
- C A place on the Internet where messages can only be read.
- D A place on the Internet where major questions are answered.

---

3 What is a cursor?

- A A drunken sailor on the town.
- B The place where you exit the program/application you are in.
- C The flashing/non-flashing line/icon that shows where you are working on the screen.
- D Someone who uses the Internet frequently and with great skill.

---

4 Which of these does the Internet embrace?

- A E-mail and browsers only.
- B Usenet and E-mail only.
- C Browsers, E-mail, and the World Wide Web.
- D All of the above.

---

5 What is a modem?

- A A device that connects your computer to other computers.
- B A device that connects your computer to a telephone line.
- C A device that generates images.
- D A device that allows you to access your E-mail without being connected to the Internet.

---

6 What does HTML stand for?

- A Hyperstudio Testing Multiple Languages
- B HyperTest of Multiple Lines
- C HyperText Markup Language
- D HyperText Mailto Link

---

7 Which is NOT a search engine?

- A Infoseek
- B Dogpile
- C Yahoo!
- D HotByte

---

8 What is a URL?

- A A web site's address.
- B The owner of a web site.
- C A redirection service.
- D Specialized software for the web.

and Internet knowledge. You can then work toward addressing gaps in their skills, much as you would in traditional literacy instruction.

At the beginning of this book we noted that the introduction of technology into the classroom led to increased use of collaborative learning experiences. This means that some of your assessments will involve looking at how students are performing as they work on literacy projects together. We also noted the influence of constructivism on classroom learning experiences. This means you will need to assess your students as they try to learn things on their own. Assessing small groups' as well as individual students' learning and productivity can be a challenge, and you will want to establish clear criteria for doing so.

Technology Standards (NETS) and Thematic Units

Although several different sets of standards (see chapter 3) can be used to develop instructional units and also for assessment of what has been learned in these units, here we focus on the ISTE standards. The ISTE publication *National Educational Technology Standards for Students: Connecting Curriculum and Technology* (2000) describes, in detail, thematic language arts units that include a variety of computer and Internet activities. Among these thematic units are the following:

- **Awesome Authors.** This project, an author study, incorporates a planned online visit (or a videotape visit) with the author. Students locate and organize information, and they create questions they would like to ask using Inspiration as an organization tool. This is designed for grades Pre-K–2. (p. 36)
- **Brrrr, It's Alive.** Students locate information about cold-weather animals and produce an electronic report. As part of the process, students create riddles about animals. This is designed for grades Pre-K–2. (p. 40)
- **Wall of Fame.** When studying the biography genre, students find online information about famous people, enter the people's dates on a timeline they create, contribute to a list of characteristics that made the people famous or great, and create a graphic element (personal symbol) for the specific person they study. Students present their findings electronically. This is designed for grades 3–5. (p. 44)
- **You Were There!** The historical fiction novel *My Brother Sam Is Dead* by James and Christopher Collier is used to teach point of view (POV). Students create a word-processed editorial from either the British or Colonial point of view. Students select one of the Boston Massacre victims and work in groups to create a multimedia presentation about the victim. This is designed for grades 3–5. (p. 48)
- **Birthstone Project with a Multimedia Twist.** Students write autobiographies (including birthstone information), prepare multimedia presentations of

the information they locate, and create a web site. This is designed for grades 6–8. (p. 52)

- **Creating a Heroic Character.** Students study heroes online and compile a list of characteristics of heroic people. They also create a number of questions they could ask heroic people, and they try to answer those questions from online or print information they locate. Instruction in using detailed images in writing is part of the project. This is designed for grades 6–8. (p. 56)

Examples of English language arts thematic units for grades 9–12 are also included in the ISTE examples (see **http://www.iste.org/**). The IRA/NCTE literacy standards (see chapter 3) are keyed to each one of the language arts thematic units and are an important part of the Multidisciplinary Resource Units found in the ISTE book. The ISTE examples make it amply clear that language arts and technology standards are easily integrated in instruction during thematic units. Evaluation is a natural and necessary part of thematic work, just as it is with any other learning experiences.

You can evaluate student projects that grow out of thematic work in terms of how well students are meeting both literacy and technology standards on which the units are based. For instance, in the "Awesome Authors" unit, you can assess the quality of the questions students create as well as their interactions with the authors, and you can assess their use of Inspiration. For the "Brrr, It's Alive" unit, you can assess student riddles and reports, as well as students' use of the features in the presentation program they use to make their electronic reports. For the "Wall of Fame" unit, you can assess not only the content students contribute, but also assess their online research skills while using a web browser. In addition, you can evaluate the graphic elements students create as well as their use of a paint program to create them. Thematic units tied to standards give you abundant opportunities to assess both process (technology use) and product (content) in authentic learning contexts, so we highly recommend that you integrate generous amounts of technology into your unit plans.

Using thematic units can help you create opportunities to assess both process (technology) and content (literacy).

Assessing Multimedia Presentations

Computers connected to viewing systems such as a computer video projector permit students to give presentations, and you should assess not only the content of their presentations, but the presentations as well. You can use many of the pointers found in chapter 7 to help students make effective presentations. You can also use those suggestions to help you create checklists or to develop rubrics to assess the acceptability of students' presentation techniques. Let students know what you are expecting of them early in the school year by sharing and explaining such checklists and rubrics, and use these as the starting point at individual assessment conferences throughout the year.

You can assess various aspects of student presentations:

- **Preparation.** Look for evidence that the student conducted adequate research on which to base the presentation.
- **Methods of delivery.** Look at the methods and materials the student uses to convey ideas to others (e.g., Inspiration, PowerPoint, live Internet, etc.) and how well they use them.
- **Clarity of deliver.** Look for the logical and comprehensible organization of information.
- **Style of deliver.** Look at speech, gestures, poise, effective use of props or equipment.

By creating checklists or rubrics for these and other aspects of making presentations that are based on advice you give students, you will create useful assessment instruments.

To conclude, assessment opportunities are bountiful when you use technology in your classroom. Check the menus of any software programs you use to determine if they have built-in assessments. Consider the possible ways you might use any of your programs as tools for assessment. We recently learned that some teachers are using Inspiration and Kidspiration, programs that are designed as graphic organizers, specifically to assess individual students' knowledge. Students read a book or story and then create graphics with the software to reveal what they know and remember. In some cases, teachers create templates of story elements (e.g., plot, setting, characters), and students reveal their knowledge of these things by adding to the diagrams. This is a very creative use of a program for assessment purposes.

SUMMARY

- Assessment involves both gathering and evaluating data about a student's performance.
- Formal standardized tests and ongoing informal classroom assessments are quite different ways of appraising students' performance.
- Informal assessments are linked to actual classroom experiences.
- Assessments should inform and influence a given student's future instruction.
- The standards movement is heavily influencing what is being assessed in schools.
- Because of standards and their pervasive influence, technology usage must be assessed.

- Technology can deliver assessments, help you create authentic assessments, and preserve assessments for long periods of time.
- Using thematic units helps you meld together literacy and technology capabilities.

ACTIVITIES

1. Locate (online if possible) and examine your state's literacy and technology standards.
2. Choose a standard and plan literacy and technology experiences to help students meet it.
3. Create a checklist or rubric for evaluating a student's electronic presentation.
4. Make a list of ten things a student might place in an electronic portfolio.

SOFTWARE

Informal Reading Comprehension Placement Test, Educational Activities, All
Thirteen selections are used to determine comprehension levels, and 104 items measure word meanings. The instrument is based on three readability formulas.

Learner Profile, Sunburst Technology, All
This program lets you decide what you want to assess, lets you enter your observations, and generates reports using the information you input.

Learning Styles Inventory, Educational Activities, All
Students respond to forty-five statements in nine learning style sub-areas. Graphs show individual or class profiles. (Available also in Spanish.)

Portfolio Builder, Visions Technology in Education, 3 and up
Students can create multimedia portfolios with this software.

QuizWorks, Current Works, 6–8
Teachers and students can create quizzes. Can be used to encourage interactivity through playing games.

Rubricator, The, Strategic Learning Technologies, Teacher
This software will help you design and use rubrics.

FOR FURTHER READING

Burns, P. C., & Roe, B. D. (1999). *Informal reading inventory: Preprimer to twelfth grade* (5th ed.). Boston: Houghton Mifflin.

Chase, M., & Jensen, R. (Eds.). (1999). *Meeting standards with Inspiration: Core curriculum lesson plans.* Portland, OR: Inspiration Software, Inc.

Harris, J. (2000). Activity design assessments. *Learning & Leading with Technology, 27*(7), 2–45.

Levinson, E., & Surrat, J. (2000). The education killer app is coming. *Converge, 3*(5), 74–75.

Sun, J. (2000). How do we know it's working? *Learning & Leading with Technology, 27*(7), 32–35, 41, 49.

EPILOGUE

Where Is Technology Taking Us?

INTRODUCTION The rapid deployment of technology over the last decade or more has had a profound influence on schooling, on what it means to be literate, and on how teachers interact with students. In this century, students will have access to more information than have any other students before them. They must learn to locate, assess, and use information wisely. As students become more independent, self-sufficient learners—as they must—teachers have got to become better facilitators of learning, helping students pursue their interests and career paths.

Developing students' literacy abilities in the digital age is an important and challenging job, and you will have the excitement of seeing students' attitudes and abilities flourish. To be an effective teacher, you must be skilled at using and teaching about technology in order to help students master the capabilities they need. Indeed, your teaching job may well depend on your knowledge of technology because school boards and principals are demanding technology competence in both new and continuing teachers.

Technology's Influences on Schooling

The amazing rapid growth of the Internet and the WWW is a clear indication that people everywhere recognize the importance of telecommunications for teaching, learning, locating information, and having fun. Consider these two items:

- There were more than sixty million web site addresses (URLs) and nearly seventy-five million domain names registered worldwide by 2002.
- On an average day, people are predicted to send about thirty-five billion e-mail messages by the year 2005.

The attraction or mystique of web-based documents has already changed the reading habits as well as the buying habits of many people. For instance, some print newspapers are struggling with sales because fewer people are buying them; some people would rather get their news at online sites that are frequently updated. Devices for downloading e-books are quickly gaining in popularity. In addition, e-commerce has blossomed, with people buying everything from books to airline tickets. Thus, technology's impact has been highly visible in business and entertainment.

Having better technology in classrooms heavily impacts literacy instruction.

Technology has had less of a major, systemic impact on literacy education up to now, but its use in language and visual arts activities is gaining strength in schools. As they get computers and Internet access in their classrooms, increasing numbers of teachers are able to integrate technology into their daily routines. This is important because school life must include the kinds of technological experiences students are having out of school. Students must not feel as if they "stepped back in time to an antiquated age of dim, fuzzy images from outdated projectors. Otherwise, woe to the teacher who's responsible for . . . [their] learning and is trying to keep . . . [their] attention," says Louis Lento (1999, p. 43). It is not just a matter of competing with cell phones, television, electronic games, and the Web. Students certainly enjoy all of those devices, but network-capable laptop computers allow learning to occur everywhere, and that is important to more and more students. Be a proponent of technology. One way to do so is to urge your legislators to support technologies that you can use to help students develop literacy capabilities. Your efforts may help bring about real, systemic changes in teaching and learning. Consider these examples:

- Florida High School, a virtual high school, offers more than sixty courses to more than 8,000 students, and Kentucky Virtual High School offers courses to students around the state.
- Alabama On-line High School has required courses and several elective courses accessible statewide.
- Fairleigh Dickinson University students are now required to take one course a year online.

Schools, colleges, and businesses are demanding better technology skills because they see them as extremely necessary learning tools. It is increasingly clear that you must help students become more computer savvy as they move through the elementary and middle school grades. As you help them develop literacy skills, you are also helping them gain ownership of the powerful learning tools they definitely need as they move to high school and beyond.

CHANGING ROLE OF SCHOOLS

As we have noted, some high schools are already engaging students in distance learning, and it is most likely that at some time in the near future, elementary and middle school teachers will need to learn about and use distance learning equipment and techniques, also. You already engage in collaborative learning activities with teachers and students in other locations.

Schools will become less isolated as students telecollaborate with people elsewhere.

Where students are already engaging in telecollaborative projects, the changing nature of schooling is evident. Students *like* to communicate with students at a distance, to use online electronic references, and to make electronic presentations to others either in person or online. Students seem to be attracted to technology that lets them communicate with the world outside their own schools. Schools may use technology to overcome isolating students within one location and open new worldwide vistas for them.

CHANGING ROLE OF PUBLISHERS

For publishers, "print delivery will transform into Web-based delivery" (Levinson & Surrat, 2000, p. 74). When author Stephen King published a novella exclusively on the Internet in the year 2000, it confirmed for publishers that it *is* possible to make a profit selling online books. Publishers were moving slowly to gauge marketing potential for online books but redoubled efforts to make their materials available online faster after that electronic offering's success.

E-book readers, electronic devices into which you can load electronic novels, are becoming popular because of their valuable features, many of which are similar to those in word-processing programs. You can scroll through text, search for keywords or phrases, insert comments, underline, change fonts and colors, and use built-in dictionaries. Photos, graphics, and animations add nonverbal messages, and audio and video clips can enrich comprehension. The ability to increase font size is very helpful for people with visual problems, and future students will benefit from being able to carry one e-book device rather than the heavy print books that presently weigh down students' backpacks. Students will also gain because publishers will be able to frequently update nonfiction materials.

You can easily download books and other e-materials from the Web to read on e-book devices. The devices are still fairly expensive, but

Electronic devices and materials enable "anytime, anywhere learning" minus heavy books.

second- and third-generation devices are getting better and have added features. About the size of a small book or notebook, the readers are light and contain rechargeable batteries that last several hours. To learn a great deal about e-book readers and related topics, see **http://www.digital output.net/edittopic5wl.html.** Here are some ideas to ponder:

- Libraries report that e-book devices they make available to the public are very popular.
- Young children appear to take to e-books quite naturally, and they are quickly gaining in popularity with the public.
- Microsoft ClearType is a typeface created to use with Microsoft Reader. It is designed to be much clearer to read than many other fonts and styles. It has a dictionary and highlighter.
- Classwell Learning Group offers, for grades K–12, teaching aids, content, and services.
- Microsoft predicts that e-book sales will overtake paper by 2009.
- Students are checking out books at amazing rates and are using the NetLibrary eBook Reader at **http://www.netlibrary.com** to read books that are in the public domain.

Efforts to improve lightweight, portable e-book devices and indications of their acceptance lead us to agree with other educators who predict that e-books will become ubiquitous. "In the not-too-distant future all works will be electronic" say Bull, Bull, Blazi, and Cochran (1999–2000, p. 56), and they add, "Virtually all new works are now submitted to publishers in electronic form, and older works are being rapidly converted to electronic formats in academic sites such as the Electronic Text Center [at the University of Virginia]." Older readers are slower to accept e-books, but the emerging generations will not have this difficulty, with the possible result that more young people will read more widely.

Two other publishing trends are pertinent to the future of the interconnectedness of technology and literacy. One trend is the major movement of companies to position themselves as online application service providers (ASPs), who provide educational products and services to schools that reside on the ASP's—not the school's—server. Schools and districts are able to *lease* instead of buy software and services at affordable prices. The second trend is publishers' push to take advantage of online delivery of products while abandoning nondigital products and even the more recent CD-ROM business they, the publishers themselves, encouraged. It has become almost as reliable to download files from the Internet as it is to use information on CD-ROMs, and publishers have discovered that they can cut expenses drastically when they do not have to package and distribute physical products, much less deal with the personnel required in order to do so. You can access educational products and files by downloading them or by using a publisher's server to house your data. The convenience is compelling!

CHANGING ROLE OF SELF-RESPONSIBILITY

Learners' self-responsibility and critical thinking has become more vital at earlier ages.

A major theme in this book is that students must become critical readers, listeners, and interpreters of nonverbal messages, as well as critical thinkers from the earliest grade levels on. Electronic devices and the Internet surround students today, and new technologies will enable them to access even more voluminous amounts of electronic materials. You must take every opportunity to help students gain skills and confidence in their ability to deal competently with the materials they encounter online because neither you nor librarians, publishers, or government agencies can protect students from electronic misinformation and nasty people. Students must learn to use technology to gather and organize information, and it is your job to help them develop intelligent literacy strategies for thinking critically and using information wisely and creatively.

Technology's Influences on Literacy

The explosion of online electronic materials and CD-ROMs foreshadows that which is yet to come. In less than a decade, the metamorphosis of online text has been amazing, and the quality of online graphics rivals the most beautiful print artwork. Primary source never-before-accessible materials are now common, and many nations are sharing their museums and other resources with the entire world. Online news is on par with radio and television for its currency. Many students fully understand that they have genuine audiences when they collaborate and share ideas with other students in remote locations. Still unanswered is the struggle over control of the Internet. There will surely be debates about this issue for many years to come.

MORE, BETTER, AUTHENTIC, INTERNATIONAL, AND CURRENT ELECTRONIC MATERIALS

E-materials will improve when educators gain technology skills to improve them.

The production of more and better electronic devices and materials is inevitable. People want to have an online presence, and it is becoming easier and easier to do so. Educational web sites will be of higher quality because of competition for awards, the recognition of excellence, and the improvement in teachers' abilities to create web sites. There will be better understanding of how to deliver interactive educational content. There will be more pride of ownership. Commercial sites will offer more free materials because companies want to attract more potential customers to their sites. As additional government agencies' documents go online, people will be able to analyze information and ideas and produce original works based on them.

Not only is there a large presence of web sites in English, but writers and speakers of other languages are increasingly placing materials online. Web sites with nonalphabetic characters such as Chinese symbols used in writing are increasing. English sites are being translated into other languages to accommodate people around the world. The universality of the Web is one major factor adding to its value; another is its changeability.

Here is one example of technology that points out how the ability to change the content of electronic documents is a priority. Two companies, Xerox (**http://www.parc.xerox.com/parc-go.html**) and E Ink (**http://www.eink.com**), are independently developing digital displays with very clear images on a surface resembling ink on paper. This new "paper" can be updated instantly through electronic signals. This means that such things as news, directions, and weather forecasts can be shown and *changed immediately* as events occur. While reading a document, readers can see the electronic paper change as they activate a device to receive updates. E Ink already makes indoor signs for retailers such as J.C. Penney, which can send signals to stores to make instant changes in prices of sale items.

MORE SHARING AND COLLABORATION

Telecollaborative projects will become ubiquitous.

The ease of sending documents as attachments to e-mail and the ease of placing documents and other electronic materials online make it possible for two or more people to work collaboratively with ease. Elsewhere, we described telecollaborative activities that students and teachers have been using, and we believe that as more classrooms gain additional computers and connectivity to the Internet, these valuable joint projects will increase exponentially. The production of this book is an excellent example of telecollaboration. I have never been in the same physical place as the various editors and production people who have brought this work into being; everything was completed through telecollaboration.

MORE THREATS OF CENSORSHIP AND CONTROL

Censorship and control of web materials will remain controversial.

Debates about how much control should reside in the hands of legislators and others with high-stakes interests in the information industry will continue for some time. Issues about freedom of speech and individual responsibilities must be examined. For instance, the Children's Internet Protection Act is a federal law mandating that schools have Internet filters in place, and this troubles groups such as the American Library Association and the American Civil Liberties Union. Filters are supposed to filter out web sites that are inappropriate for children, but they also filter out useful sites containing certain words. Sites containing the words "breast cancer," for example, would be filtered.

Censorship has long been a part of some countries' history, but it is increasingly difficult for such countries to shield their inhabitants from electronic reading materials, particularly those people who have wireless technologies that can access the Internet via satellites. It is too early to determine how long a "wide open" Internet will persist. A related concern is the possibility of cybersnooping by agencies, businesses, or parents, given that cell phones may become electronic homing devices. Consider these examples:

- Spector (see **http://www.spectorsoft.com/**) records "snapshots" of computer screens and replays them to interested snoopers to show what programs people have opened, what web sites they visited, their chat room conversations, and all keystrokes and e-mail activity.
- Cell phones are able to receive downloads from webcams (cameras sending continual signals to the Internet) in their homes.

Several of these new or up-and-coming electronic devices have great potential for helping people, perhaps even saving their lives. The thought that many new devices offer opportunities for others to find out so much about individuals, however, is perturbing.

MORE EMPHASIS ON THE HUMAN SIDE OF TEACHING AND LEARNING

Unfortunately, too many people equate the memorization of facts with learning and understanding. Technology is helping educators better realize that it is impossible to know all of the facts about everything. Sometimes, learning is about knowing how to find facts, but, more important, learning is a continuing lifetime process, and people need strategies to be able to learn on their own throughout their entire lives. People also learn in social situations, and schools help students learn about themselves in the contexts of their lives. Connie Louie, of the Massachusetts Department of Education, answered the question, "In the future, will there be schools as we know them today?" by saying, "There will be a place for students to go. It may not be a traditional classroom, but it will be somewhere with a teacher because they'll still need a teacher to facilitate learning—the human factor has to be there" (Brown, 2000, p. 55).

You are more important than ever as the human factor in education.

Teachers will continue to be needed to help students who require advice and direction, assistance in clarifying and interpreting ideas, and assurances they are doing things well and in productive ways. Social and emotional developments throughout school occur through constant interactions with teachers and other students, but technology cannot deal with such matters other than to enable communication. As pre- or in-service teachers helping students develop literacy capabilities, you already know how to direct students to online and offline reading materials so they can deal with a personal problem. *You know* that discussions about pertinent topics which sometimes arise incidentally while talking about stories or nonfiction selections are more helpful to students than any facts or figures in those materials. *You represent* the human, personal side of teaching, and this role is becoming even more valuable in the information age.

Technology's Influences on Teaching

Technology is helping educators adopt supportive roles. As librarians have done historically, teachers today are helping students learn how to find, analyze, use, and create knowledge. Technology allows students to collaborate and share as never before, making learning a more interactive endeavor. Teachers and students alike can work together as coinquirers about many topics, and teachers can use their knowledge and wisdom to help students think productively and engage in educationally sound investigations.

Whoever said, "If you are worried that technology will replace you, you should be!" was correct. Teachers who believe their job is mainly to transmit knowledge to students should be replaced by someone else. Much of the important learning in schools is facilitated by interactions between teachers and students, and that will not change regardless of technology's influence.

You will become better at facilitating learning as students pursue their interests.

Teachers using technology to enhance literacy development have discovered that their roles quickly evolve into being more of a facilitator of students' learning. According to Skarecki and Insinnia (1999, p. 24), "being the sole source of information and using the 'stand and deliver' approach to education doesn't serve the students of today." As technology evolves at a faster and faster pace, new jobs replace old jobs, and students will need to develop intellectual flexibility in order to move from one job to another. "We're trying to teach a generation of children who will be completely reeducated six or seven times in their lifetime—that is, they'll make six or seven complete career changes. To do this successfully, they must become independent problem solvers and lifelong learners" (Skarecki & Insinnia, 1999, p. 27).

TEACHERS MUST EXPERIENCE WHAT AND HOW STUDENTS ARE READING

MTV made a major impact on television programming for younger people. The style of jiggly cameras, fast collages, and counterbalancing words and music gave a new look and feel to popular music on television. Adults, including many teachers, were unaccustomed to the major departure from the music television shows of the past, and they were uncomfortable with the need to process information coming at them simultaneously from competing visual and auditory signals. So, they avoided MTV instead of trying to understand what young people were experiencing. Adults stopped experiencing what youngsters became accustomed to viewing.

You must experience what and how students read, listen to, and interpret electronic messages.

You need to experience what and how students are reading when they read from CD-ROMs, the Web, e-books, handheld devices, and any other technologically based electronic tools they encounter in the future. While there may not be a great deal of text to video games, you should experience those as well because they typically bombard users with images in ways you may not have experienced. We hope that the definition of literacy we use in chapter 1 will encourage you to think about and experience the technologies students use outside of school that have such major impacts on their attention spans, their attitude toward literacy development, and their ability to attend to polysymbolic messages in their environment. If you experience what they experience, you will be better able to understand students, communicate with them, and help them learn.

TEACHERS MUST CREATE CLASSROOM EXPERIENCES TO TAKE ADVANTAGE OF NEW TECHNOLOGIES

Your leadership will guide students in learning to use technology well.

You have used pencils, pens, crayons, watercolors, paper, worksheets, and print books to teach literacy skills, and there are hundreds of activities you may have already developed using these older technologies. Now, you can use newer technologies to engage students in many of the same activities. Encourage students to use technology to learn everything from developing phonemic awareness to becoming independent critical readers. There are plenty of electronic materials to read using CD-ROMs and the Web. Students will learn facts, make inferences, study vocabulary, and engage in most of the traditional reading behaviors while working in electronic media. In addition, they will learn to track their thought processes as they navigate through hypertext and other new electronic formats they encounter. Students will learn to produce messages electronically, creating speeches and presentations in programs designed to help them organize, make ideas visual, and share their ideas with others. Using the multiple features of electronic materials, students will learn to construct meaning for others to see and hear, and they will learn to have an active voice in deciding what they want to learn. They will take advantage of the portability of texts using small electronic devices and learn to use electronic features—such as quickly and easily searching through text using keywords. Without your leadership and guidance in using the new learning technologies, students might still learn some of these things, but probably not in ways that are rich in educational value or as thoroughly. You can model effective strategies for searching the Internet or a CD-ROM. You can help students value the use of databases and spreadsheets to sort and analyze collections. You can guide students as they organize and create reports, stories, and web sites. You can open students' minds to understanding that they have literacy skills that go way beyond those used when they interact with paper print. You and students will profit from your efforts to educate them in the use of the newest learning technologies. You not only can help students do these things better, but you can help them do better things using the major helpful features that are part of modern electronic technologies.

In Conclusion

There have been cries for systemic changes in education for decades, and frustrated politicians and parents want accountability. They often react by demanding better student performance on high-stakes tests, pushing for vouchers to move students to private or other schools, and encouraging people to open charter schools. They are not happy to learn that computers sometimes sit in classrooms for long periods of time without being used. They are not happy to hear that students are permitted to use computers as a "reward" after they get their "real" work done. They are not happy to learn that students play computer games or surf the Web visiting sites that have no relevance to your curriculum. They are not happy with teachers who cannot use computers well for instruction and who do not help students use them for learning.

About two-thirds of today's teachers are not comfortable using the Internet and computers, but as professional development efforts gain ground, this percentage should drop dramatically, as it must. Letting more generations of technologically deprived students leave public schools is intolerable. Computers have had a profound effect on the world, and with new technologies emerging, teachers and students will have to make every effort to keep up. Pre- and in-service teachers must make technologies an integral part of teaching and learning or, as Bruce Balen said to Catherine Keefe, a reporter for the *Orange County Register,* teachers would "act as foolishly as the sillies who kept scribbling books on vellum after the printing press was invented in the 1400s" (Keefe, 1994, p. D5). You owe it to students to keep up with emerging technologies, and as Donald Leu (1997, p. 65) remarked, "No matter how technologically challenged anyone of us feels, each of us must enter this new world and make every attempt to keep up with the changes taking place in what literacy means."

One of the pioneers of technology in education is Seymour Papert, who sees the potential for major changes in schooling because of the use of technology. He encourages teachers to imagine various scenarios about schooling. Papert speculates that grade levels might disappear when "age segregation" is not used to group people. He ponders the idea that classrooms may fall by the wayside as people realize that students learn in all kinds of settings, and he suggests that traditional ideas about curriculum may be replaced because not everyone has to acquire the exact same knowledge (Papert, 1998). Papert feels certain that technology will have a major effect on schooling because of "Kid Power," noting that

> the real army that will make the system change is filled with troops of kids. Kids who have grown up with computers at home will be less and less inclined to let parents or teachers get away with loose talk and backward ideas. They will be less and less willing to buy into a school system that offers learning that is inferior to what they can experience outside. (p. 12)

One way or another, the growing use of technology will impact every teacher and every student. Technologies are being created for the future that will have profound effects on many aspects of life both in and out of school. Consider these:

- MIT and IBM are conducting research using *affective computers* that detect the emotional state of a person using them. Sensors read vital signs such as heart rates and rates of breathing, and modify the activities on the computer accordingly. The sensors are embedded in a computer mouse or built into belts, jewelry, or other items worn by the computer user. As you read, the content adjusts to your emotions, altering the reading experience.
- Logitech has created the iFeel MouseMan, a computer mouse that lets you "feel" different textures as you move it across a web page. The company believes that web pages in the future will incorporate the sense of touch, and this could add an exciting new dimension to reading online as you "feel" a pillow or "touch" a wall.

Having a computer is becoming more and more crucial for learners. High school and college-bound students are increasingly facing pressure to own computers, and K–8 students must be prepared to use them when they go on to higher grades. You may need to prepare students to be part of first a virtual high school and then a virtual university. Think of the independent literacy and study habits students will need, including the ability to collaborate while working cooperatively with other students whom they will never meet. Some schools are requiring students to have laptops and are shutting down school computer labs.

It is important to realize that both the context and content of literacy will change in the coming years, and literacy as defined in chapter 1 will continue to be critical in the lives of all people. "The shift from print to the computer," Jay David Boulter says in Korolenko (1997, p. 27), "does not mean the end of literacy. What will be lost is not literacy itself, but the literacy of print, for electronic technology offers us a new kind of book and new ways to write and read." Korolenko notes that oral storytelling did not die when Gutenberg created the printing press and Korolenko reminds us that novels did not go away when films became popular. Literacies simply evolve!

Glossary

acceptable use policy (AUP) School policies regulating what students may and may not do working at school computers.
advanced organizers Short summaries designed to overview and provide structure to upcoming materials.
affective Pertaining to the emotional aspects of thinking.
anachronism Something out of its correct historical time.
analogy approach An approach that utilizes consonant or vowel substitution to help students transfer knowledge of phonic elements in one word to another word.
analytic approach An approach that keeps phonemes in the context of whole words.
applets Programs downloaded from the Internet and executed on one's own computer.
assessment The process of collecting information about a person's understandings, skills, and abilities as well as making judgments about that person's performance.
authentic assessment Assessing students as they engage in routine day-to-day literacy activities.

Boolean logic The logical operators, based on Boolean algebra, used to limit searches. Typically AND, OR, and NOT.

CD-RW (compact disc, rewritable) A compact disc (CD) onto which you can place files. You can then view the files.
character web Often, a graphic with lines drawn from a character's name or image to words or phrases descriptive of that character.
cloze strategy A strategy in which letters or words are deleted from a passage and students make use of their general knowledge or phonemic knowledge to fill in acceptable replacements.
cobweb sites Web sites that are very much outdated.
computer video projector A device for projecting computer images onto a screen.
constructivism The theory, practice, or belief that people construct meanings for themselves.
contiguity Related to proximity.
creative dramatics Unrehearsed, extemporaneous acting of known stories.
creative reading Reading that involves relating ideas to other ideas and making inferences and intuitive leaps.
critical listening Actively being aware of a speaker's logic, attempts to persuade, and/or motivations.
critical reading Evaluating while reading and comparing ideas with standards as well as making conclusions about accuracy, appropriateness, and timeliness.
cropping Cutting out unwanted or unneeded parts of an image.
CyberHunt An activity in which people access identified web sites to search for specific information.

deductive strategy A teaching strategy in which the teacher shows a letter and makes the sound associated with the letter.
diacritical markings Marks added to letters to indicate specific phonetic values.
dramatic play Acting that simulates real-life experiences such as washing a car.

e-materials Verbal and nonverbal messages that are electronically generated.
evaluation Your judgment of student performance based on the information you collect.

flash A file format that permits authors to place animations and interactivity on web pages.
formative evaluations Evaluations made throughout an ongoing activity.

genre Distinctive types or forms of, for instance, art or children's literature.
graphemes Letters on a page or computer screen.

gutter Added space in a margin for binding pages without interfering with the text.

hackers People who use their computer expertise to tamper with data or programs.
headers Coded identification information placed at the top of web pages.
holistic scoring Judging something as a whole and assigning a score from 0 to 4 based on preestablished criteria.
hornbook Usually, a small wooden paddle on which letters, words, or sentences were printed.
HTML The acronym for hypertext markup language, which uses tags to mark elements to indicate how web browsers will make them appear.
hypertext Coded words or graphics in electronic text, which, if you mouse click on them, link you to a different portion of verbal text, sound, or visual material located elsewhere in the same document, another web site, or another file.

independent DRTA A self-directed Directed Reading-Thinking Activity.
independent reading Reading that is not teacher directed.
inductive strategy A teaching strategy in which students discover and understand (induce) a grapheme-phoneme relationship from examples in whole words.
Internet literacy Understanding the organization and form (e.g., image, text, audio, video) of information found on the Internet.
interpretive reading Constructing meaning through making inferences and intuitive leaps.
invented spelling Children's attempts to write words using rudimentary knowledge of sounds and letters.

keyboarding Typing on a computer keyboard, including the function and other keys.
K-W-L A strategy that has readers describe what they already know and what they want to learn as well as reveal what they have learned.

landscape mode A horizontal page layout.
literal reading Reading primarily for factual understanding.

media literacy The ability to identify, interpret, and construct in multiple communications formats (e.g., video, music, art).
metasearch engines (metacrawlers) Computer programs that search several other search engines in parallel and report results from each of those engines.

navigation aids On a web site, buttons or other links that help you move to various parts of the site.
netiquette Etiquette conventions when communicating via a computer.

orthography The representation of sounds using graphic letters.

PDF (portable document format) A system, created by Adobe, that enables viewing of documents using Adobe's Acrobat Reader.
Phonemes The smallest units of sound in oral language that distinguish one word from another.
phonemic awareness Understanding phonemes and such elements as rhymes.
phonics A system for teaching students to link the sounds of a language with the graphic symbols used to represent those sounds.
plug-ins Small software programs that add functionality to larger software programs.
point of view (POV) Understanding something from a specific perspective.
portrait mode A vertical page layout.

recoding Changing something from one symbol system to another without understanding. For example, you recode when you appropriately pronounce words you see in print but do not know what they mean.
recursive Moving back and forth through various stages of the writing process.
rubrics Scaled sets of criteria that clearly define a range of acceptable and unacceptable performances on a task.

scaffolding Providing support until a task can be completed independently.
scan Reading lightly to get the gist without an intent to memorize.
search engines Computer programs that locate specific sites on the World Wide Web.
server A computer with software designed to handle e-mail, web sites, and other administrative electronic communications.

SGML/TEI (standard generalized markup language–text encoded initiative) Like HTML, SGML is a system of enabling users to define the structure of their electronic documents.
sight words Words people recognize instantly without using decoding skills to analyze them.
skim Searching text for specific kinds of information such as names or dates.
spelling conscience Having a desire to spell words correctly at all times.
spelling consciousness Being aware that one has spelled words correctly or incorrectly.
storyboarding Indicating what a reader or viewer will eventually see and/or hear in a constructed message when it is created.
streaming audio Sound that plays through a computer's speakers directly from the Internet while the file is being transmitted.
study Carefully reading texts with an intent to understand and remember.
summative evaluations Evaluations made after an activity is finished.
synthetic approach An approach that starts by teaching students individual letter/sound pairs and, later, the blending together of sounds.

technology Computers and the systems that enable the Internet and World Wide Web.
techspeak The use of esoteric technology-related terms.
telecollaborative Collaborative learning experiences which involve communicating over the Internet.
telecommunications literate The ability to quickly locate, collate, analyze, and act upon electronic messages as well as construct new ideas and electronic messages.
temporal Related to time.
temporal contiguity Observing two or more things together at nearly the same time.
thumbnail illustrations Miniature images that, when clicked on, call up larger versions. They let you view images without spending the time required to download very large computer files.
TLAs Acronyms that consist of three letters.
translation engines Software programs that translate texts from one language to another.

Uniform Resource Locators (URLs) The identification address of a web site.
URLs (Uniform Resource Locators) The identification address of a web site.

visual literacy The ability to interpret other people's nonverbal messages and to construct effective visual messages to convey ideas to others.

web browser Software that lets you view web pages. Netscape Communicator and Microsoft Internet Explorer are web browsers.
webliography A listing of web addresses.

XML (Extensible Markup Language) A condensed form of SGML.

References

Agnew, P. W., Kellerman, A. S., & Meyer, J. (1996). *Multimedia in the classroom.* Needham Heights, MA: Allyn & Bacon.

American Library Association. (1998). *Information literacy standards for student learning.* Chicago: ALA.

Aukerman, R. C. (1971). *Approaches to beginning reading.* New York: John Wiley & Sons.

Bailey, G. D., & Blythe, M. (1998). Outlining, diagramming & storyboarding or how to create great educational web sites. *Learning & Leading with Technology, 25*(8), 6–11.

Barrett, H. C. (2000). Create your own electronic portfolio. *Learning & Leading with Technology, 27*(7), 14–21.

Barrett, H. C. (1998). Strategic questions: What to consider when planning for electronic portfolios. *Learning & Leading with Technology, 26*(2), 6–13.

Baugh, I. W. (1999–2000). To keyboard or not to keyboard. *Learning & Leading with Technology, 27*(4), 28–31.

Bitter, G. B., & Pierson, M. E. (1999). *Using technology in the classroom* (4th ed.). Boston: Allyn & Bacon.

Boulter, J. D. (1991). *Writing space: The computer, hypertext, and the history of writing.* Hillsdale, NJ: Erlbaum.

Brown, J. K. (2000). Leadership, technology and schools. *Converge, 3*(3), 54–57.

Brunner, C., & Talley, W. (1999). *The new media literacy handbook: An educator's guide to bringing new media into the classroom.* New York: Anchor Books.

Bull, G., Bull, G., Blazi, L., & Cochran, P. (1999–2000). Electronic texts in the classroom. *Learning & Leading with Technology, 27*(4), 46–49, 56.

Burns, P. C., Roe, B. D., & Ross, E. P. (1999). *Teaching reading in today's elementary schools* (7th ed.). Boston: Houghton Mifflin.

Coley, R. (1997). *Technology's impact* [Online]. Available: http://www.electronic-school.com/0997f3.html [August, 2000].

Cooper, J. D. (2000). *Literacy: Helping children construct meaning* (4th ed.). Boston: Houghton Mifflin.

Cramer, R. L. (1998). *The spelling connection: Integrating reading, writing, and spelling instruction.* New York: Guilford Press.

D'Ignazio, F. (1996–1997). Build a virtual library on disk. *Learning & Leading with Technology, 24*(4), 60–62.

Dalton, B. (2000). Exploring literacy on the Internet. *The Reading Teacher, 53*(8), 684–693.

Dexter, S., & Watts-Taffe, S. (2000). Processing ideas: Move beyond word processing into critical thinking. *Learning & Leading with Technology, 27*(6), 22–27.

Douville, P., & Finke, J. (2000). In N. D. Wood, K. D. Wood, & T. S. Dickinson (Eds.), *Promoting literacy in grades 4–9: A handbook for teachers and administrators* (pp. 370–381). Boston: Allyn & Bacon.

Eagleton, M. B. (1999). *Hypermedia composition in a seventh-grade language arts classroom.* Unpublished doctoral dissertation. Tucson, AZ: The University of Arizona.

Ellsworth, B. (1997). *Keyboarding for kids on the computer.* Chandler, AZ: Ellsworth Publishing.

Fernandez, M. (1999). Electronic versus paper. *Learning & Leading with Technology 26*(8), 32–34.

Flatley, R. (No date). *Visual literacy* [Online]. Available: http://dtc.pima.edu/psychology/Visual_Literacy.html [2000, May 24].

Fox, B. J., & Mitchell, M. J. (2000). Using technology to support word recognition, spelling, and vocabulary acquisition. In S. B. Wepner, W. J. Valmont, & R. Thurlow (Eds.), *Linking literacy and technology: A guide for K–8 classrooms* (pp. 42–75). Newark, DE: International Reading Association.

Gage, N. L., & Berliner, D. C. (1998). *Educational psychology* (6th ed.). Boston: Houghton Mifflin.

Grabe, M., & Grabe, C. (2000). *Integrating the Internet for meaningful learning.* Boston: Houghton Mifflin.

Guinn, J. (2000, May 18). Pulp to plastic: E-books' promise. *The Arizona Daily Star,* p. E2.

Harris, J. (1997–1998). Wetware: Why use activity structures. *Learning & Leading with Technology, 25*(4), 13–17.

Heese, V. (2000, May/June). E-classroom. *Scholastic Instructor, 109*(8), H81.

Heinich, R., Molenda, M., Russell, J. D., & Smaldino, S. E. (1999). *Instructional media and technologies for learning* (6th ed.). Upper Saddle River, NJ: Prentice-Hall.

Heistand, M. (2000, May/June). Radio to the rescue. *Scholastic Instructor, 109*(8), 10–11.

Hodges, B. (1999). Electronic books. Presentation software makes writing more fun. *Learning & Leading with Technology, 27*(1), 18–21.

Horban, D. (1998). Technology & writing. *Learning & Leading with Technology, 25*(7), 32–33.

Hugo, J. (1996). *Visual literacy and software design* [Online]. Available: http://www.uasbilitysa.co.za/vislit.htm [2000, May 24].

International Society for Technology in Education. (2000). *National educational technology standards for students: Connecting curriculum and technology.* Eugene, OR: ISTE.

International Society for Technology in Education. (1998). *National educational technology standards for students.* Eugene, OR: ISTE.

Johnson, N. J., Giorgis, C., Bonomo, A., Colbert, C., Conner, A., Kauffman, G., & King, J. (2000). Language of expression. *The Reading Teacher, 53*(7), 600–608.

Johnston, A. (1997–1998). The Internet pyramid. *Learning & Leading with Technology, 25*(4), 36–37.

Jongsma, K. (1999–2000). Vocabulary and comprehension strategy development. *The Reading Teacher, 53*(4), 310–312.

Kahn, J. (1996–1997). Help! I only have one computer. *Learning & Leading with Technology, 24*(4), 16.

Kamil, M. L., & Lane, D. M. (1998). Researching the relationship between technology and literacy: An agenda for the 21st century. In D. Reinking, M. McKenna, L. D. Labbo, & R. Kieffer (Eds.), *Handbook of literacy and technology: Transformations in a post-typographic world* (pp. 323–342). Mahwah, NJ: Erlbaum.

Kauffman, D. L., Jr. (1980). *Systems one: An introduction to systems thinking.* Minneapolis, MN: Future Systems.

Keefe, C. (1994, August 26). Computers can't replace kids' books. *The Arizona Daily Star,* p. D5.

Kloza, B. (2000, May/June). CyberHunt 7. *Scholastic Instructor, 109*(8), 69–70.

Korolenko, M. D. (1997). *Writing for multimedia: A guide and sourcebook for the digital writer.* Belmont, CA: Wadsworth Publishing.

Labbo, L. D. (2000). 12 things young children can do with a talking book in a computer center. *The Reading Teacher, 53*(7), 542–546.

Laframboise, K. L. (2000). Said webs: Remedy for tired words. *The Reading Teacher, 53*(7), 540–542.

Land, M., & Turner, S. (1997). *Tools for schools: Applications software for the classroom* (2nd ed., p. 291). Belmont, CA: Wadsworth Publishing.

Lapp, D., Flood, J., & Fisher, D. (1999). Intermediality: How the use of multiple media enhances learning. *The Reading Teacher, 52*(7), 776–780.

Lapp, D., Flood, J., & Ranck–Buhr, W. (2000). Visual literacy: Some important considerations for tomorrow's classrooms. In N. D. Wood, K. D. Wood, & T. S. Dickinson (Eds.), *Promoting literacy in grades 4–9: A handbook for teachers and administrators.* (pp. 317–330). Boston: Allyn & Bacon.

Lee, G. (2000). Technology in the language arts classroom: Is it worth the trouble? *Voices from the Middle, 7*(3), 24–32

Lento, L. (1999). Presenting the future in today's classroom. *T.H.E. Journal, 26*(6), 43.

Leu, D. J., Jr. (1997). Caity's question: Literacy as deixis on the Internet. *The Reading Teacher, 51*(1), 62–67.

Leu, D. J., Jr., Karchmer, R. A., & Leu, D. D. (1999). The Miss Rumphius effect: Envisionments for literacy and learning that transform the Internet. *The Reading Teacher, 52*(6), 636–642.

Leu, D. J., Jr., & Kinzer, C. (2000). *Effective reading instruction, K–8* (3rd ed.). Columbus, OH: Merrill.

Levinson, E., & Surrat, J. (2000). The education killer app is coming. *Converge, 3*(5), 74–75.

McKenzie, J. A. (1999). Beyond technology: Literacy is the true game. *eSchool News, 2*(8), 32.

McNabb, M. (2001). Literacy skills and the Internet. *Learning & Leading with Technology, 28*(6), 46–49.

McNally, L., & Etchison, C. (2000). Strategies of successful technology integrators: Part 2—Software tools. *Learning & Leading with Technology, 28*(3), 6–9, 17.

Meltzer, B. (1999–2000). Kiss clip art goodbye. *Learning & Leading with Technology, 27*(4), 22–27.

Milner, M. (2000, October 8). Cyber-scents may be in the air. *The Arizona Daily Star,* p. A19.

Moline, S. (1995). *I see what you mean: Children at work with visual information.* York, ME: Stenhouse.

Moore, F. (2001). Storage changing so fast it even obsoletes the future. *Computer Technology Review, 21*(1), 1, 28, 34.

Moursund, D. (1997). Alternate histories. *Learning & Leading with Technology, 25*(3), 4–5.

National Center for Missing & Exploited Children. (1998). *Teen safety on the information highway.* New York: NCMEC.

National Center for Missing & Exploited Children. (1994). *Child safety on the information highway.* New York: NCMEC.

Norman, M. (2000, March). Don Tapscott: Man with a message. *Converge, 3*(3), 50–52.

Northwest Regional Educational Laboratory. *6+1 TRAITS of writing rubrics and definitions* [online]. Available: http://www.nwrel.org/assessment/department.asp?d=1 [2001].

Norton, D. E., & Norton, S. E. (1999). *Through the eyes of a child: An introduction to children's literature* (5th ed.). Upper Saddle River, NJ: Prentice-Hall.

Ogle, D. M. (1986). K-W-L: A teaching model that develops active reading of expository text. *The Reading Teacher, 39*(6), 564–570.

Oliver, K. M. (1997). Getting online with K–12 Internet projects. *Tech Trends, 42*(6), 33–40.

Palinscar, A. S., & Brown, A. L. (1984). Reciprocal teaching of comprehension-fostering and comprehension-monitoring activities. *Cognition and Instruction, 2,* 117–175.

Papert, S. (1998). Let's tie the digital knot. *Technos, 7*(4), 10–12.

Paulson, F. L., Paulson, P. R., & Meyer, C. A. (1991). What makes a portfolio a portfolio? *Educational Leadership, 48*(5), 60–63.

Rakes, G. C. (1999). Teaching visual literacy in a multimedia age. *Tech Trends, 43*(4), 14–18.

Ramsey, I. L. (No date). *Choosing stories for storytelling* [Online]. Available: http://falcon.jmu.edu/~ramseyil/storychoose.htm [2001, April 14].

Reissman, R. (1999). Student-reviewed software. *Learning & Leading with Technology, 26*(5), 22–24.

Reissman, R. (1998). Great Aunt Sophie's American journey. *Learning & Leading with Technology, 25*(8), 28–30.

Sampson, M. R., Valmont, W. J., & Allen, R. V. (1982). The effects of instructional cloze on the comprehension, vocabulary, and divergent production of third-grade students. *Reading Research Quarterly, 17*(3), 389–399.

Scolari, J. D., Bedient, D., & Randolph, T. D. (2000). Too few computers and too many kids: What can I do? *Learning & Leading with Technology, 27*(6), 28–30.

Short, K. G. (1997). *Literature as a way of knowing.* York, ME: Stenhouse.

Simonson, M. R., & Thompson, A. (1997). *Educational computing foundations* (3rd ed.). Upper Saddle River, NJ: Prentice-Hall.

Skarecki, E., & Insinnia, E. (1999). Two views of technology: Revolutions in the classroom. *Learning & Leading with Technology, 26*(7), 22–27.

Snowman, J., & Biehler, R. (2000). Psychology applied to teaching (9th ed.). Boston: Houghton Mifflin.

Stauffer, R. G. (1969). *Teaching reading as a thinking process.* New York: Harper & Row.

Sullivan, J. (1998). The electronic journal: Combining literacy and technology. *The Reading Teacher, 52*(1), 90–92.

Swearingen, R., & Allen, D. (2000). *Classroom assessment of reading processes.* Boston: Houghton Mifflin.

Tapscott, D. (1999). *Growing up digital: The rise of the net.* New York: McGraw-Hill

Taverna, P., & Hongell, T. (2000). Meet Harriet Tubman: The story of a web site. *Learning & Leading with Technology, 27*(6), 42–45, 62.

Taylor, T. W., & Ward, I. (1999). *Literacy theory in the age of the Internet.* New York: Columbia University Press.

Technology's role in evaluation and assessment. (2000). *Learning & Leading with Technology, 27*(7), 6–7.

Thurlow, R. (2000). How do I begin to use technology in my classroom. In S. B. Wepner, W. J. Valmont, & R. Thurlow (Eds.), *Linking literacy and technology: A guide for K–8 classrooms* (pp. 19–39). Newark, DE: International Reading Association.

Tierney, R. J., Readence, J. E., & Dishner, E. K. (1999). *Reading strategies and practices: A compendium* (5th ed.). Boston: Allyn & Bacon.

Tompkins, G. E. (1990). *Teaching writing: Balancing process and product.* Columbus, OH: Merrill Publishing.

Tower, C. (2000). Questions that matter: Preparing elementary students for the inquiry process. *The Reading Teacher, 53*(7), 550–557.

Truett, C., Scherlen, A., Tashner, J., & Lowe, K. (1997). Responsible Internet use. *Learning & Leading with Technology, 24*(6), 52–55.

Vacca, R. T., & Vacca, J. L. (1998). *Content area reading: Literacy and learning across the curriculum* (6th ed.). New York: HarperCollins.

Valmont, W. J. (1972). Spelling consciousness: A long neglected area. *Elementary English, 49*(8), 1219–1221.

Valmont, W. J. (1976). *See-listen-think.* New York: McCormick-Mathers.

Valmont, W. J. (1995). *Creating videos for school use.* Boston: Allyn & Bacon.

Valmont, W. J. (2000). What do teachers do in technology-rich classrooms? In S. B. Wepner, W. J. Valmont, & R. Thurlow (Eds.), *Linking literacy and technology: A guide for K–8 classrooms* (pp. 160–202). Newark, DE: International Reading Association.

Vardell, S. M. (1998). Using read-aloud to explore the layers of nonfiction. In R. A. Bamford & J. V. Kristo (Eds.), *Making facts come alive: Choosing quality nonfiction literature K–8* (pp. 151–168). Norwood, MA: Christopher-Gordon.

Weeg, P. A. (1999). *Kids@Work: Math in the cyberzone.* London: Beaumont Publishers.

Wepner, S. B., & Ray, L. C. (2000). Using technology for reading development. In S. B. Wepner, W. J. Valmont, & R. Thurlow (Eds.), *Linking literacy and technology: A guide for K–8 classrooms* (pp. 76–105). Newark, DE: International Reading Association.

Wood, J. M. (2000). Author, author! *Scholastic Instructor, 109*(8), 64–66.

Yoder, M. B. (1999). The student webquest. *Learning & Leading with Technology, 26*(7), 7–9.

Young, T. A., & Vardell, S. M. (1993). Weaving readers theatre and nonfiction into the curriculum. *The Reading Teacher, 46*(5), 396–406.

Index

QUICK REFERENCE GUIDE

TECH TIPS